Ultimate Attainment in Second Language Acquisition

A Case Study

Ultimate Attainment in Second Language Acquisition

A Case Study

Donna Lardiere
Georgetown University

Routledge
Taylor & Francis Group

NEW YORK AND LONDON

Camera ready copy for this book was provided by the author.

Table 3.2 and Table 3.3 on pp. 76 and 78 respectively are from "Case and Tense in the Fossilized Steady State," by Donna Lardiere, 1998, *Second Language Research, 14*(1), pp. 16 and 18 respectively. Copyright 1998 by Hodder Arnold. Reprinted with permission.

Table 3.4 on p. 79 is from "Dissociating Syntax from Morphology in a Divergent L2 End-state Grammar," by Donna Lardiere, 1998, *Second Language Research, 14*(4), p. 369. Copyright 1998 by Hodder Arnold. Reprinted with permission.

Table 4.9 and Table 4.9 on p. 115 are from "Revisiting the Comparative Fallacy: A Reply to Lakshmanan and Selinker," by Donna Lardiere, 2003, *Second Language Research, 19*(2), pp. 133 and 134 respectively. Copyright 2003 by Hodder Arnold. Reprinted with permission.

First published 2007 by Lawrence Erlbaum Associates, Inc.

Published 2015 by Routledge
711 Third Avenue, New York, NY 10017, USA
2 Park Square, Milton Park, Abingdon, Oxon OX14 4RN

First issued in paperback 2015

Routledge is an imprint of Taylor & Francis Group, an informa business

Copyright © 2007 by Lawrence Erlbaum Associates, Inc.

Cover design by Kathryn Houghtaling Lacey

Library of Congress Cataloging-in-Publication Data

Lardiere, Donna.
    Ultimate attainment in second language acquisition : a case study /
    Donna Lardiere.
        p. cm.

Includes bibliographical references and index.

ISBN 0-8058-3456-7 (cloth : alk. paper)
ISBN 1-4106-1547-2 (e book)
1. Second language acquisition.   I. Title.
P118.2.L369   2006
418—dc22   2006013946
                                         CIP

ISBN 13: 978-1-138-83993-9 (pbk)
ISBN 13: 978-0-8058-3456-7 (hbk)

Contents

Preface

Sometime in the early 1980s—probably 1981—I was introduced by my college roommate to a smart, stylish, vivacious, and gregarious friend of hers whom she had met at the restaurant where they both waitressed part time. Thus began my acquaintance with "Patty," which, over time, bloomed into a friendship that has lasted now for over two decades, through major life events and changes for both of us, as well as (somewhat miraculously) through all my queries, requests, and pestering for more data, and the eventual completion of this book.

When I taped my first recording of Patty, in 1986, at an impromptu brunch with her and my college roommate, I did not have the slightest intention of beginning what has since turned out to be one of the longest-running longitudinal case studies in the area of second language acquisition (SLA) that I am aware of; I was simply completing an assignment for an introductory course in bilingualism. By the time I thought of carrying out such a case study many years later, that particular course paper had long been consigned to oblivion, but happily, I still had the tape. One of the things that struck me on relistening to it (in addition to nostalgia for that era of leisurely brunches with old school friends) was how little Patty's English grammar seemed to have changed in all the time since we had first met. But was that impression in fact correct? And if so, why hadn't it changed? This book represents my stab at answering these two questions, although admittedly with only partial success, and with rather more of an answer to the first question than the second. Still, I believe it is a small step forward in an area where comparably-detailed L2 case studies of ultimate attainment were simply unavailable when I began this project, and will surely still be much needed in the future.

There is no doubt that I have been intellectually influenced in my focus of inquiry by Chomsky's (1986) *Knowledge of Language*. The task of describing the nature of the formal properties of attained language knowledge is logically prior to accounting for how such knowledge could have come to be attained. Moreover, I was interested in studying Patty's own idiolect of English in I-language terms. That is, I wanted to try to characterize various aspects of the particular idiolect she had actually attained and internally represented—her knowledge of "what makes sound and meaning relate to one another in a specific way, what makes them 'hang together', a particular characterization of a function, perhaps," and her "notion of structure" (Chomsky, 1986, p. 27).

I have limited my scope of investigation to those formal areas in which much work in generative linguistic and language acquisition theory has yielded relatively highly articulated analyses and hypotheses. At the time I started writing this book, most of these analyses were in the areas of syntax and morphosyntax, particularly regarding the acquisition of functional categories and the features associated with them. Since then, investigation into the nature of formal phonological representations in SLA has made considerable inroads into the "syntactocentrism" (to borrow a term from Jackendoff, 1997) that has monopolized so much of generative SLA research, and empirical inquiry into the nature of L2 formal semantic and pragmatic representations has begun to yield interesting findings as well. Such results will undoubtedly guide and inform other researchers' more comprehensive case studies in the future.

This book was written almost entirely during the summers of the past several years, and I gratefully acknowledge the generous summer research grants I have received from the Graduate School of Georgetown University. Rebekha Abbuhl, Dee Cain, Myong-Hee Choi, Joaquim Kuong and Dominik Rus helped out with various aspects of data transcription, coding, and statistical analyses, and Ashley Fidler assisted with preparation of the manuscript. My initial contact at Lawrence Erlbaum Associates was Judi Amsel, who regularly chatted with me at conferences and wondered when I would decide to turn my study into a book. Cathleen Petree has seen it through to completion with care, patience, and yet more patience, and Sara Scudder provided helpful advice throughout the editing and production process. Several colleagues have made valuable comments on various pieces of the study at various stages of development: Heather Goad, Zhao-Hong Han, Roger Hawkins, Elaine Klein, Peter Patrick, Clifton Pye, Bonnie Schwartz, Margaret Thomas, and Lydia White. David Birdsong and Lydia White read and commented on the entire manuscript, and so I especially thank them. I am grateful for the love and support of my family and friends, even those who nagged me. Finally, obviously, this work would not have been possible without Patty, who endured with characteristic grace, humor, and patience my incessant prying and poking around in her personal language space. This book is dedicated to her, with deepest gratitude.

1

Some Preliminary Issues in Adult L2 Ultimate Attainment

The impetus for this study arose from a long-standing acquaintance with Patty, a Chinese-American naturalized immigrant whose typical everyday exposure to the English language is, in many respects, very similar to mine and has been so for well over two decades. It is true that our daily exposure to technical jargon is different—hers in corporate accounting and mine in academic linguistics—but otherwise we each live, work, and play with native English speakers in the northeastern United States in an English language environment which is by and large urban, educated, and professional. We see many of the same films (although she has probably seen more of them), read the same newspapers, and watch the same newscasts and commercials on TV. We listen to the same radio stations while driving. We read English-language fiction and nonfiction and occasionally exchange with each other those books that one or the other of us has particularly enjoyed. We browse the Internet and read and send e-mail. We subscribe to magazines. We each socialize at dinner parties and backyard barbecues, sometimes the same ones. We are both avid bargain hunters and not shy about negotiating prices with store clerks and managers and yard-sale hosts (although she is much better at it than I am). We both have undergraduate and graduate degrees from American institutions in the same northeastern U.S. metropolitan area. We read cookbook recipes, telephone bills, prescription labels, bank and credit card statements, menus, road maps, advertising and travel brochures, birthday cards, income tax forms, food and product labels, traffic signs, billboards, concert schedules, wedding invitations, and refund and cancellation policies, all in English. We each read a lot of memoranda at work and attend a lot of meetings to discuss the memoranda.

Despite these similarities, the language we both speak in this environment—English—in some ways sounds quite different from each other. Unlike me, Patty is a non-native speaker of English, acquiring it largely after her arrival in the United States more than 25 years ago at the age of 22. As with many second or foreign language (L2) learners whose language learning has commenced after childhood, Patty's English contains phonetic, morphosyntactic, and lexical forms that in some ways sharply diverge from those produced rather more uniformly by the particular community of native English speakers with whom she interacts daily.[1] The nature and extent of this divergence, as well as the extent of overlap and similarity, are the subjects of this study.

Sorting Through Some Terminology

The apparent persistence of such divergent forms in Patty's grammar, in the face of ongoing rich target-language input (presumably the same input that would suffice to bring a young child's grammar into eventual conformity with target norms), is known as language *fossilization* (Selinker, 1972; Selinker & Lamendella, 1979). A brief example of a "fossilized" speech sample from Patty after she had already lived in the United States for about 10 years, taken from her conversation with two native English speakers, is shown in (1).

(1)   [1]PAT: You know, *I call B. this morning* and *nobody answer*. And *I start* to worry.
      [2]NS1: Do you have his phone number where he is?
      [3]PAT: Well, *he either stay* in Eliotville, because he said *he call me last night,* and he never did.
      [4]NS2: He said he'd call you?
      [5]NS1: He said he would?
      [6]PAT: Yeah, he would. In the morning, *I talk to him* from Eliotville, and then *even if he stay over Eliotville, he will give me a call,* you know?

---

[1] I use the phrase "rather more uniformly" advisedly here, aware that some degree of variability of performance and indeterminacy of intuitions exists among native speakers as well (e.g., Birdsong, 1989; Klein, 1998; Larsen-Freeman, 2006). However, it would be clearly disingenuous to maintain that the degree of variability exhibited in Patty's production of English is of the same type and magnitude as that exhibited by the community of native speakers with whom she interacts daily. I further discuss the notion of "target norm" in the next section.

[7]NS1: Yeah.

[8]PAT: And *then I call her house* and *nobody answer.*

This sample highlights the variability with which certain obligatory grammatical elements are produced. Note, for example, the frequent omissions of verbal inflection and the error in pronominal gender, as illustrated earlier, as well as the attempt by both native speakers at lines [4] and [5] to clarify the intended meaning of Patty's preceding utterance, which is missing a modal auxiliary.

The term *fossilization* is often distinguished from *stabilization*, the latter term generally used to indicate a more permeable, temporary knowledge state (in more common parlance, something like a "plateau"). For example, Selinker and Lakshmanan (1993) suggest that certain stabilized states can lead to either fossilization or further development. (I return to this suggestion in chap. 7.) Long (2003) points out several difficulties with the terminology and favors a research focus on stabilization in contrast to fossilization. He argues that *fossilization* as a theoretical construct cannot simultaneously encompass both synchronic and diachronic variability because such variability renders the claim of permanent divergence from nativelike norms essentially unfalsifiable. Moreover, he argues, the meaning of fossilization includes that of stabilization (with the difference being that fossilization implies permanence), and yet the dictionary definition of stabilization includes the descriptor "unfluctuating" (p. 489), interpreted by Long to mean disallowing variability.

I agree with Long that diachronic variation over a certain developmental span (i.e., the learner produces Form A at some developmental stage X but Form B at some later developmental stage Y) is inadmissible evidence of fossilization. However, synchronic variability, a hallmark of adult second language performance, is well known to persist at advanced proficiency levels and indeed, even at the steady, or end state, of acquisition.[2] To the degree that such variability diverges significantly from that exhibited by native speakers, it does not necessarily "bleed the construct [of fossilization] of any remaining meaning" (p. 510), as Long (2003) writes. Indeed, Long cites one view of variation as "fundamental to any postulated definition of fossilization" and that fossilization would have to include a kind of

---

[2] The term *steady state*, or S_s, is used by Chomsky (1986) to describe the fully developed mental grammar of a native speaker. The term *end state* is preferred by Birdsong (1999). Neither term should be construed as implying that certain aspects of language learning, such as the addition of new vocabulary or idiomatic expressions, are no longer possible for either native or non-native speakers.

"head-banging variation" within a general context of cessation of development (p. 526). Putting aside the unflattering imagery, I agree that the status of (synchronic) variability in a so-called fossilized grammar is, as Long points out, a major unresolved issue. I focus in detail on the variability of a particular morphological inflection—namely, past-tense marking—in Patty's production data in chapter 4, and I return to a more conceptual discussion of variability in chapter 7.

Regardless of the terminological choice between *fossilization* and *stabilization* to describe an end-state grammar such as Patty's, what is even more important for my purposes here is to recognize that both terms implicitly entail a comparison with a *target norm*, itself a highly problematic notion. A target norm can only be a fairly crude shorthand way of referring to a set of hypothesized grammatical constructs of a language from the researcher's perspective, not the learner's. The notion of *target* is somewhat misleading in that it implies a teleological endpoint to acquisition, that is, that the learner will somehow (tacitly) "realize" when this goal has been attained such that further grammatical learning can now cease. In other words, the learner must know in advance precisely what has not yet been acquired and thus still needs to be learned.

This strikes me as implausible. It is certainly possible for a learner to have some metalinguistic understanding of some learning problem—I realize in some vague way, for example, that I have difficulties with the correct choice and placement of clitics in Italian and with tone sandhi in Chinese. But if I knew (exactly) what these should be in all relevant contexts, then I would, in fact, *know* them even if I could not always accurately control them in production. More worrisome, however, is the near-certain likelihood that there are many aspects of Italian and Chinese that I do not even know that I don't know! Thus, it is impossible to speak in any meaningful sense of an ultimate nativelike target from the learner's perspective, because that target is always moving, so to speak.

Similarly, the term *interlanguage*, implying some globally vague intermediate knowledge state "on the way" somewhere between knowledge of the L1 and ultimate mastery of the L2, shares some of the problems associated with the notion of *target*. In describing Patty's end-state knowledge of English, which clearly differs in some respects from that of a native English speaker, I prefer the term *idiolect*. Although I occasionally use the conventional *IL* acronym in referring to her L2 grammar, I have something closer in meaning to *idiolect* in mind—her individual knowledge state (or *I-language*, in Chomsky's terms) of English.[3]

Therefore, in this and the following chapters, although I use the terms *(non-)targetlike* and *(non-)nativelike* in describing Patty's English production, it should nonetheless be kept in mind that such usage necessarily implies something along the lines of: 'From the researcher's perspective this is what appears to be the case in comparison to what we have observed or hypothesized about native speaker grammars.' (In chap. 4, I discuss some possibly troublesome implications of researcher perspective with respect to lexical aspect in Patty's data; see also Lardiere, 2003a.) Similarly, I continue to rather loosely use the term *fossilization* (*pace* Long, 2003) to describe those aspects of Patty's grammar which appear to differ from the observed or hypothesized properties of native-speaker grammars (including in terms of variability or non-categoricalness), and for which there is no indication of further diachronic development over the observation period; however, Long's terminological caveats should also be kept in mind.

Finally, a word about the term *ultimate attainment*, as contained in the title of this work. I use this phrase to refer to the state of knowledge actually attained at the end or steady state of grammatical development, which may or may not be nativelike. Over the course of the following chapters, it will become clear that Patty's English idiolect—her state of ultimate attainment in that language—diverges from nativelike competence in some respects and completely converges in others.[4]

What Can a "Fossilized" End-State Grammar Tell Us About the Language Faculty?

The divergence in ultimate attainment from native speaker grammars we observe among adult language learners is theoretically interesting because it is (inversely) related to a well-known question concerning what type of

---

[3] What I have in mind is reminiscent of Aronoff's (1994) description of *Michal*, an idiolectal variant of Hebrew representing the later stages of attrition of the L1 of its sole speaker (named Michal), a native Israeli Hebrew-speaking child who moved to an English-speaking environment at the age of 2;6, and who, over a period of 2 years, acquired English and lost Hebrew.

[4] Similarly in this regard, Birdsong (2004) writes that ultimate attainment "refers to the outcome or endpoint of acquisition" and should not be confused with or taken as meaning "synonymous with 'nativelike,'" although nativelikeness is one of the observed outcomes of L2A" (p. 82).

linguistic information is extractable from the environment. Referring to this question as Plato's Problem, Chomsky (1986, citing Bertrand Russell) asked: How can we know so much, given such limited evidence? Specifically, it has been amply demonstrated by now that (native) speakers of a language appear to end up with a much richer, more abstract system of knowledge than could possibly be induced from only the observable evidence in the environment—a problem known as the *poverty of the stimulus*.

To give a more concrete example, native speakers of English know that the sentence in (2), involving the displacement of a *wh*-element to sentence-initial position from its interpreted position as the subject of a relative clause, is ungrammatical, whereas the sentence in (3) involving similar *wh*-movement of the same phrase from the subject position of a subcategorized subordinate clause is perfectly fine:

(2)   *Which professor did Mary read the book on functional categories had written?

(3)   *Which professor* did Mary think had written the book on functional categories?

Given that sentences such as (3) occur in the input, what prevents an English learner from (over)generalizing the possibility of movement of the *wh*-phrase *which professor* to a sentence such as the one in (2)? How does an English speaker learn that the sentence in (2) is absolutely impossible? The answer given by Chomsky was essentially that such constraints on possible sentences are not learned; rather, they are a reflection of the way human brains are biologically predisposed to organize and represent linguistic knowledge. Such constraints are thought to collectively make up Universal Grammar (UG), and their precise formulation can be viewed as an attempt by generative linguists to model the human capacity for acquiring certain formal properties of possible natural language grammars. The principles of UG have been argued to make up (at least part of) a Language Acquisition Device (LAD), severely restricting the learner's hypothesis space in the course of grammatical development.

In the case of fossilization, we might ask whether maturational changes in the LAD affect either the extractability of information from the input or the hypothesized constraints on grammatical acquisition, and whether such changes can account for the apparent inability to detect, compute, or otherwise internalize certain aspects of linguistic input that are (ultimately) perfectly accessible to very young children. In fact, assuming optimal exposure conditions of sufficient duration—a point to which I return below—nonnative speakers immersed in the second language environment are exposed to the same linguistic input, and in this sense face the same poverty-of-the-stimulus problem as native speakers. One might well imagine that adult learners' grammatical representations of the target language fail to be constrained by UG, thus leading to fossilization. However, in my view, this seems unlikely.

The UG-constrained characteristics of natural languages, such as hierarchical structure dependence, displacement (such as *wh*-movement), the autonomy of linguistic modules (e.g., phonetics, phonology, morphology, syntax, semantics), the presence of functional categories and features, and the subjecting of grammatical relations and operations to highly restrictive structural and locality conditions (e.g., c-command, subjacency, etc.)—in other words, the essential *formats* of linguistic representations within UG—appear to be largely intact in second language knowledge. This has been amply demonstrated (to the extent it can be) by a large number of studies investigating a wide range of formal aspects of language (e.g., Dekydtspotter, Sprouse, & Anderson, 1997; duPlessis, Solin, Travis, & White, 1987; Kanno, 1997; Martohardjono, 1993; Schwartz & Sprouse, 1994, 2000; Schwartz & Tomaselli, 1990; Thomas, 1991a, 1991b; Tomaselli & Schwartz, 1990; Vainikka & Young-Scholten, 1994; White & Genesee, 1996; and many others).

To take one example, Martohardjono (1993) tested native speakers of Chinese, Indonesian, or Italian learning English on their knowledge of the ungrammaticality of sentences such as the one shown earlier in (2) and repeated below as (4):

(4)   **Which professor* did Mary read the book on functional categories had written?

The results indicated that, like native speakers, the non-native speakers in all three groups rejected more strongly ungrammatical sentences such as the one in (4) (i.e., "strong" violations), at a higher rate than somewhat more acceptable sentences involving more weakly constrained *wh*-movement (i.e., "weak" violations) such as the one in (5):

(5)   **?Which professor* did Mary think that had written the book on functional categories?[5]

---

[5] The difference between the sentence in (5) and the nearly identical (but grammatical) sentence in (3) shown earlier is the presence in (5) but not (3) of the complementizer *that*, resulting in a *that*-trace violation, a type of weak violation of constraints on extraction from a subject position of a subordinate clause in English.

This distinction between strong and weak violations of constraints on
wh-movement was theoretically motivated within a UG framework and thus
predicted to occur. Although there were differences in the absolute percentages of rejection among the non-native groups (reflecting some lingering
influence of their native L1s), and between these groups and the native
speakers, Martohardjono (1993) showed that the relative rate of rejection
between the types of sentences in (4) and (5) was statistically significantly
different for all the non-native groups as well as for the native speakers,
suggesting that all groups had knowledge of the relevant constraints.[6] In
chapter 5, I show that Patty appears to display similar knowledge of constraints on *wh*-movement despite the fact that such movement is not overtly
evident in her native Chinese.

Returning to the nature of fossilized production, such as in the sample
shown earlier in (1), we often find variability or omission of elements such
as tense and agreement marking, and other functional elements such as
prepositions, auxiliaries, articles, and so on, for which in fact there is abundant overt evidence in the input. If it is indeed the case, as the studies cited
earlier have suggested, that adult learners are able to acquire grammatical
knowledge of the second language for which there is little or no evidence in
the primary linguistic data available to them, what prevents learners from
acquiring elements of the target language that *are* overtly evident? Here we
encounter the flip side of Plato's Problem, as noted by Hale (1988). This is,
namely, the question of why one knows so little, given so much evidence.[7]

---

[6] Schwartz and Sprouse (2000) rightly point out that, even though the technical details of
the syntactic framework Martohardjono assumed in her study have changed in the meantime, the conceptual problem addressed by Martohardjono remains the same: "No matter
how the constraints on [*wh*-] extraction are framed, there is a clear poverty-of-the-
stimulus problem involved in acquiring the distinction between strong and weak violations, since they both refer to essentially non-occurring syntactic patterns. [...] The fact
that Martohardjono's L2 acquirers display knowledge not only of the unacceptability of
strong violations, but also of the distinction between strong and weak violations, is a very
strong indication that L2 development is constrained by UG" (p. 177). See Schwartz and
Sprouse for additional examples and discussion.

[7] Chomsky (1986) referred to this particular question as *Orwell's Problem*. He posed it in
a political rather than linguistic context, and assumed that it involved a qualitatively
different type of knowledge. Hale (1988) acknowledges the different context, but nonetheless remarks that "it is at least conceivable that there is an element of Orwell's problem in the second language acquisition situation" (p. 32). Although I don't use the term
Orwell's Problem here (but see Selinker & Lakshmanan, 1993, who do), I agree with
Hale that a specifically linguistic instantiation of the problem can be pursued, in particular via the issue of fossilization. The interesting question, of course, is whether the fram-
(Continued)

It is this seemingly paradoxical problem that I attempt to explore in this book.

The issue of (non-)convergence with the target could in principle be distinct from the question of whether or not the learner's developing or end-state IL is constrained by UG, as has often been noted in the literature. Hilles (1991) observed that UG is not synonymous with the LAD, although it is likely subsumed under it. UG is a necessary but insufficient condition for acquisition; if learners had only UG, they could not learn their language (p. 306). Borer (1996) writes that it is "perfectly possible for an output grammar to be constrained by UG, although the process of acquisition is informed by an independent acquisition device" (p. 719). Similarly, Bickerton (1996) points out that UG is "normally restricted to the categories and processes of core syntax, while the language faculty embraces any aspect of the organism that helps make language acquisition possible" (p. 716). Carroll (2001) observes the necessity of describing and explaining how the grammatical periphery, or the "flotsam and jetsam of specific language systems" is acquired (p. 40). In other words, it is certainly possible that second language learners have grammars that are constrained by UG in those domains in which UG applies, but nonetheless fail to conform to nativelike target norms in other domains.

To the extent that UG-like knowledge has been convincingly demonstrated in the SLA literature, we might in fact hypothesize that the investigation of what has *not* been fully acquired at the steady state given optimal exposure conditions potentially illuminates the nature of the (rest of the) LAD, as well as the limits of the scope of UG and associated phenomena such as critical- or sensitive-period effects. According to this sort of hypothesis, we would expect the "categories and processes of core syntax" to be intact, whereas other so-called "interface" areas could be more likely to be affected by factors such as those related to maturation or prior language experience (whether representational or processing-related; see e.g., Sorace, 2003 for just such a suggestion). We might not be surprised, for example, at the relative fragility of the correspondence rules or algorithms by which semantic or syntactic categories are morphophonologically expressed. As is shown throughout the remaining chapters of this book, Patty's data largely conform to this expectation. At the same time, the data also suggest that the way in which the notion of UG parameters has been conceived in generative acquisition research (at least for L2 research, but perhaps even for L1

---

ing of a linguistic version of Orwell's Problem involves a qualitatively different type of knowledge than the type hypothetically postulated as a solution to Plato's Problem.

research) should probably be revised. I have more to say about this in the following chapters, especially chapter 7.

Finally, one of the leading research questions for SLA study within a generative framework is determining the extent to which first and second language acquisition are similar or different, and why L2 acquisition often appears to be "behaviorally distinct" from L1 acquisition (Borer, 1996, pp. 718–719). As Borer points out, such a comparison can be undertaken only if we know what the steady state of L2 acquisition is (we presume to have a much better idea of the steady state of L1 acquisition), and therefore, that should be the first question to be resolved. Similar to the approach taken in native-language acquisition research, we know what is acquirable by examining what has actually been acquired and working backward to try to figure out how that type of knowledge could have been acquired in principle. This book attempts to take that first step—namely, that of describing in some detail some aspects of a single learner's L2 steady-state grammar.

Why a Case Study?

As mentioned earlier, the original motivation for carrying out this case study was a desire, mainly born of simple curiosity throughout my long-standing acquaintance with Patty, to discover more about the formal nature of her English idiolect. Since then, however, I have been further convinced of the value and validity of such a study by arguments presented in Caramazza (1986), who writes that "only the single-case method allows valid inferences about the structure of cognitive systems from the analysis of impaired performance" (p. 41). I think it is worth reviewing these arguments in some detail. (All page number citations in this section are from Caramazza, 1986, unless otherwise noted.)

In order to determine what counts as the most appropriate or relevant evidence that bears on a particular area of inquiry, Caramazza reminds us, we need to clarify our ultimate theoretical objectives. Caramazza's own interest is in the use of studies of the performance of atypical (e.g., aphasic or brain-damaged) patients "to inform and constrain theories of normal cognitive processing" (p. 52). (In analogizing from Caramazza's clinical context to the adult SLA context—assuming such an extension is possible, sensible, and fruitful—I substitute [adult L2] *learner* for *patient* in outlining his main points.)

In relation to Patty, it should be made clear from the outset that I have not attempted to establish the basis for any sort of effective pedagogical intervention that could be applied either specifically to her or more generally to native Chinese-speaking adult learners of English, or even more generally to adult SLA of any type. Of course, this would certainly be a worthy objective, and I would be delighted if the data reported here were to eventually contribute in some way to such an endeavor. But ultimately I am more interested in questions about the representational nature of language in general, and of a specific I-language—Patty's English idiolect—in particular, and in what the latter can tell us about the former. Following Caramazza, we might allow that the ultimate goal toward which nearly all acquisitionists strive to contribute is the (collective) formulation of a functional architecture of the human mind/brain, which specifies the componential structure of a cognitive system (p. 47).

According to Caramazza, two crucial features of some model M (e.g., a theory about some cognitive subsystem) are assumptions of *transparency* and *universality*. The assumption of transparency, within our generative SLA context, holds that the cognitive system (or, more precisely, our model of such a system) of a fossilized language learner is, in its essence, the same as that of a "successful" (i.e., normal L1) language learner except for some local "disruption" or "modification" that may lead to impaired performance. This modification does not, however, result in "the *de novo* creation" of a fundamentally different system of cognitive operations that bears "a nontransparent relationship" to M (p. 52).

In the adult SLA context, note that we cannot automatically assume transparency (although I do not think it is an unreasonable assumption). Rather, it needs to be established to the extent it can be (and has been) by studies of the sort mentioned earlier, which suggest that the essential format of linguistic representations within UG appears to be essentially similar in both first and second language knowledge. As we proceed through the remaining chapters, I hope to show that the data from Patty appear to support the transparency assumption, in that the English idiolect she has acquired is a natural human language and is even remarkably nativelike in certain domains, with local modifications leading to non-nativelike performance in other domains.[8] (Within the SLA context, cf. Beck's (1997, 1998) *Local Impairment Hypothesis*.)

The second assumption—that of universality—holds that M is true of the "normal" human mind/brain in general and thus true for *any* individual

---

[8] Caramazza (1986) observes that, in principle, the transparency assumption could hold even if such modifications were nonlocal (i.e., more general and extensive); however, in practice, given the "tremendous complexity of the systems we are dealing with" (p. 52), we may only be able to draw meaningful conclusions under the more restrictive condition of locality.

normal mind/brain in particular (p. 49; italics original). This assumption critically, although perhaps tacitly, underlies the justification for obtaining experimental group data, in that we assume that the averaged performance of the group "essentially reflects" and is representative of the performance of any one individual in the reference population from which the group is drawn. As Caramazza notes, however, we cannot construct "a parallel argument" for learners with impaired performance, because the task of correctly identifying and classifying the relevant reference population in relation to our model is highly problematic (p. 54).

The first problem we encounter is the difficulty in guaranteeing essential homogeneity in the relevant respects. In the adult SLA context, we could conceivably (and plausibly, in my view) account for fossilized L2 outcomes in terms of some difference, for example, a disruption or local modification (as above) in the cognitive systems of adult learners compared to those of native speakers of a language. However, according to Caramazza, we would be justified in averaging the performance of group subjects only if we could assume that the nature of this modification or difference in the particular cognitive system of each learner is "identical in all theoretically relevant respects" (p. 54). This problem strikes me as especially acute in the adult group SLA context, where learners may have radically differing initial conditions: different L1s (one or more), prior knowledge of additional L2s with varying degrees of proficiency in different skill areas, different ages of exposure to the target language, varying degrees and types of prior instruction in the target language, differences in the amount and quality of input in the target language, varying social conditions under which the target language is produced, and even different competencies among the various sub-components of researcher constructs like "language aptitude" (e.g., see DeKeyser, 2000) or "field (in)dependence" (e.g,. Chapelle & Green, 1992). At this point, we are not even sure what constitutes a "relevant respect" although age of exposure and knowledge of the L1 must surely be high on the list. (See Han, 2004 for the most recent and extensive overview of the fossilization literature and arguments that these two factors are paramount, and additional discussion later in chapter 7, this volume.)

And therein lies another problem. Caramazza argues that we can only determine whether the relevant conditions are identical a posteriori—that is, after actually observing each learner's performance (in a learner-by-learner analysis), and that there is no independent a priori classification schema that can be used to justify the assumption of homogeneity and thus allow valid inferences from group data (pp. 54–55). Moreover, we need to provide independent justification for considering our specific learner categories as *theoretically basic*, with no possibility of "statistically relevant partitions" into further subclasses of categories (p. 56).

Furthermore, even if the group reference class is "perfectly homogeneous," Caramazza argues, or were we to weaken our homogeneity criterion such that all group members belong to some antecedently specified reference population, such as native Chinese-speaking adult learners of English, we could still only obtain probabilistic statements. For example, we could only address questions of the sort, "What is the probability that [learners] of type R manifest property *y*?", but not questions such as, "Is it the case that [learners] of type R necessarily manifest property *y*?" (pp. 56–57). A related point is made by Yin (1994), who writes that the case study is the "preferred strategy" when posing "how" or "why" questions (p. 1).

It may well be the case that certain objectives within the SLA context can be met using probabilistic statements obtained from group studies. For example, we might be interested in the likelihood that certain language-planning policies will affect members of a particular reference population (which could make use of survey data from questionnaires), or in the extent to which certain laboratory or classroom-based interventions are likely to be effective for a given population (which would require experiments). However, Caramazza contends that the posing of probabilistic questions is fundamentally not relevant to the constructing of a "theoretically coherent account of the structure of cognitive systems" and thus the group study method is "inappropriate." In other words, our ultimate theoretical concerns do not lie in the *intrinsically probabilistic relationship* (less than 1.0) between some antecedently specified learner type and an observed pattern of performance (pp. 56–57).

A commonly voiced objection to case study research is that one cannot construct a theory on the basis of a single case. Both Yin (1994) and Caramazza (1986) address this concern, the latter going so far as to label it "a monstrous misapprehension of what single case study methodology is all about" (p. 60):

> No one has proposed that we construct a *different* theory for each case studied, just as no one would propose that we construct a different theory for each experiment with a group of subjects or patients. What *is* being claimed is that the performance of each [learner] potentially provides relevant evidence for a model. (Caramazza, 1986, p. 60, italics original)

Yin (1994) makes a similar observation in relation to the (non-)generalizability of case study data, observing that scientific theories are only rarely based on single experiments, but rather on a multiple set of experiments:

[C]ase studies, like experiments, are generalizable to theoretical propositions and not to populations or universes. In this sense, the case study, like the experiment, does not represent a "sample," and the investigator's goal is to expand and generalize theories (analytic generalization). ... In analytical generalization, the investigator is striving to generalize a particular set of results to some broader theory. (Yin, 1994, pp. 10 & 36)

According to Yin, the case study relies on and benefits from the prior development of theoretical propositions to guide data collection and analysis and is useful in the further development or testing of a theory. I return to the issue of theory development in a later section of this chapter.

The best remedy for overcoming worry that the results from a case study are too overspecific or idiosyncratic, Caramazza (1986) suggests, is by doing more of them, or by being sure to carry out within-subject individual data analyses if group studies are carried out. The greater the total body of evidence accumulated, the more we can reduce the "potentially deleterious effects" of any individual idiosyncratic performance as a proportion of that evidence. We expect that, as more findings from individual studies become available, the pattern of results should ultimately converge on the "best" theory, whereas discrepant results should diverge from each other, proportionally weakening the value of any single discrepant result (pp. 61–62). Finally, we are reminded to pay special attention to the range and type of variation exhibited among "normal" controls (in our case, native speakers). This last point is taken up at some length within the SLA context by Birdsong (2006).

In principle, given that within UG research the primary focus of inquiry is on the intensionally defined formal properties of language as represented within an individual mind/brain, or I-language, following Chomsky (1986), we are obliged to direct our attention to individual data even when conducting group studies. We might think of a collection of individual grammatical representations, or individual I-languages, as constituting a "Language" (i.e., an E-language) to the extent that there is some (as yet undefined, possibly undefinable) criterial degree of overlap among those representations in relevant respects; we can scarcely assume or expect complete identity of representations between even native speakers of the "same" language. Though Patty and I speak to each other often and generally without difficulty, this book is ultimately a kind of preliminary attempt to explore to what extent we are speaking the same language when we do.

Why Study Patty?

One might reasonably hypothesize that the failure to achieve a nativelike representation of an L2 grammar is a function of an impoverished input environment, and thus this factor needs to be controlled for to as great an extent as possible in SLA research on ultimate attainment. There is a nice discussion by Birdsong (1999) on the need for researchers who are truly interested in ultimate attainment to look at *only* those learners in "exogenous circumstances favoring language acquisition, not at any and all who have had some exposure to an L2 or who have tried to learn a foreign language" (p. 14). Birdsong cites an approximate figure of over 6 million utterances directed to a young child acquiring an L1 over the first 5 years of life, and notes that the proportion of L2 learners exposed to such massive input would likely constitute only "a small fraction of the universe of 'second language learners' " (pp. 14–15). His own research is informed by participants who have been immersed in their L2 environment for a substantial length of time, with a minimum of 3 to 5 years. Other researchers (e.g., Long, 2003) suggest studying those L2 learners whose length of residence is considerably longer—from 5 to 10 years.

But even a long length of residence may in itself be insufficient to ensure access to circumstances favoring language acquisition. Carroll (2001) writes that we do not really know the extent to which L2 learners "spend their days immersed in their own thoughts against a background rumble of noises which make no sense to them, and emerge only occasionally to participate in speech exchanges mostly involving highly ritualised language" (p. 2). Moreover, she claims, SLA researchers are remarkably naive when it comes to the "linguistic lives of L2 learners, most of whom are not and never will be fully linguistically integrated into the societies they have joined" (p. 178).

Carroll (2001) does not provide any independent criteria for what it would actually mean to be "fully linguistically integrated," and one can imagine different dimensions or facets of such integration, including sociocultural ones. For example, might an English as a second language (ESL) learner (of a certain age, perhaps) living in the United States within a linguistic community much like Patty's be expected to know, say, some of the lyrics to the song *If I Only Had a Brain* from the film *The Wizard of Oz* to be considered truly and fully linguistically integrated into that community? In the absence of such a measure, we are probably stuck with relying on observations of the learner's ordinary, everyday behavior and interactions with those who live and work within the native English-speaking linguistic community she or he has joined.

In this sense, Patty is a near-ideal candidate for study; as mentioned earlier, nearly all of her daily interactions—not only within her community and workplace but also within her more intimate circles at home and with her friends—are conducted in English and have been now for well over two decades. It is impossible to estimate the millions of English sentences to which she has been exposed since her arrival in the United States (including the written ones she has encountered throughout her undergraduate and graduate degree programs and in daily newspapers, etc.), but surely it overwhelmingly surpasses the estimate by Birdsong for children during their first 5 years of life. A more in-depth biographical (actually, autobiographical) portrait of Patty is presented in the next chapter, along with some discussion of her motivation to learn English and her assimilation into the target language community.

The bulk of this book, however, focuses on Patty's acquisition of various formal grammatical categories, features, and constructs that have been well described in linguistic theory and the acquisition literature. The length of the data-collection period and comparison of the data at different points over this time period enable us to establish whether a likely steady state has been achieved (rather than our simply assuming it, based on her length of residence in the target-language community), or whether further language development appears to be still ongoing within specific grammatical sub-domains.

A Note on the Data

Most of the data in this book consist of naturalistic production data that come from three audiotaped conversations with Patty, as well as about two dozen written e-mail samples and written answers to written interview questions. The first recording (Recording 1) was made in 1986 when Patty was 32 years old and had been living in the United States for about 10 years. The next two recordings (Recordings 2 and 3) were taped about 2 months apart in 1995, almost 9 years later, during which time she was immersed in a nearly exclusively English-speaking environment. At that point, she had been living in the United States for over 18 years.

Recording 1 is about 34 minutes long and was made at the apartment I was then sharing with one of her closest friends (a mutual friend through whom I first became acquainted with Patty). It is the most spontaneous and naturalistic of the three conversations and includes discussion by Patty of some of her philosophical and religious views with the interviewer (me) and the close mutual friend. Recording 2 is about 75 minutes long, was made at Patty's home, and consists mainly of an autobiographical narrative in response to interview-like questions about her language background and life history. Recording 3 is about a half-hour long and was also made at Patty's home. It includes Patty's husband in the conversation, during which they provided some details about how they met and decided to get married, and some observations about language learning in general and Patty's English in particular. The third recording is more comparable to the first recording in terms of length, degree of informality and spontaneity of the conversation, and the inclusion in the conversation of another interlocutor very close to Patty (i.e., her close friend in Recording 1 and her husband in Recording 3). The data from these recordings were transcribed, independently checked against the tape by another rater with a strong background in phonetics and phonology, and then rechecked. The first recording was independently transcribed at two different times (10 years apart), with the two versions checked against each other and the final version checked and rechecked against the tape.

The written samples come primarily from e-mail messages collected over a period of about 6 years, from early 1997 through 2002. These samples, although possibly more self-consciously monitored as they were written, are nonetheless chatty, colloquial and apparently spontaneous—perhaps as close to natural conversation as written text can be. Most of them are quite short. Some were directed to me personally, and some were sent out to a circle of friends, and mainly concern various informative bits of news, plans, and so on.

Note that these e-mail samples were collected after the third spoken recording was made. As is discussed in chapter 4, for some aspects of Patty's English there are significant differences between her spoken and written production. To help ensure that these differences are actually attributable to the difference between speaking and writing, rather than the possibility that her knowledge of English changed so significantly in the years following the third recording, data from yet another audiotaped conversation (Recording 4) are introduced in chapter 4 in relation to Patty's rate of past-tense marking. This recording was made in 2002, toward the end of the period for which most of the e-mail samples were collected. It is fairly short (approximately 20 minutes long) and was again made at Patty's home, with her husband and daughter present in the room, but only occasionally participating in our conversation. At that point, Patty had been living in the United States for over 25 years. Unless otherwise specified, however (as in chap. 4), the spoken data reported on throughout this book are generally drawn from Recordings 1 to 3.

In addition to these recordings and e-mail samples, there are additional written data, including written answers elicited from Patty in response to written interview questions. There are also Patty's responses to varied grammaticality judgment tasks administered at different time periods, which are described in the following chapters as appropriate.

A Note on the Role of Linguistic Theory in this Study

Models of generative grammar provide, at the very least, some well-articulated and detailed descriptions of many grammatical phenomena of interest in exploring the issue of ultimate attainment in SLA. Within this powerful analytical framework, it is possible to draw on a fairly precise vocabulary of terms and notions for modeling the formal aspects of language. As pointed out by Jackendoff (1997), such formalization permits us to be "more abstract, rigorous and compact in stating our claims" (p. 4). The constructs of UG are presumably not the same as actual mechanisms of language learning (see Wexler & Manzini, 1987, and especially Carroll, 2001, with whom I agree on this point). Nonetheless, these constructs provide us with a way to hypothesize about the content of what has or has not been acquired, a necessary first step in our attempts to formulate a model of the acquisition of a grammar.

For example, the past decade has seen a proliferation of SLA studies that depend on the distinction drawn in linguistic theory between the lexical categories N (noun), V (verb), and A (adjective) and functional categories D (determiner), I (inflection or INFL), and C (complementizer).[9] The functional categories are associated with various formal features such as finiteness, tense, aspect, mood, definiteness, number, and so on that vary in their morphological expression across languages. This cross-linguistic variation, conventionally formulated in UG theory in terms of *parameterization*, has provided a way to frame certain questions and formed the basis for several hypotheses in both first and second language acquisition, but especially in SLA in relation to proposals about the extent and nature of L1 influence (transfer). (See White, 2003b, for a comprehensive overview of many of these proposals.)

Where appropriate throughout the remaining chapters, I present data from Patty within the context of some of these hypotheses as a means of evaluating them using a case-study approach. It should be mentioned that current generative theory is undergoing constant revision, a process to which both L1 and L2 acquisition findings can contribute, along with re-

---

[9] In the traditional generative literature, P (preposition) is usually also considered lexical, but see Baker (2003) for compelling arguments against classifying it as a lexical category.

search from related fields of inquiry such as psycholinguistics, neuroscience, creole genesis, and language evolution and change. It is assumed that readers are familiar with the basic outlines of UG theory (mainly principles-and-parameters theory and notions of phrase structure). I have tried to limit discussion of technical details to those that are necessary for establishing the background context and describing the phenomena under investigation that have given rise to the relevant acquisition proposals. For those readers who may be less interested in theoretical linguistic concerns, I have tried to be lavish in providing examples from the data, so that the reader can get as full a sense as possible of what Patty's English idiolect is like.

Goals and Outline

Overall, the two main objectives of this book are the following: First, to characterize formal aspects of a particular L2 end-state idiolect—that achieved by an informant whose exposure to the L2 has been optimal and of sufficient duration to establish that these aspects of her grammar have indeed longitudinally stabilized. It is hoped that this description contributes to a collective effort within the field of SLA to isolate and identify some of those aspects of L2 knowledge that seem particularly vulnerable to fossilization as well as those that are likely to be more fully acquired. Second, we would like to see whether the findings can be accounted for under recent proposals in the theoretical and language acquisition literature. In this (as in previous) work, I especially concentrate on determining the nature of the relationship between knowledge of abstract grammatical features and production of the morphological and syntactic forms typically assumed to constitute evidence for those features.

The remaining chapters are organized as follows: Chapter 2 introduces background information about Patty, much of it provided autobiographically in her own words within the context of my interviews with her. The second part of the chapter relates this background to questions and claims about the role of motivation and assimilation into the target-language community in determining the state of ultimate attainment in SLA. Chapter 3 investigates at some length the acquisition of the abstract feature of finiteness, set within the context of much literature in both first and second language acquisition linking this fundamental yet elusive formal feature to other properties of grammar. This chapter draws on and further develops arguments and ideas presented in some earlier work (Lardiere, 1998a, 1998b, 2000). Chapter 4 focuses in depth on a particular morphological expression—past-tense marking—including detailed type-token analyses.

Various acquisition hypotheses are evaluated in relation to how well they can account for the observed data. Chapter 5 considers syntactic word order and movement phenomena as articulated within generative linguistic theory—in particular, verb raising and *wh*-movement and the effect of locality (e.g., subjacency) constraints on such movement. Chapter 6 then turns to features associated with nominal determiner phrases (DPs), such as definiteness and number. Chapter 7 concludes with some discussion about theories of fossilization and ultimate attainment, including the role of native language influence and maturational (or so-called "critical period") effects.

2

Introducing Patty

In this chapter, I first introduce the reader to Patty by presenting a brief bio-graphical sketch. This biographical background information is then used in the second part of the chapter as the basis for considering the role of affect and motivation in Patty's acquisition of English specifically, and in fossili-zation more generally.

Some Background Information About Patty

To give the reader a more precise and vibrant picture of Patty's English language use and of her story in her own words, I have taken the liberty of liberally interspersing in italics some of her own quotes from her transcripts about her background, taken from the second and third interviews with her, recorded after she had been living in the United States for more than 18 years.[1] In addition to providing background information about the infor-mant, the rather detailed picture presented here allows us to refer eventually to affective factors and better evaluate the extent to which such factors may have played a role in the outcome of Patty's English proficiency.

Patty was born in 1953 in Indonesia, although her parents were Chinese and spoke Chinese at home and in their local community. Both parents spoke two Chinese languages: Hokkien and Mandarin. Patty reports that she usually spoke Hokkien at home, although occasionally Mandarin, especially with her mother, who was a (Mandarin) Chinese language teacher. At the

---

[1] A note about the transcript symbols: # indicates a repetition or self-correction, an un-bracketed ellipsis notation indicates a pause usually followed by some kind of reformulation, and a square-bracketed ellipsis indicates a true orthographic ellipsis where further conversational material follows or intervenes, which has been omitted here.

age of 2, she began attending a nursery school where her mother taught and where Chinese rather than Indonesian was spoken:

> *Uh, since my mom was a teacher, so I start sch [sk]... to going to school, like nursery. Uh, start going to school with her when I was two.*

In addition, her family employed an Indonesian maid, from whom she learned some Indonesian as a young child. Therefore, Patty claims that by the time she was 3, she was already essentially trilingual in Hokkien, Mandarin, and Indonesian, with Hokkien her dominant family language:

> *Because we have a maid also, who is Indonesian who speak, uh, Indonesian to me. So I guess, you know, I learn it when I was little. At two uh, at two or three. I already, uh, like uh, automatically like, we spoke two languages in our household. Or three sometimes.*

Patty's primary schooling was in an Indonesian public school, where Indonesian was the language of instruction and where she acquired literacy in that language.

> *[A]ctually I was brought up in Indonesian school, so I wrote and speak fluently in Indonesia. Also, um, you know ... but I do not write in Chinese, I only uh, speak.*

During this time, her mother taught her how to write some Chinese characters, but Patty indicates that it was not until she was about 12 that she began to learn how to read and write Chinese in earnest:

> *Well, I already know # knew, you know, I'm not ... like maybe I knew about hundred character, but not as many as I should. Like simple thing, because my mom teach us after school hour. [...] And then, uh, after twelve, after twelve to thirteen, I take, uh, I start to took it seriously.*

At this point, she began keeping a journal in Chinese, writing in it every day, and sharing it with her Chinese violin teacher, a mentor and tutor whom she credits with correcting her written Chinese and helping her quickly acquire more advanced literacy in that language:

*And then I have my teacher, who's my violin teacher, and she # he
would look at my journal and give me correction. And that is how I
improve very very f... uh, you know, like incredibly fast.*

She also notes that in the fifth or sixth grade, at around the age of 9 or
10, some English-language lessons were introduced at school, consisting
mainly of simple vocabulary:

*Yes, we start to learn English. And we have a book. Just for vo-
cabulary, and you know, very simple, like "umbrella."*

In 1965, a military coup in Indonesia led to a period of massive political unrest there. Ethnic Chinese were among those especially targeted as
suspected communist sympathizers in an anticommunist purge and massa-
cres that eventually resulted in hundreds of thousands of deaths in that
country. In a governmental effort to promote a common national identity
and repress ethnic identity, Chinese schools were closed, Chinese-language
newspapers and books were banned, and signs written in Chinese were for-
bidden; in 1967, the public celebration of Chinese New Year was also
banned.

*So I ... well uh, when I was thirteen, from thirteen to fourteen
there's political change in Indonesia. So my school, which is Indonesian school, was closed. [...] And uh, I eventually also get into
the Chinese school for maybe six month. And then school was
close.*

At the age of 14, Patty left Indonesia to go to China; as she explains:

*Because of the uh, patriotic # patriotic. Because uh, in 1965 Indo-
nesia, uh, they kill a lot of Chinese, and then Chi # China also send
a lot of boat to the refugee who want to go back to China.*

She arrived in China in 1968, at the age of 14, during that country's
cultural revolution. She had wanted to become a dancer and had planned to
stay with a cousin who was a dancer in the Peking Opera, but quickly dis-
covered that that would be impossible in the political climate there. She
then moved to a dormitory in Shanghai to be near another cousin and because she hoped the standard of living would be higher there. In excerpts
from her own extended, vivid recounting:

She's in Peking and she was a dancer in a Peking Opera, so she perform and always send me the picture. [...] She came all the way down to Canton to pick me up. But then I saw everything is really uh ... it's like a turbulen[Ø] there. There's a cultural revolution, and there's nothing going on. [...] And I cannot be a dancer either, because there's nothing going on there, and uh, the school was uh, half close, the only thing that, you know ... everyday uh, the student just get together, you know, like, have a meeting, and they would just uh, talk about, um ... like the teacher, how do you call that, like, uh, put the teacher in front of the crowd and then just, you know, either ... sometime they kick him, and you just have to be "yes, yes, yes" all the time, you know? So it's very scary in a way. You don't know who you should associate with, he or she may be the next line # in line, and you see a lot of teacher who # who have a very good education, and suddenly they are the one who clean your bathroom, and they clean uh, everything. [...] So ... and then after awhile close # uh ... school[s/'s] close, and uh, actually we have all the worker came to be a teacher and all the worker[s?] sit around, you know, on the desk, and have paper in front of them, and they just read [/rid/] the paper. [...]

And also what I want, like not even think about dancing but um, everyday I don't know how to ... um, there's no school, I cannot even practice violin because I cannot even play any notes, any Western music. Um, I can only play like seven song uh, by # by you know, chairman's uh, wife, so there's seven # seven opera that you can only listen to and there's only two movie to go to and uh, sometime[s?] Sunday I would just stay in bed all day, and I would just get out to go to uh, dinner and then came back home and just lay in bed again. Um, you just so cold in the winter.

Patty lived in China for 2 years—until she was 16. In 1970, with the help of her grandmother and some family friends, she was able to get out of mainland China and move to Hong Kong, where she now had to begin to use both English and Cantonese in her new high school:

So I ... well, I was suddenly have to wri[te?] # try English, and also um, read English. We don't spoke that much English, because uh, we have oral with uh, with couple English woman, but it's very very slow. [...]

[I]n English school they have two Chinese literature and Chinese history that you have to # that you have to ... uh, mandatory that you have to take. And they'll # they're even read [/rid/] in

*Cantonese, so, I have to tell my ... because there's a poem that you
have to memorize, I just tell the teacher that I ... there's no way for
me to # to spoke, I mean I # I hardly learn to speak Cantonese and
how can I read in Cantonese? [...] When they want you to memorize you have to stand up and you memorize from, you know, the
whole poem, beginning to the end, so you have to # you have to
really, you know, spoke it loud. And I just don't # don't think I can
do that in Cantonese, so they let me spoke it in Mandarin.*

Aside from the Chinese literature and history courses, English was the
primary language of instruction in Patty's other courses at school in Hong
Kong. She emphasizes that her first year in school there was very difficult;
that it was obviously hard for her to understand what her teachers were saying in English, and that she needed special attention, which she was able to
get from a family friend who helped her with English. She notes that, by the
end of her first year in Hong Kong, she had become very fluent in Cantonese; however, English was still a major problem:

*I have friends from Indonesia also speak Hokkien, and also have #
have a lot of friends um, who is Hong # Hong Kongese, well, who
is Cantonese, so uh, after about a year I'm very fluent in Cantonese. So I start um, both languages, but it is almost not ... um, I
don't have any uh, friend who spoke English. So, I would say I ...
after school I didn't speak English at all. And also when you were
at school, you just listen mostly, because you sit there and then,
you know, the teacher would just like, explain things, you know,
this and that ... comprehension ... uh, you don't have a chance to
really speak in English, and I remember we have one, maybe one
... uh, maybe once a week we have oral class which we have English woman sit around and then we spoke English to her. And I remember it's really hard for me because my # my mind would think
about, you know ... it's like, you think about it and then you spoke,
so your lang... # your sentence is not like fluently, it's like in a #
um, in a different section.*

Patty also explicitly comments on how much more difficult it was for
her to understand English spoken by native English speakers, rather than by
her Chinese teachers:

*Uh, I hear better with the Chinese person who speak English than
a native, because I catch it much better, and I remember when I
went to uh, see movie, and I # I have to read subtitle because I*

*cannot hear anything they say. [...] Yeah, and then I have um, I
have a math teacher who is English, and I did so poorly in my
math because half the class I didn't understand what he's talking
about in the class, and uh, that's my lowest point in math. Because
I don't know why I understand Chinese better when they spoke
English.*

After 3 years in Hong Kong, Patty finished high school. She then
worked for another 3 years there at an import-export company, during
which time she says she spoke no English at all. In high school, she had met
and eventually become engaged to a Vietnamese immigrant, S., with whom
she spoke only Cantonese—a second language for both of them. However,
after graduating, S. emigrated to the United States with his family; so, during her last year in Hong Kong, Patty began applying to schools in the
United States so that she could join him. She took the TOEFL, which was
required for admission, twice; although she does not remember the scores,
she says she did rather poorly, but somewhat better on the second try. She
was eventually accepted at a small junior college in the city where her boyfriend's family lived.

*Because it's uh [/a?] requirement to came to United ... I # I was
applying to junior college here, and then it's requirement to took
uh, the TOEFL test. And I don't think mine score is very high, but I
just barely pass the # uh, the # the minimum.*

Patty arrived in the United States in 1976, at the age of 22. Her recol-
lection of her first year in school in the United States is very positive:

*[I]t's a wonderful uh # wonderful uh, memory because uh, I have
the most wonderful teacher there. Professor? Yeah. Um, that's why
it ... I change my major on my first year to accounting. After all
I'm not, uh... or after all, my math is really good! I just uh, find out
that uh, I'm very good in # at math and I really like it a lot. And I
have a very good uh, psychology teacher, um, and it's all in Eng...
um, I think I # I really learn a lot from the first year, to listen, uh,
and then get use to it.*

After arriving in the United States, Patty lived in her fiancé's house-
hold, which was situated in an urban Asian neighborhood, and where the
primary language spoken among family members was Vietnamese. She did
not know Vietnamese, but rather used Cantonese with them as the primary
lingua franca. She also primarily used Cantonese throughout the neighbor-

hood, for example, for ordering in the local restaurants, shopping, etc. But, of course, she was using English exclusively at school. She recalls that her fiancé's sister spoke the best English in the family and often helped her with her schoolwork:

> *I was living with S's parents and who spoke no English. We spoke uh # we speak in uh, Cantonese. And her sister, who is a physical therapy, and she spoke more English. And she have a very good background, um, so, I have a chance to listen um, to her. And on my first year college, uh, she really help me a lot. When I need to do my composition, uh, which I s... I have a # I have most # mostly difficulty to write than to read [/rid/].*

Within a year of arriving, Patty had also taken on a waitressing job at a large, downtown restaurant where the entire staff was Asian or Asian-American, but not necessarily Chinese—although there was at least one Taiwanese waitress who spoke Mandarin Chinese; there were also several Japanese, Thai, and Malaysian immigrants, along with a Japanese-American waitress and a Hawaiian-born waitress who were both monolingual American-English speakers. The lingua franca at work was English. Most of the customers were Americans, and she credits the job with providing her an additional opportunity outside of school to interact with Americans. She had also begun to take dance classes and to occasionally play violin in a local university orchestra; in these activities again, she began meeting and socializing with more Americans. About her orchestral violin playing, for example, she says:

> *Yeah, I did that for... I did that until 1980, and then I'm more serious in dancing, so I give up, uh ... actually I have a ... I also take lesson in violin, with P.* [a professional violinist in one of the well-known local orchestras] *[...] and um, I do not like to play in front of people, and she keep asking me to get a concert. And since I'm not going to do any concert, so it's like ... so I # I stop taking the class after awhile.*

Patty did indeed become more involved in dancing, an interest she has continued to pursue, and she has participated in numerous local dance performances throughout the city.

The small junior college Patty was attending closed after her second year there, and she transferred to a local 4-year university, from which she received her bachelor's degree in accounting. She subsequently also completed a master's degree in 1982, then began working full-time as an accountant in a local computer-leasing and office-supply company. She and S. married, although they continued to live with his family, and were subsequently joined there (at various times) for extended stays by her brother and one of her cousins, who had come over to the United States to attend school. During this time, then, until about 1985, Patty was speaking primarily English outside her home (e.g., school, work, dance class, and various social events), primarily Hokkien with her own relatives at home, and primarily Cantonese with her husband and his family members at home, with English now the primary language used when everyone was together. Her husband's professional training and career in the United States as an architect likewise provided him with abundant interaction with Americans, and both he and Patty spoke English in social situations with Americans. In the meantime, they had also bought a house in the suburbs and moved out of their inner-city Asian neighborhood, so that English became the primary language of their neighbors and local community as well.

In 1985, Patty and her husband separated and Patty moved out to live by herself in another suburban neighborhood. They subsequently divorced about a year later. During this period, Patty estimates she was speaking English about 80% of the time and Chinese (either Cantonese, Mandarin, or Hokkien) about 20%:

> *I move out '85 and then I live in, um ... by myself for a year. [...]*
> *Maybe 80 to 20. Is it? Yeah. Yeah. Because I don't speak Chinese*
> *that much. Uh, my Cantonese after I left S. was really uh ... the*
> *only person I talk to maybe [/may be?] C., you know?*

It was also during this time, in 1986, that the first recording of Patty's conversation was audiotaped. She had been living in the United States for just over 10 years.

Patty became temporarily involved in a self-actualization organization in 1987 and met her second husband, A., a native-English speaker, there; they married in 1989. She describes how they met in that context:

> *It's a very intense ... we spend from twelve noontime to twelve uh,*
> *midnight, everyday for the next five days. [...] So it's like we ...*
> *because during the training you have to reveal a lot of your past,*
> *your emotion, your um, like, uh, everything you deal with, trust, uh,*
> *a lot of issue in life, so [...] three days is like two years, huh? [...]*
> *I think I br... I # I # I was have a breakthrough in # in uh, this*
> *training, right?*
>
> *Anyway, so, uh, first time, uh, I remember my dance company*
> *have a party ... [pr] # uh, promo, I think, so I invite A. to the party*

and then meanwhile there's ... I was dating um, a man that I met in a club previous week. So he was waiting for me all this night, until like almost twelve I was late because of the training. I don't know what time I # I'm gonna be there, so he left and he was very upset and he sit by himself, alone. So by the time A. and I uh, arrive there he left already, so ... and the party's kind of uh, you know, at the end, so we were dance for like, couple dance, right? [To her husband] *[...] Well, that's five days later you ask me if I want to be your steady girlfriend. [...] And then uh, so we did [g]... uh, we decided to get marry.*

A's family is highly educated, his English is "standard," and he is talkative and extremely articulate. Apparently, in the early stages of his relationship with Patty, he tried to help her improve her English. She recalls:

I guess I speak more English because, uh, when I came home he's the only person I spoke to, right? I spoke more English. And at beginning, he try to correct me a lot, about my English, about my pronunciation, right? But then after awhile, he just give up. He did not try to do it anymore.

Patty's husband A. is neither a linguist nor an academic, but he is keenly aware of his own native-speaker knowledge of English despite not remembering formal terms or prescriptive grammar rules. The following conversational excerpt reveals that Patty in fact did learn such terms and rules and may have consciously tried to apply them:

A: *You know what I remember it being funny when we would um ... when I would correct your English? Like, I know what's correct. Generally. I mean, I have a pretty good knowledge but I don't know what the names of ...*
P: *It's my pronunciation?* [= "pronounce-iation"]
A: *No, you ... I # I would correct you, and* [to interviewer:] *she'd go "Well no, you're wrong" because of this rule of English grammar, this past participle ..., present tense of the ..., past of that ... I'd go "What are you talking about? You're wrong ..."*
P: [Laughing] *Past participle ...*
A: *... You can't put those words together, you know? That doesn't fit. I just know how things are supposed to sound. So I probably had pretty good teachers, or I have great powers of osmosis.*

At the time of the third tape-recorded interview, in 1995, Patty had been living in the United States for over 18 years. She had assumed American citizenship as soon as she became eligible. She had been married to A. for 6 years, and was working in a managerial position within her company. The nearly 9 years between the first and third recordings were spent in complete immersion in an American English-speaking environment—at home, at work, in her community, and in most social situations. During this time, her primary Chinese-speaking contact was with a cousin living in a different part of the state who is similarly married to an American and immersed in a completely English-speaking environment. Patty estimated that she spoke with her cousin by telephone approximately weekly and visited her approximately monthly. In private conversations, they tend to speak to each other in Hokkien, but use English in social situations when friends or other family members are present. Patty has also kept in touch, although somewhat less regularly, with a close childhood friend who also speaks Hokkien and Mandarin and lives in a distant state.

When asked whether she ever encounters language-related difficulties at work, Patty replied that she sometimes has a little trouble understanding telephone messages, although she felt she was getting better with more common American surnames:

> *A. left me a message, [...] and I hear it so many time! I cannot get the three uh, digit. [...] I hear it so many time, I # I call and it's always wrong number, so I ... three # three times I try it, and I give up, and then I'm ... I # I # I copy it to my friend [...]. And she say that she have to listen it ... she have to listen twice, but she got the number right. [...] And I still have ... sometimes if people call me and uh, left me message, I still have a hard time sometime to hear their name. [...] Before, I realize that a year ago, or two ago, when they told me their last name I have a ... the ... I have a hard time. But now I'm mostly I don't have that, uh ... like if they ... if # if I know, like, you know, "Collins" or, uh, they say it and I just write it down I know how to spell it, you know? Like I have less, uh, hard time than # than before. [...] You know, uh, they have one last name was so long, some of them.*

To date, Patty's language environment has remained nearly exclusively English. Within the past few years, she has become quite friendly with an elderly Chinese couple (both doctors), occasionally socializing with them exclusively in Mandarin; another cousin has recently moved into the area, with whom Patty speaks primarily Hokkien in private, and English in public. Thus, although her home and work environments remain exclusively

English-speaking (including now her interaction with her young daughter in addition to her husband), Patty's social environment occasionally includes Chinese speakers as well. It remains to be seen whether this will have any significant effect on her English over time.

On The Role of Motivational and Affective Factors

It is often assumed that fossilization occurs because learners have progressed to a point where they are communicatively competent "enough" to handle the linguistic demands of interaction with the target language community at whatever level of engagement they are motivated to pursue. When learners reach that point, the enormous expenditure of conscious effort required to progress further may simply outweigh any perceived benefit. The following is a representative example of this view, as expressed in an online TESL discussion forum:

> Fossilization is proof of a stable linguistic system. We all "fossilize". When we reach a point at which we are functioning perfectly well in our linguistic community, we cease to develop, grammatically speaking. We may add a few new vocabulary items, but we don't add too many other new structures. The exception to this is … [l]earning directed from personal motivation. We perceive a difference between our linguistic performance and that of the community around us. This can happen for second language speakers or for first language speakers wishing to adopt a new dialect. Contrary to popular belief, it *does* happen. A wonderful pop-culture example is the singer Celine Dion—(French Canadian). On her first appearance on US TV about three years ago, in very basic English explained her desire to "cross-over" to US audiences. Now three years later, there's barely an accent detectable.[2]

A few interesting questions immediately arise here. First of all, although fossilization does imply the persistent or permanent stabilization of one's linguistic system (at least in some domains), and this sort of final- or steady-state knowledge also characterizes native as well as non-native speakers, it cannot mean only that. What would still need to be explained is why native speakers converge far more uniformly on the target language, that is, in much closer conformity with the input, and with each other, than the typical adult second language learner.

---

[2] Posted to the TESL-L Electronic Discussion Forum on January 4, 1993, by Maggie Sokolik, cited here with her permission.

Second, how is "functioning perfectly well" to be self-evaluated by both native and non-native speakers? Extending the construct of fossilization to native speakers on the basis of self-assessed degree of functioning (or acculturation) within a particular community is highly problematic.[3] If such self-assessment held as well for *native speakers*, we would likely encounter far more striking grammatical variation among native speakers within a given linguistic community than we actually do; for example, we might expect the steady-state representation of, say, syllable structure or definiteness features or unaccusativity by extremely shy, anti-social, or hostile introverts to deviate noticeably from that of "better functioning" members of the community. Clearly, we need to distinguish the (nativelike) representation of more formal aspects of a grammar from pragmatically driven communicative competence. The very fact that communicatively competent second language learners *can* function perfectly well even with an apparently divergent L2 grammatical system is evidence that nativelike attainment is to some extent quite independent of the ability to function in a given linguistic community. Moreover, it is not clear at all—and strikes me as highly unlikely—that young children determine whether or not they are functioning perfectly well enough at any point before they have actually gone ahead and acquired the grammar in question. (I return to this point below.)

Finally, why should adult language acquisition even require in the first place such an enormous and often conscious expenditure of effort and perseverance—that is, be so contingent on personal motivation—as compared to child language acquisition? A motivation-based explanation necessarily begs the question of why some aspects of linguistic knowledge seem to be so much harder to acquire than others (and therefore require much more motivation in order to overcome the difficulty in acquiring them). It cannot explain, for example, why certain morphosyntactic elements of the L2 (e.g., pronominal case selection in English) seem to be so much more easily acquirable and thus require so much less motivation to fully master, than others (e.g., 3SG -*s*). An explanation for this type of discrepancy must lie elsewhere; depending on one's linguistic and psycholinguistic framework(s), one could, for example, invoke functional utility, degree of perceptual sali-

---

[3] In a finding that adds an interesting twist to the view that when learners are satisfied with their level of attainment they stabilize, Moyer (2004) reported that L2 learners who were "relatively *dis*satisfied" with their own level of phonological attainment in the target language "tend to do little overtly to improve it" (p. 66; italics added), and were (perhaps unsurprisingly) more likely to be rated by native speakers as non-nativelike.

ence, UG (in-)accessibility, L1 transfer, processing/memory retrieval factors, or some combination of these.

In summary, then, although the degree of interaction required by a language learner within a certain linguistic community (as self-assessed) may indeed influence the extent to which that learner becomes communicatively competent, it provides little insight as to why certain formal aspects of the grammar fossilize more readily than others, and why native speakers do not similarly fossilize. In the remainder of this chapter, I build on the preceding background information about Patty in considering in greater depth one of the more prominent theories about the role of social and affective factors in second language acquisition—that of Schumann (1978, 1986, 1997), who argues, in a nutshell, that "variable success in second language acquisition (SLA) is emotionally driven" (1997, p. xv).

The basis for Schumann's claim lies in earlier work that viewed second language acquisition as the product of acculturation, in which the crucial variable was degree of integration within the target language community. In this *acculturation model*, states Schumann (1997), "the learner is seen as acquiring the second language to the degree he or she acculturates to the target language group" (p. xviii). Among the forces influencing acculturation are group dominance patterns centered around political, cultural, technical, and/or economic superiority, and integration strategies ranging from preservation to adaptation to assimilation. Because these forces are formulated in terms of *group* identity, it is not immediately clear how they would apply to individuals such as Patty following her arrival in North America (although we can see how they might apply to her family during her childhood years, which were spent in a classic language contact situation, that of members of an affluent and sizable yet politically harassed and socially insular minority immigrant community in Indonesia).

By the time Patty arrived in the United States, she had already been living apart from her native group for 8 years during a highly formative period of her life (ages 14–22) so that it is possible her sense of original group identity was somewhat diffused at that point; moreover, she immigrated to the United States at age 22 to join a boyfriend who was not a member of that group. By that time, she had already lived in three different countries and visited a few others, and her outlook had become cosmopolitan, urban, sophisticated, liberal, open, and in certain respects, already quite Westernized. On an individual level, Patty's integration pattern in the United States has been assimilative—that is, adopting the lifestyle and many of the values of the target language group—claimed by Schumann to foster maximum acculturation and "thus a high degree of language learning" (p. xviii).

In addition to social group factors, there are individual affective factors influencing second language acquisition that center around attitude and motivation. For example, having a positive attitude toward target language speakers would lead to greater contact with those speakers and thus better foster target language acquisition (p. xviii). Motivation may be *integrative* (having an interest in the speakers of the target language) or *instrumental* (having "more utilitarian goals" such as getting a job, p. xix). Schumann notes, however, that it has proved difficult to measure the social and psychological components of acculturation and assess its changes over time within individuals. We return later to the issue of assessing attitude and motivation in Patty's case specifically.

Several previous studies have attempted to account for observed (non-)acquisition of a second language within the framework of the acculturation model. Perhaps the best known of these, and most relevant for our purposes, is the 3-year case study by Schmidt (1983) of Wes, a Japanese artist who immigrated to Hawaii as an adult. Schmidt writes:

> [I]n our frequent assessments of nonnative speakers as having just enough English to communicate in limited situations, there is an assumption that if communicative needs were greater and psychological and social distance less, much greater control of the grammatical structures of the target language could have been acquired without formal instruction. This assumption is made explicit in Schumann's "acculturation model"... which claims that two groups of variables, social and affective, cluster into a single variable of acculturation which is the major causal variable in SLA, i.e. that the degree to which a learner acculturates to the target language group will control the degree to which he acquires a second language. (p. 139)

Schmidt's (1983) study, then, attempted to provide evidence for the acculturation model in a case where his subject's social and psychological distance from the target language group was low and his communicative need and degree of interaction high, thus predicting facilitated acquisition of English. Schmidt additionally addressed the issue (left vague in Schumann's work) of identifying exactly *what* was acquired, extending his analysis to cover sociolinguistic as well as more formal grammatical aspects of English.

To the extent that they could be assessed, the overwhelming majority of relevant factors comprising social and psychological distance should have facilitated acquisition in Wes's case; these include communicative need (high), type and amount of interaction (high), social dominance and interaction patterns (equal and adaptive, respectively), L1 group enclosure/cohesiveness (low), attitudes toward the L2 group (positive), intended length of residence (indefinite or permanent), culture and language shock (low), empathy/social outreach (high), inhibition/fear of appearing foolish (low), motivation type (integrative and also instrumental), motivational drive for communication (very high), and preferred learning style (naturalistic). Possibly negative factors include cultural dissimilarity (Japanese vs. [Hawaiian-] American) and very low motivation for formal language study (e.g., classroom or other tutored study).

A word about age is in order here—although several researchers have found age of arrival/exposure to the target language environment a significant predictor of ultimate attainment in the L2 (e.g., Bialystok & Hakuta, 1994, 1999; Birdsong, 1999, 2006; Birdsong & Molis, 2001; Flege, 1999; Johnson & Newport, 1989, 1991),[4] Schmidt points out that within the acculturation model, age-related effects can be reduced to affective factors, for example, "problems of attitude, motivation, language and culture shock, and so on" (p. 141). Thus if affective factors are favorable, as in Wes's case, the effect of age should be neutral with regard to acquisition. I return to this point shortly.[5]

---

[4] The studies cited here differ as to whether ultimate L2 proficiency continues to decline in a linear relation to AOA beyond a specified critical period. See Birdsong (1999) for additional discussion.

[5] In a recent study of factors most highly correlated with nativelike attainment of German as a second language (as judged by native speakers from speech samples), Moyer (2004) found the following to be significant at the $p \leq .01$ level: bilingual (vs. monolingual) childhood, (earlier) age of onset (AO), length of residence (LOR), personal desire to acquire the target language, learners' satisfaction with their own phonological attainment, self-rating of spoken German, amount of formal German language instruction, amount of "indirect" (German-medium) instruction in subjects other than German language study, and frequency of spoken interaction with native speakers. Of these, the top five in descending order of significance were: satisfaction with own phonological attainment, length of residence, personal desire to acquire the target language, age of onset, and indirect formal instruction in subjects other than German language study. Moyer also treats the influence of age of onset as "essentially connected to psychological, social, and instructional aspects of the learner's experience" (p. 96), although she observes that the role of AO alone does exert an independent main effect and cannot be dismissed. Moreover, Moyer found that, in her study, similar to the findings of Johnson and Newport (1989), no one with an AO beyond 15 obtained a nativelike rating.

In Patty's case, AO would appear to exert the strongest influence among Moyer's "top five" variables, because (as I discuss further shortly) Patty would rank highly on personal desire to acquire the target language, length of residence, and amount of indirect instruction, yet would almost certainly be rated by native speakers as "definitely nonnative" on Moyer's assessment scale. Regarding the factor of self-satisfaction with phonological attainment, it is noteworthy (and comports with Moyer's findings) that Patty has occasionally expressed dissatisfaction with her own English pronunciation. This is the variable that correlated most highly with attainment in Moyer's study, and yet Moyer herself notes that it may simply be a realistic assessment of one's current abilities, *(Continued)*

Schmidt (1983) found that Wes showed far more development in the acquisition of sociolinguistic aspects of language use than in grammatical competence over time. He notes that over the 3-year observation period during which Wes's interaction with native speakers was "extensive and intensive," there was nonetheless a general lack of progress in the acquisition of morphosyntax such that, among the grammatical morphemes analyzed, and using 90% correct in obligatory contexts as the criterion for acquisition, nothing moved "from unacquired to acquired status" by the end of that period (pp. 145–146). Moreover, the "rather dismal picture" presented by Schmidt's grammatical morpheme analysis extended to other areas of the grammar as well, including a lack of productive subject-auxiliary inversion in questions, expletive subjects, relative clauses, and passives. In sum, Schmidt writes that Wes's English language development "in terms of what is generally considered to be the heart of SLA, the acquisition of productive grammatical rules, has been minimal and almost insignificant" (pp. 150–151).

As Schmidt points out, however, the failure of Wes to acquire much of the grammatical component of his second language cannot be due to social distance factors, poor attitudes toward native speakers, or lack of integrative motivation. Therefore, although such factors may be important for the development of communicative competence, they seem to have little effect on improving grammatical competence. That is, Schmidt concludes that the degree of acculturation as defined within the acculturation model seems *not* to be the primary factor in accounting for variable linguistic achievement in SLA (p. 169); moreover, the ability of Wes to communicate well despite his lack of grammatical control suggests that grammatical competence is at least partially independent of other components of communicative competence (p. 172).

At this point, let us focus a bit more closely on the role of motivation in Wes's L2 attainment (by the end of the observation period). Schmidt notes that motivation was the most difficult variable to assess, depending on whether that assessment should necessarily include the willingness and/or ability to engage in conscious *formal* study of the language quite aside from immersion in the target language environment and extensive interaction with its speakers. That is, Wes had strong integrative motivation and was

---

"and therefore not particularly informative or of great explanatory value" (p. 76). She also observes that this self-satisfaction factor is "connected significantly" to opportunities for contact and interaction with NSs (p. 76); however, this correlation would fail with respect to Patty, because the magnitude of such contact and interaction in her case is totally beyond question.

"committed to learning English through natural interaction" with native speakers, but was essentially uninterested in formal classroom study and was clearly more concerned with communication than with the analytical study of form (p. 143).

However, as Schmidt points out, it is important not to confound the variable of affect with that of formal instruction, as this would trivialize the affective argument. He writes, "The claim that acculturation and affective factors are the major causal variable in SLA, with instruction playing only a minor role, can only be empirically justified if the model recognizes the possibility of individuals with positive affect but no instruction" (p. 173), concluding that adults seem not to be able to acquire the grammar of their L2 through interaction alone.

The role of motivation also continues to occupy a central position in more recent studies aimed at understanding its psychological and neurobiological underpinnings (Pulvermüller & Schumann, 1994; Schumann, 1997). Within Schumann's (1997) framework, learner outcomes are determined by an individual's stimulus-appraisal mechanism, associated in particular with a region of the brain known as the amygdala, which "assesses the motivational significance and emotional relevance of stimuli" and accordingly allocates attention and memory resources to language learning (p. xix). Such appraisals then lead to "action patterns that enhance or inhibit language acquisition" (p. 21), and underlie what has been considered "motivation" in SLA. Schumann writes that "the brain makes stimulus appraisals, and patterns of appraisal constitute motivations" (p. xx), and also that motivation "may simply consist of patterns of stimulus appraisal" (p. 237). Because appraisal systems are a product of the past developmental and emotional experiences of an individual learner, each is unique, accounting for the wide range of variance found in adult learner outcomes. Within this model, there seems to be little significance attributed to the role of L1 transfer in SLA, or to linguistic universals, except to the extent that groups of learners, "for cultural reasons, occasionally make similar appraisals about language learning" (p. 2). I return to this point below.

Again, we find ourselves back to the question of *why* the variable of motivation should be so crucial in determining ultimate attainment in adult SLA; that is, why such an enormous amount of conscious effort and perseverance should be so necessary in the first place, unlike in child language acquisition, and why some aspects of language are apparently so much more difficult to acquire than others. In fact, in examining a bit more closely the case studies provided by Schumann, one can discern evidence for another factor in language learning of perhaps equal or even greater significance than motivation and emotional affect, referred to by Schumann as *aptitude*. According to Schumann (citing [J.] Carroll, 1965, 1981), aptitude includes learner characteristics such as phonemic coding ability, associative memory for vocabulary acquisition, grammatical sensitivity, and "inductive language learning ability" (i.e., "the capacity to determine patterns of meaning and form in a language sample" (Schumann, 1997, pp. 154–155). That seems to cover quite a large chunk of language learning. Schumann observes that aptitude is not independent of stimulus appraisal, and that one is likely to find language learning pleasant and self-enhancing *if* he has high aptitude and "learns with facility." However, lack of aptitude is likely to generate withdrawal from language learning: "It is probably extremely rare for people to become proficient or expert in an area for which they lack aptitude" (p. 155).

It appears, then, that what Schumann is referring to as aptitude may be the more important and logically prior factor to motivation in language learning. Certainly, the less aptitude one has, the greater the motivation would be needed to persevere in the face of continuing difficulty, shame, and frustration; without aptitude, the language learning process is likely to be "so long and so insulting to one's self and social image, that the effort would be abandoned" (p. 155).

We might assume that the various subfactors of aptitude cited by Schumann, such as phonemic coding ability, associative memory, grammatical sensitivity, and inductive language learning ability, are available to very young children (which seems to be determined after the fact; for instance, by looking at the relative uniformity of the steady state achieved in these respects by native speakers). In other words, we might conclude that they have "perfect" aptitude. We would then be in a position to see why children apparently do not require any particular degree of motivation to acquire these aspects of their native language.[6] That is, given that stimulus-appraisal systems are a function of developmental emotional experience and are thus unique to individuals, we would expect the outcome of child language acquisition to be much less uniform if such appraisals constituted a primary variable in the acquisition of the phonemes, vocabulary, grammar, and patterns of meaning-form correspondences in their L1. However, we can also now discern a possible explanation for why Wes demonstrated a deficit in at least one of these abilities—grammatical sensitivity—

---

[6] Pulvermüller and Schumann (1994) assume that "healthy children exposed to one language are always motivated to learn it" (p. 688). Within Schumann's more recent stimulus-appraisal approach, however, it is not clear how the very mechanism that is used to account specifically for the wide variance in ultimate attainment among adult learners could similarly be applied to children in accounting for their "inevitable" acquisition of their native language (p. 682). More on this follows in the text.

independently of and despite his high degree of integrative motivation and positive emotional attitude toward native English speakers and toward communicating with them in English: apparently poor aptitude in this regard. It thus looks as if some sort of (mainly grammatical) aptitude, or some subset of associated abilities, is a truly necessary condition for nativelike success in acquisition; that all normal children have it in acquiring their native language; and that it appears to diminish (most likely in differential or *modular* respects) as a function of increasing age among adult language learners (e.g., Birdsong 1999, 2006).

Pulvermüller and Schumann (1994) model the distinction between grammatical ability and motivation in language learning as the specifying of [±g] (grammatical) and [±m] (motivational) features. respectively. They propose that the feature [–g] characterizes all late language learners; that is, all learners beyond the hypothesized critical period for acquisition "will always show some problems with the acquisition of phonological and syntactic rules and units" (p. 688).[7] Motivation, or the [±m] feature, however, may be variable among late learners, such that these learners can be characterized as either [+m, –g] or [–m, –g] according to whether they are motivated or unmotivated.[8] Thus, the authors claim, "the large variance in language abilities found in late learners reflects their degree of motivation, which can vary dramatically among adults" (p. 689).

Let us return now to Patty's case and ask what a model based on affective factors can and cannot account for. Like Wes, Patty appears to have been highly integratively motivated and, having immersed herself within and even eventually marrying a member of the target language community,

---

[7] The authors note that their proposal is not sufficiently developed to explain exceptionally good language learning among adults, who would presumably have to be characterized as [+g, +m]; Birdsong (1999) points out that this population is not insignificant, constituting perhaps about 10% to 15% of those immersed in the target language for a substantial length of time (3–5 years, based on his study of French SLA), and therefore should not be dismissed as "peripheral" (Birdsong, 1999, p. 15). Pulvermüller and Schumann suggest that such exceptional acquisition can be explained by individual variation in either "myelination and plasticity of the language cortex" or "exceptionally strong dopaminergic input to the forebrain" (leading to new "assemblies" or connections with earlier learned elements that are associated with positive emotional states; p. 720). Because neither Wes nor Patty appear to be among this minority percentage, at least in some obvious respects, I let the matter rest here for now.

[8] The authors of course recognize the non-binary nature of syntactic abilities and motivation, and thus propose a modification by which the feature values are actually assigned in a continuum from 0 to 1, without, however, indicating how these more precise values are to be calculated.

clearly demonstrated an apparently positive attitude toward that community. Unlike Wes, she did have some formal training in English, both in Hong Kong and after arriving in the United States, and in both places English was the medium of instruction for other classroom subjects as well. It is true that there was no particular integrative reason for her to learn English while in Hong Kong; however, there was an instrumental one: initially, to do well in her studies, and eventually, to obtain the minimal TOEFL score needed to gain admission to an American university so that she could join her boyfriend in the United States.

Therefore, it seems quite clear that we can ascribe to Patty a very high degree of motivation, characterizing her generally as [+m], although, in accord with Schmidt's observations about Wes's emphasis on communication over formal study, a more fine-grained assessment is elusive. Patty's eventual discontinuation of English language study per se was at least in part a consequence of severe time limitations imposed by full-time study of the material needed to satisfy the requirements for her undergraduate and graduate degrees, working more than full-time (often at more than one job) in an English-speaking milieu, and participating in music and dance activities in addition to having a rich social life with English-speaking friends. How are we to weigh the relative contribution of these activities as opposed to continued formal language study when assessing degrees of motivation (see footnote 8)? The assessment problem seems especially acute given that the illustrative assessment questionnaires provided by Schumann (1997) are clearly geared toward stimulus appraisal within the foreign language classroom environment, and thus are not obviously applicable to situations such as Patty's—that of an immigrant to the United States in a target-language immersion context.[9]

Furthermore, let us reconsider the earlier concerns of Schmidt (1983) about the confounding of affect with formal instruction as "the major causal variable in SLA" (p. 173). Schumann (1997) includes a case-study profile of an L2 learner of French, Barbara Hilding (BH), whose motivation, from an interactional standpoint, appears comparable to Patty's in several respects. This learner studied French in Grades 6 to 12, "but learned very little" and had been "a competent but uninspired student" while completing her BA degree. However, on meeting and developing a romantic relationship with a francophone boyfriend, she became highly motivated to learn French in order to "be able to understand the French language and culture

---

[9] See, for example, Clément, Dörnyei, and Noels (1994); Dörnyei (1994); Gardner (1985); Schmidt, Boraie, and Kassabgy (1996); Tremblay and Gardner (1995), among others.

and interact with native French speakers" (p. 167). Quite unlike Patty, this learner succeeded in mastering her L2 so well that she eventually went on to become a French professor. Schumann writes that, given her apparent aptitude for language learning (assessed, of course, on the post hoc basis of her ultimate attainment in French),

> ... nevertheless, she failed to learn French when she was exposed to it in junior high school, high school and college, but she did learn French when she was exposed to it in her late twenties. She accounts for the difference by the fact that, in secondary school and college, she appraised French as irrelevant to her life goals and irrelevant to her social image in terms of what was expected of her by valued others. She reports that she found French classes neither motivating nor pleasant and, in general, her teachers were uninspiring.
>
> In her late twenties, when she developed a relationship with her French-speaking boyfriend, the situation changed. The relationship created a need. Learning French became important in order to communicate with him, his family, and friends, and to understand French culture. Her autobiography indicates how her need led to enormous effort. She highly appraised her French classes, the language laboratory, and the interactions with her boyfriend as conducive to what had become her goal—to master the French language and to participate in the French experience. (p. 169)

Now, recall Patty's situation. Although she was heavily exposed to English and studied it in high school, as in BH's case, it was also at that time irrelevant to her life goals and social image in Hong Kong, where most of her friends spoke Cantonese and none spoke English. On immigrating to the United States, however, that situation changed. If anything, her need to acquire English must have been even stronger than BH's to acquire French, because finding work and continuing her education—her survival, really—completely depended on it. She moreover reports that her first year of college study in the United States, including ESL classes, was a wonderful experience. Her social circle became primarily English-speaking, and, of course, she eventually also became romantically involved with, and subsequently married, a native English-speaking American. Her relationship with her own young daughter is an English-speaking one. Thus, the depth and extent of her integrative motivation is surely beyond doubt.

What about aptitude? BH reports that the differential success she achieved at separate times studying French could not be due to aptitude, because that would have remained constant over time; nor could "the age advantage" have played a role, because she succeeded at the later period of study (in her late 20s) rather than the earlier one (p. 166). However, it appears likely that Patty also has a general aptitude for language learning, as she managed to become completely fluent in Cantonese within a year or so of having started learning it at the age of 16, and despite the fact that the formal study of Chinese literature in Cantonese was originally difficult for her in her classes in Hong Kong, as she mentioned in her autobiographical narrative.

Rather, it is quite clear that the main difference between Patty and BH's outcomes lies in the extent of formal metalinguistic study of the target language within their respective "highly integratively motivated" interactional contexts. BH notes that she spent 4 to 6 hours *daily*, including weekends, in the language lab, spent "many hours every night on [her] homework, playing the incomprehensible bits on the tapes over and over again, reading dictionaries and verb books in the bathroom" (pp. 160–161), and also "began the serious study of French linguistics (phonology, morphology, and syntax as well as history of the French language)" (p. 167). She writes:

> Of course, it can be argued that I devoted greater quantities of time and attention to the task of learning French the second time and thus achieved a superior level of proficiency. However, the very act of spending so much focused time on the task came out of a high level of motivation. (p. 166)

But, of course, this is precisely the theoretical confound between motivation and formal study that concerned Schmidt (1983), illustrated quite sharply by the contrast between BH and Patty. Whereas integrative motivation and a desire to interact with native speakers was extremely high in both cases, perhaps even higher in Patty's case than in BH's, the difference in their respective ultimate attainment seems much more directly related to the specific ways in which this motivation was channeled. That is, the variable more directly responsible for BH's success is formal study, including the phonology, morphology, and syntax, of the target language, providing tentative support for Schmidt's conclusion that adults seem not to be able to perfectly acquire the L2 without such intensive study.

Also, the kind of integrative motivation BH demonstrated seems quite different not only from that of Patty (and Wes), but from that of young children as well, who uniformly enjoy success in primary language acquisition. However, without more refined means of measuring degrees and kinds of motivation, there seems to be no way to test Pulvermüller and Schumann's (1994) claim that it is degree of motivation which is responsible for the large variance in abilities among adult learners (p. 689).

Comparing Patty with Wes within Pulvermüller and Schumann's (1994) framework, for example, we would presumably characterize them both as [+m, −g]. In some rather vague, global sense, both certainly do exhibit non-nativelike aspects of English in their production data, and both were also highly motivated to learn English. But that is just about all we can say, and it does not seem like much. Even if the comparison could be made more valid, say, by matching length of exposure or other factors, there would still be interesting differences between their grammars that we would not be able to account for, and for which the difference presumably lies somewhere in the degree of "negativeness" of [−g] rather than the positive degree of the [+m] feature, because both exhibited a high degree of motivation.

In fact, it is quite telling, I think, that even though both Patty and Wes are clearly not comparable with regard to years of L2 exposure, age of arrival in the United States, constancy and exclusivity of English input, English literacy, general educational level and degrees obtained, L1, and probably a variety of other factors, including the particular ways in which knowledge is represented and organized in the brain of a visual artist as opposed to an accountant, in this framework we are essentially left without anything much to say about their respective L2 acquisition of English except that in both cases the outcome has been non-nativelike despite high motivation. Both can be described theoretically within the framework as [+m, −g], as, presumably, could BH, whose outcome was quite different. In other words, although Pulvermüller and Schumann characterize variance among late learners as primarily a function of [+m] versus [−m], there seems to be no way to operationalize or account for "within-[+m]" variance. Likewise, there is no way to capture varying degrees of "[−g]-ness" among adult learners (because this is linked explicitly to age until puberty, and in this case both Patty and Wes began their acquisition of English after a hypothesized critical period beyond which, according to Schumann, we should not expect to find continuously declining, linear effects on grammatical aptitude or ability as a function of increasing age, but, rather, only differences in motivation).

Furthermore, within the stimulus-appraisal model, there may be no way in principle to account for between-learner grammatical variance on the basis of, say, L1 influence, or location in a sequence of universal developmental stages, because each learner's motivational makeup and aptitude are completely individual and unique and thus inherently uncategorizable:

> The appraisal mechanism guides SLA. It appraises the teacher, method, and syllabus, as well as the target language, its speakers, and the culture in which it is used. Because each appraisal system is different, each second language learner is on a separate motivational trajectory. Consequently, inconsistency across individuals in the measurement of affective factors and SLA proficiency is to be expected. When consis-

tency is found, it is only because groups of people, for cultural reasons, occasionally make similar appraisals about language learning. (Schumann, 1997, p. 2)

But if so, we find ourselves in a bit of a quandary—not only regarding the falsifiability of the model and its ability to generate and test explicit predictions, but also regarding the exact domain or level of analysis at which stimulus appraisal should be taken to apply in the language-acquisition process.

Schumann writes of high versus minimal levels of attainment, of failure or success in acquisition, and the emotional appraisal of entire learning environments in very, very broad terms. There are no explicit criteria for "successful acquisition." (In fact, I was unable, on trying to apply the acculturation/stimulus-appraisal model to Patty, to determine whether her level of acquisition would be regarded within this perspective as "high" or "successful.") But how then do we account for more specific aspects of language form acquired (or not acquired)—that is, what role, if any, does stimulus appraisal play at a more fine-grained level of formal analysis on the part of the learner (or evaluation of variance on the part of the researcher)?

We find, for example, that, although there is considerable variance between Patty and Wes on their respective rates of overall past-tense marking, both Patty and Wes consistently mark past tense at a higher rate on irregular verbs than on regular verbs.[10] It seems unlikely, however, that this particular cross-learner consistency in past-tense marking is due to their having made similar emotional appraisals about regular versus irregular past-tense asymmetry for cultural reasons. Presumably, therefore, stimulus appraisal does not apply at this level of analysis in the acquisition process. And indeed, Schumann (1995) writes that "words, sounds, and morphological and syntactic items do not have to carry emotional associations independently as linguistic units," noting that when these items occur embedded within an entire "stimulus situation or stimulus array" that is positively evaluated by the learner, they will be "preferentially perceived, attended to, and, with sufficient exposure, acquired" (p. 61).[11] In this case, however, given the ac-

---

[10] I discuss Patty's past-tense marking in much greater detail in chapter 4.

[11] Schumann was responding here to Eubank and Gregg (1995), who observed that most words do not have positive emotional associations, yet are learned nonetheless (p. 51). Eubank and Gregg were in turn responding to Pulvermüller and Schumann's (1994) claim that linguistic elements become associated with the positive emotional evaluation of the learning situation: "Sounds, words, or larger syntactic structures co-occur frequently with positive evaluation of a teacher, the teaching setting, the learning materials, *(Continued)*

tual production data, we would seemingly be forced to the conclusion that, for some cultural reason, both Patty and Wes positively appraised (and thus preferentially perceived and attended to past tense in) exactly and only those situations and/or cultural contexts in which one formal class of verbs, but not another, was presented in the input or stimulus array—a quite amazing coincidence if it were really true.

Rather, it is far more likely that the stimulus-appraisal model is simply incapable of accounting for any particular grammatical knowledge—that is, in terms of suggesting what particular knowledge is more or less likely to be acquired or not. For that deeper, more interesting level of refinement, I agree with Eubank and Gregg (1999) that we will need to turn to linguistic theory (p. 88), as well as acquisition theories that afford deeper coverage of the aspects of grammatical knowledge under consideration. Looking at the past-tense production data in this case, for example, one could quite plausibly initially hypothesize that, because the L1s of both Patty and Wes do not permit final consonant clusters, there might be some effect of L1 phonological transfer that induces the omission or deletion of regular past-tense affixes when adding these would result in a cluster.

In other words, in order to even formulate the hypothesis, we require (at least) a theory of syllabification and a theory of language transfer. Neither of these appears to have an articulated place yet in the aptitude and motivation components of Schumann's (1997) or the [±g, ±m] features of Pulvermüller and Schumann's (1994) frameworks.

In the remaining chapters, I primarily focus on some of these more fine-grained aspects of Patty's grammatical representation of English, in particular those for which more articulated theories of grammatical knowledge and acquisition are available. One highly interesting finding, perhaps unexpected in a fossilized L2 grammar, is that, despite conveying a rather global impression of divergence from nativelike speech in some obvious respects, certain elements of Patty's production data nonetheless appear completely nativelike, including some that are highly complex and abstract. It is this striking within-learner differential competence in the L2 steady state, or "persistent *selective* fossilization" (Hawkins, 2000), in which some aspects of grammatical (within-[±g]) knowledge seem perfectly acquired and others far from so, that this case study seeks to describe and, ultimately, try to account for, and for which affect-based models such as those discussed here seem to offer little help.

---

or, for naturalistic language learning, the native speakers and aspects of the cultural context" (p. 708).

Finally, I would draw the reader's attention to those aspects of *first* language acquisition which Schumann (1997) suggests fall more directly within the realm of the stimulus-appraisal mechanism—namely, pragmatics, social reasoning, and communicative competence. For example,

> [T]he role of affect in first language acquisition is in the acquisition of pragmatics because attachment and pragmatics seem to be subserved by the same neural system that underlies stimulus appraisal, affect regulation, and social reasoning. ... We might predict that damage to this system ... would affect discourse pragmatics. (p. 202)

Following Locke (1995), Schumann assumes that primary language acquisition is determined by two distinct neural systems—one that governs social cognition (presumably underlying or corresponding to the [+m] feature of Pulvermüller & Schumann, 1994) and a separate grammatical analysis module (presumably corresponding to the [+g] feature) that identifies and analyzes recurring elements in utterances and constrains their form (Schumann, 1997, pp. 192–193). Of course, it is apparently this grammatical module that is thought to become severely attenuated—perhaps altogether quite useless—for second language acquisition beyond the critical period (becoming [–g] in adults) within Schumann's framework. Schumann states, however, that the former system—the "specialization for social cognition"—continues to operate throughout life as language is used in different social contexts (p. 193).

Interestingly, this far more direct role of affect in guiding the social and pragmatic use of one's native language appears compatible with the findings for Wes by Schmidt (1983) in a second language—that is, the finding that Wes's sociolinguistic competence in his L2 far exceeded his grammatical competence. The same could be said for Patty as well, who, judging by her level of professional and personal accomplishment and integration into the target language community, can obviously communicate effectively. In other words, the direct correlation between positive emotional affect and pragmatic sociolinguistic competence posited by Schumann for primary language acquisition also appears to hold well beyond the critical period—a fact which again suggests that degrees and kinds of motivation (and/or affect, however these are to be distinguished) need to be more clearly refined and articulated within the stimulus-appraisal model. Schumann (1997), aware of the problem, writes:

> Motivation to learn a second language is studied separately from pragmatic decision making in one's native language, but both may result from how we appraise agents and events in terms of our sense of nov-

elty, familiarity, and pleasantness and in terms of our goals, coping ability, and self and social image. (p. 237)

In sum, I would finally suggest that such broad brush strokes in this model paint an overly vague picture of second language acquisition at a rather uninformative level of generality. Long (2003) similarly observes that the arrays of social and psychological factors argued for by Schumann "have repeatedly failed to account for age-related success and failure in SLA at the level of individuals ... and groups ... and have no obvious potential, either, for explaining differential success within the same individual at the level of linguistic domain or grammatical structure" (p. 516). Schumann's affective model smudges and blurs what are likely to be very real distinctions among different kinds of knowledge in both first and second language acquisition, as well as the distinct sources of that knowledge. In the following chapters, I hope to provide a much more detailed and nuanced picture of Patty's grammatical knowledge—one that is dependent on detailed theoretical descriptions of the linguistic phenomena to be investigated.

3

Knowledge of Finiteness

In this chapter, we begin our detailed investigation of some of the more formal aspects of Patty's knowledge of English by first turning to her acquisition of the finiteness distinction in English. In the first part of the chapter, I discuss the nature of finiteness in general and previous acquisition findings; then I focus more specifically on the data from Patty. There is a large and interesting literature on the acquisition of finiteness, both in L1 and L2 acquisition. My intent here is not to present an exhaustive summary of the findings to date, but rather to provide enough of a context in which to interpret Patty's data within the second language acquisition context and in comparison with data from first language acquisition studies. Although this chapter briefly touches on Patty's past-tense marking, obviously relevant to the issue of finiteness, Patty's acquisition of past tense is treated separately in more detail in the next chapter. Likewise, although I introduce the related issue of verb raising here, I also deal with verb raising and adverb placement in more depth in chapter 5. For now, we are primarily concerned with the abstract formal notion of finiteness, how it can be acquired, and whether Patty has acquired it.

Sections I and II focus on more formal and conceptual issues associated with finiteness and the sorts of evidence available for it in the linguistic environment in different languages. I review some of the theoretical issues that have been raised with respect to finiteness, especially the existence of so-called optional or root infinitives in child L1 acquisition and the hypothesized relationship between inflectional morphology and the abstract feature of finiteness. Readers primarily interested in SLA may fast-forward to Section III, where I review some of the relevant SLA literature, and then on to Section IV, where I provide an overview of Patty's own data in relation to her acquisition of the finite/nonfinite distinction in English.

I. Defining Finiteness

The particular grammatical feature to be examined in this section is that of *finiteness*—an intuitively fundamental distinction between clause types, but one that varies in the extent of its morphological expression across languages. What, exactly, is finiteness? It is a formal grammatical property that has been characterized as a "notion ... far from being well defined" (Koptjevskaja-Tamm, 1993, p. 29). Typically, the finite clause is one whose verb or auxiliary forms bear morphological marking for categories such as agreement and tense/aspect and can in principle serve as the only verb form in an independent (matrix) clause, whereas nonfinite forms, such as infinitives, participles, and gerunds, cannot be the only predicate of matrix clauses (Koptjevskaja-Tamm, 1993, 1994; Trask, 1993).

Within the acquisition literature, *finiteness* has been defined, for example, by Meisel (1994) as "depending on the presence of agreement and tense" (p. 90) or, more precisely, of agreement *or* tense, since Meisel argues that only one of these two elements may suffice to instantiate finiteness, with agreement developing first among the German/French bilingual children he studied. Eubank (1994) writes that "saying that some verbal element is finite reduces to an epiphenomenon that results from the presence of particular value specifications [for Tense and Agreement—DL]; in the same way, the infinitive simply involves a set of different value specifications" (p. 374).

It seems to hold generally cross-linguistically—and more specifically for the languages under consideration here—that languages which do have distinctive verbal or clausal infinitive (or other nonfinite forms) indeed do not permit these to function as the sole predicate of main declarative clauses.[1] However, many languages allow subordinate clauses to be nonfinite. For languages without distinctive finite or nonfinite forms, such as Chinese, in which verbs exhibit neither agreement, nor tense marking, nor infinitive forms, and appear in the same uninflected form in all clause types, one might question whether the notion of finiteness even makes sense at all (e.g., Koptjevskaja-Tamm, 1993, 1994). I return shortly to the

---

[1] I disregard here utterances generally analyzed as elliptical, such as the following (although of course they certainly make up a non-negligible part of the primary linguistic data to children):

Q. What's John doing?
A. *Scooping out the litterbox.*

issue of finiteness in Chinese, because it is relevant to a discussion of Patty's data.

II. Considering the Input: Kinds of Evidence for Finiteness

Verbal Inflection and Clause Position: English

Finiteness is often presented as a characteristic of verbs, because it is the verb that often bears the morphological reflex(es) of finiteness in the form of tense and/or agreement marking. In English these verbal morphological reflexes include past-tense marking and nonpast agreement with 3SG subjects. However, except for the suppletive forms of the paradigm for *be*, no person/number distinctions for nonpast verb forms other than 3SG are marked. Modals, typically considered finite, are also unmarked for agreement in English and select bare verb complements. Let us consider, then, the problem confronting the English-speaking child who would depend on the inflectional morphology on verbs in the environment—in particular main lexical (thematic) verbs—to acquire the distinction between +/– finite. Consider, for example, the following sentences:

(1) a. Mommy loves Baby.
     b. Mommy and Daddy love Baby.
     c. Mommy will give Baby a cookie.
     d. Does Baby want a cookie?
     e. Wanna cookie?

(2) a. Mommy was kissing Santa Claus.
     b. I saw Mommy kissing Santa Claus.

Looking at the main lexical verbs in the examples in (1), we can see that if it were really the inflectional morphology on the verb itself that determined finiteness, we might wonder what would prevent the child from concluding that the inflected verb in (1a) *Mommy loves Baby* is finite, but *non*finite in (1b–e). Likewise, what role could inflectional morphology on the thematic verb *kiss* play in informing the child that *kissing Santa Claus* is a predicate in a finite clause in the sentence *Mommy was kissing Santa Claus* in (2a), but nonfinite in *I saw Mommy kissing Santa Claus* in (2b)?

Thus, it is quite clear that, although verbal morphology may reflect (clausal) finiteness, the notion of finiteness is not likely to be a feature of the thematic verb itself; elements such as the copula, modals, and auxiliaries, to the extent they are present in a clause, are in fact more reliable indicators of finiteness, and these are located outside of the verb phrase (VP) in the higher domain of IP or even in CP (as in the case of questions in English, or as the determinant of V2 position in German matrix clauses, to be discussed below).

Tense marking has been claimed to appear later than agreement in child early grammars, because its acquisition is likely to be contingent on the more gradual development of the corresponding semantic interpretations of tense (and/or perfective aspectual) distinctions, rather than with the purely formal feature of finiteness per se (Meisel, 1994; Wexler, 1994). Although past-tense marking may, in fact, be one indicator of finiteness in English, its absence, of course, does not entail the opposite—that nonpast clauses are nonfinite. That is, there is not a unique, one-to-one feature-form correspondence between tense marking and finiteness.

To make matters even worse for the learner, however, in English the verbal morphological marking for finite past tense is often (and productively) identical to that for past participles, which are considered nonfinite forms; again, finiteness rests on the presence of auxiliaries related to other functional categories or features involving mood, voice, perfective aspect, and so on. Compare the following sentences in (3), typical of the input to a young child, in which past participle forms may occur in the same thematic context as the simple past form; note that (3d) is finite even though the thematic verb itself is uninflected:

(3) a. You finished your cookie.
     b. (You) finished your cookie?
     c. (Have you) finished your cookie?
     d. (Did you) finish your cookie?

Again, because the inflectional morphology on thematic verbs in English could thus easily lead the child astray, it seems at best a redundant and at worst a faulty and even confusing indicator of finiteness; that is, knowledge of the finite/nonfinite distinction in English is not readily inducible from the morphological forms of these verbs in the input.[2] Such knowledge

---

[2] Given the complexity of the input described above, I think the following question posed by Wexler (1994), loses some of its rhetorical force:

> Generally speaking, as children get older, the percentage of verbal [3SG] *s* inflections in obligatory contexts increases. But even at somewhat older ages, the children are still not producing the inflection all the time. ... [W]hy

(Continued)

must come from another source and would seemingly need to be in place already in order for the child to be able to start figuring out the appropriate morphological realization of verbs (perhaps as suggested, for example, by Borer & Rohrbacher, 1997).

As mentioned earlier, whereas subordinate clauses may be nonfinite in English (and many other languages), main clauses cannot be: Main clauses must be finite. Tense marking, like nonpast 3SG agreement marking, will not provide the child with the means to distinguish between main and subordinate clauses and the kinds of predicates (i.e., nonfinite) that are not allowed in the former; sentences in which both clauses are finite, such as *I thought you were hungry*, provide abundant input in which any morphological distinction based on appearance in main versus subordinate clauses is neutralized.

In other words, if children observe that the same kind of clauses (i.e., finite) are possible in both main and subordinate clauses, what in the input would prevent them from concluding the same about nonfinite clauses? In fact, there is a growing body of evidence suggesting that children do indeed initially assume this, during early stages of sentence production in which they sometimes produce nonfinite forms in main (or root) clauses, known as *root infinitives* or *optional infinitives* (Rizzi, 1993/1994; Wexler, 1994). (I return to this phenomenon shortly.) The point here is that the inadmissibility of nonfinite forms as matrix predicates is in fact a constraint on the (adult target) grammar requiring negative evidence not obviously available from the input, and thus appears to pose a likely poverty of the stimulus problem for the child.[3]

---

should it take such a very long time to memorize such a simple form? (p. 306)

From the grammarian's perspective the rule may be fairly simple indeed. But clearly the child's task is not simply to "memorize" a given form, but to figure out its distributional (and peculiar semantic) properties as well. Although several other explanations have been advanced for this particular delay (see e.g., Brown, 1973), it also seems at least possible, given the input, that children acquiring English are overgeneralizing the most common inflectional form of the (nonpast) thematic verb paradigm in the input in English—namely -∅. We know that overgeneralization in other domains is a robust feature of language development, is variable, and persists through early childhood.

[3] The learnability problem may in fact be compounded if one considers the frequent occurrence in the input of imperative clauses.

Inflection and Clause Position in Verb-Raising Languages

A child learning a so-called verb-raising language such as German or French would seem to have things a bit easier in the acquisition of finiteness. Not only are the morphological reflexes of person/number agreement generally more clearly differentiated from each other and/or from nonfinite forms, but crucially, verbs inflected with these agreement markers (as well as auxiliary elements) can be more reliably correlated with a particular position in the clause. Finite-marked verbs appear in raised surface positions in the matrix clause relative to nonfinite verbs—for example, preceding negative particle *pas* (and *jamais*, *rien*, etc.) in French, and in the second (V2) position in German matrix clauses, as well as preceding negative *nicht*.

Children can thus make use of this key difference in word order in attempting to gradually sort out and compile the set of morphological forms specifically associated with each position, eventually configuring the paradigms for thematic verbs in these languages. The development of verbal inflectional paradigms in verb-raising languages may therefore be understood as tied to finiteness via the mediation of an *association with a raised or nonraised position*.[4] This suggests that finite verbal inflectional morphology, to whatever extent it exists in specific languages, is indeed a reflex of a [±finite]-related feature, but not necessarily the principal determinant or trigger for the acquisition of finiteness or, in particular, for the projection of the functional category or categories associated with it. Such morphology, although reflecting finiteness, does not confer it.[5]

This view of finiteness appears to be quite compatible with the available developmental data from studies investigating the presence or absence of functional categories in the grammatical representations of young children acquiring verb-raising languages. We would expect, for example, that knowledge of the clausal position of finiteness (which is primary) should precede the acquisition of verbal inflectional paradigms (which is secondary).

---

[4] In German, the finite-marked element appears in final position in subordinate clauses. Thus, if clause position is what helps the child acquire the feature-form mapping of the verbal morphological paradigm, as I suggest here, one would also have to assume that children acquiring German induce this mapping for main clauses before subordinate clauses.

[5] See Bobaljik (2001, 2002) for additional theoretical arguments from Icelandic and Mainland Scandinavian languages in support of a view that "takes overt morphology to be a reflection (albeit a somewhat imperfect one) of the prior syntactic structure" rather than a cause of that structure (p. 31).

We also expect that those grammatical elements or forms most consistently associable with particular clausal positions should most consistently show up there. For example, copular, modal, and auxiliary elements that occur in raised positions in the input (and are thus unambiguously finite) should consistently appear in those positions in children's speech as soon as they are acquired, whereas distinctive nonfinite forms, which always occupy unraised positions, should likewise consistently show up in children's speech in those positions as well.

That is in fact what has been reported. Wexler (1994) notes that, at a stage when young children still alternate between using finite and nonfinite lexical verb forms in main clauses (where nonfinite forms would of course be ungrammatical in the adult grammar), modal and auxiliary verbs, in contrast, never appear in nonfinite form. Rather, these "always appear in finite form and they are always in the correct position" (p. 341). Similar results have been reported for German by Clahsen (1990/1991), Clahsen and Penke (1992), and Clahsen, Penke, and Parodi (1993/1994). These studies indicate that before regular subject-verb agreement paradigms have been productively acquired, modals and the auxiliary forms of *sein* 'to be' appear in their raised position in finite form and from the beginning exhibit "practically no errors" (Clahsen & Penke, 1992, p. 199).[6] Verrips and Weissenborn (1992) also observe the same for German as well as for French, and de Haan (1987; cited in Wexler, 1994) for Dutch.

By the same token, consider the consistent association of distinctive nonfinite forms in lower (unraised) positions in the clause. Wexler (1994) cites several studies of the acquisition of various languages: French (Pierce, 1992; Verrips & Weissenborn, 1992), German (Poeppel & Wexler, 1993; Verrips & Weissenborn, 1992), Dutch (de Haan, 1987; Weverink, 1990), Swedish (Platzack, 1990, Plunkett & Strömqvist, 1992), Danish and Norwegian (Plunkett & Strömqvist, 1992), all of which appear to show that the form of the verb depends on its position in the clause—finite verbs usually (and increasingly) appear in raised position whereas nonfinite forms from the start almost never do. Poeppel and Wexler (1993) found that this

---

[6] Clahsen and colleagues argue for an early stage F[inite] P[hrase] dominating VP in the child's grammatical representation, which eventually becomes a more fully specified functional category (CP) after verbal inflectional paradigms are acquired. The 3SG -*t* affix is part of the regular (thematic) verbal agreement paradigm and is also used correctly (i.e., in agreement with 3SG subjects) from the earliest utterances. There is some debate over whether the early appearance of this affix in German L1 acquisition actually represents knowledge of agreement (see Clahsen & Penke, 1992; Clahsen et al., 1993/1994; Clahsen et al., 1996; Meisel, 1994).

correlation was statistically significant for the German child whose data they examined.

Note that this contingency between verb position and verb form, although statistically significant, is nonetheless somewhat asymmetrical. Whereas nonfinite-marked verbs virtually never raise (only 3% of all verbs in raised V2 position were infinitive forms in Poeppel and Wexler's data), finite-marked verbs more often fail to raise (23% or nearly one-fourth of all verbs in clause final position).[7] Meisel (1997) observes this as well: "Most importantly, although inflected elements may occasionally fail to move and remain in final position, non-inflected elements never move, e.g. one does not find non-finite verbs in V2 position..." (p. 380).

In sum, the German L1 acquisition data show that elements that always appear in raised position (e.g., modals, auxiliaries, the copula) and those that always appear in final position (e.g., the infinitive form) are virtually always correctly located in the German child data. The children's working out of the inflectional paradigm for finite marking on verbs appears to be more gradually acquired, perhaps as a function of properties of the input (the German studies note that 3SG -t in German, probably the most frequent finite-marked present tense verb inflection, is also acquired very early).

These findings suggest that the child has indeed acquired the distinction between +/− finite on the basis of a consistent association with clausal position, prior to acquiring the regular inflectional paradigms for subject-verb agreement. However, I will return to the issue of a hypothesized relation between verbal agreement paradigms and verb raising in more detail in chapter 5. In the meantime, we may conclude that the findings of many of the L1 acquisition studies cited above suggest that the grammatical representation of young children most likely includes at least one functional category projection specified for a +/− finite distinction from the earliest stages of acquisition. Indeed, several researchers (e.g., Clahsen et al., 1993/1994 and Poeppel & Wexler, 1993), while differing in some of their

---

[7] Poeppel and Wexler (1993) considered verbs affixed with the infinitive -en ending to be nonfinite, and all other forms ("otherwise") finite (p. 6). As noted by Atkinson (1996), the latter category apparently included bare-stem forms in V2 position with no finite affix where one would be required in the adult grammar. Atkinson points out that, for cases such as these (and we do not know how many there are), "there is no signal that it is [+finite] beyond the observation that it occurs in second position" (p. 461), possibly confounding the strength of the contingency between form and position argued for by Poeppel and Wexler. (However, Prévost, 2001, in his child L2 German acquisition study, looked at bare-stem verbs as a separate category and found that they patterned more closely with finite than infinitive forms anyway in their syntactic behavior; cf. his Truncation Hypothesis studies summarized in Section III below.)

conclusions and analyses, nonetheless agree that such a projection is needed—according to Poeppel and Wexler—in order "to account for even the simplest facts of very early grammar" (p. 21).

Finally, another interesting finding in teasing apart the relative roles of verb position versus verb form comes from Pye's (2001) study on the acquisition of finiteness in K'iche' Maya, a language with "French-like" finite verb raising over NEG (p. 646). Pye reports that K'iche' children correctly raise verbs over NEG even when they fail to produce any of the required aspectual and agreement marking on such verbs, noting that "the children obey all of the constraints on verb movement except for the production of aspect and agreement inflections on verbs in raised positions" (p. 650). Pye's data suggest that the verb's position in raising languages seems indeed to be the primary indicator of finiteness and is not necessarily contingent on morphological spell-out. Unlike the languages mentioned so far, K'iche' Maya uses verbal prefixes rather than suffixes to encode its reflexes of finiteness, and thus the overt expression of required morphology may also hinge to quite a large extent on independent factors such as phonological salience, metrical stress patterns, and so on (as noted by Pye).

The Role of Case Marking on Subjects

Although finiteness may be morphologically reflected in the form of modifications for tense and/or agreement to a verb stem, the feature itself is associated, as mentioned earlier, with a functional category having scope over the VP—that is, one which is higher than the VP in the grammatical representation of phrase structure. The relation between nominative case marking on subjects and finiteness in this higher functional category has long been noted in linguistic theory; in recent versions of the Principles and Parameters and Minimalist Program frameworks (e.g., Chomsky, 1995, 1998, 1999), the feature [± finite] is associated with the functional category T[ense], head of the functional projection T[ense] P[hrase].[8] In English (and many other languages), if the finiteness feature in T is specified for the [+finite] value, a nominative (NOM) case feature on subject DPs in the

---

[8] The feature [± finite] has been argued to be located in C in V2 languages to account for verb-second effects, and thus parameterized (i.e., the Finiteness Parameter of Platzack & Holmberg, 1989). Some acquisition researchers have also argued for an early stage underspecified F[inite] P[hrase], as noted above. Giorgi and Pianesi (1997) consider T to be conflated with AGR (i.e., T/AGR) in English. For my immediate expository purposes here, these alternative possibilities can be set aside for now.

Spec[ifier] of T position is checked within the domain of T, as shown in the phrase structure diagram in (4).

(4)

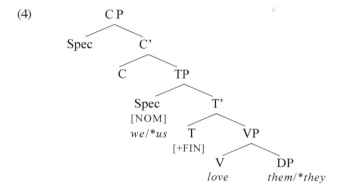

Syntactic case as conceived within these generative approaches is abstractly assigned and/or checked within particular structural configurations, and all (overt) nouns must bear abstract case. However, case may be morphologically realized or not; Chomsky (1995), for instance, writes that, although "case systems are basically similar cross-linguistically ... the differences lie primarily in their phonetic realization (the mapping to PF)" (p. 26).[9] In the languages we have been looking at so far, morphological case distinctions are overtly expressed on pronouns (and/or clitics in the case of Romance languages, and also on determiners in German). In English, such distinctions appear overtly on non-2nd person pronouns. However, subjects of infinitive clauses cannot receive nominative case and thus must be either null (PRO), as shown below in (5a), or in the case of so-called exceptionally casemarked (ECM) constructions, overtly realized in the default object case, as in (5b):

(5) a. We$_i$ want [PRO$_i$ to go]
     b. We want [them/*they to go]

In her cross-linguistic survey of finiteness, Koptjevskaja-Tamm (1994) writes that,

---

[9] For a recent discussion of approaches to case theory in the minimalist framework, particularly on the relationship between syntactic and morphological case, see Weerman (1997).

[C]ombinability with the subject is, in fact, sometimes considered as crucial for the opposition in finiteness itself. Thus, while finite verb forms typically take subjects, nonfinite verb forms (at least, in a number of languages) either cannot combine with overt subjects at all or take them in another form than in independent sentences. (p. 1245)

Thus, for acquirers of English, it is the distinctive form of pronominal subjects—that is, the presence of subject or nominative case marking on subject pronouns, that can probably serve as a more reliable correlate of clausal finiteness in the input than verbal morphology.[10]

Returning now to the issue of root infinitive (RI) clauses mentioned earlier, a statistically robust correlation has been widely observed in (non-null-subject) verb-raising languages between children's nontargetlike omission of subjects and (non-)finiteness (e.g., Bromberg & Wexler, 1995; Pierce, 1992; Wexler, 1994). In other words, a significantly higher proportion of nonfinite utterances are missing subjects than finite ones. This effect has been demonstrated for children learning Danish, Dutch, Flemish, French, and German (Haegeman, 1995; Hamann & Plunkett, 1998; Krämer, 1993; Pierce, 1992; Poeppel & Wexler, 1993). For children learning these languages, then, we might conclude that the constraint against nonfinite predicates in main clauses is directly tied to their understanding that the particular language being acquired requires overt subjects, implicating in turn the child's (UG-driven) knowledge that overt subjects must bear (abstract) case, licensed by the feature [+finite] in T.

Interestingly, this correlation between overt subjects and finiteness does not appear to hold for lexical main (thematic) verbs (which happen not to raise) in English, as pointed out by Phillips (1995, 1996), who examined these verbs in 3SG finite contexts. However, the correlation is strong for modals and copular/auxiliary *be* in English—that is, between the presence of these Infl elements and overt subjects (Hyams, 1996; Sano & Hyams, 1994; see also Phillips, 1995, 1996, for some discussion). As

---

[10] Parrott (2005), citing the variability of pronominal usage in comparative objects, predicate nominals, and coordinate structures in English, argues that the morphological form of English pronouns does not productively spell out abstract syntactic case features but rather results from a purely morphological algorithm that spells out "sisterhood to finite T" (in the case of nominative subject marking). Nothing in this alternative analysis is incompatible with the general point here, however (and in fact further supports it), which is namely that there is a contingent relation in English (and many other languages) between finiteness and the form of subject pronouns, such that the form reflects the value of the finiteness feature.

mentioned earlier, because the copula, modals, and auxiliaries always occur (in suppletive forms) in raised surface position in the clause, we have additional support for viewing the *position* of verbs rather than the morphological *form* of verbs as the more primary indicator of finiteness in acquisition. In other words, children apparently work out the association of finiteness with clausal position prior to (and perhaps initially independently of) acquiring the inflectional paradigms of thematic verbs.

Is There a Finiteness Distinction in Chinese?

Finally, let us consider the existence and acquisition of a finiteness feature in a language like Chinese, which was mentioned earlier as having verbs that exhibit neither tense nor agreement marking and appear in their basic uninflected form in both matrix and subordinate clauses; nor is there any kind of distinctive case marking on nouns or pronouns (which may be null). As mentioned earlier, one might question whether it even makes sense to posit finiteness in such a language. Whereas root declarative sentences in Chinese are indeed argued to be finite (e.g., C.-T. J. Huang, 1984; Y. Huang, 1994; Progovac, 1993), what is more controversial, however, is whether there is a true finiteness *distinction*, entailing the contrastive existence of nonfinite clauses as well. Li (1990) has argued that Chinese does indeed have a finiteness distinction, by providing evidence of subtle syntactic differences among subordinate clauses that are complements of *persuade*- (i.e., object control) versus *tell*-type classes of verbs, which appear to subcategorize in Chinese for infinitive versus finite clauses, respectively. The types of evidence supporting this distinction include the licensing of negative polarity items across infinitive but not finite subordinate clauses, the possibility of (overt) subjects occurring in finite but not infinitive clauses, the possibility of topicalization out of the subject position of finite but not infinitive clauses, and the possibility for certain modal verbs—argued to be grammaticized future tense markers—to appear in finite but not infinitive clauses. Let us digress briefly to look at these in turn, because a finiteness distinction in this language would have important implications for the acquisition of knowledge of finiteness, as I discuss below.

First, consider the evidence from negative polarity items, which when licensed by negation must co-occur with the negation element within the same clause for *tell*-type verbs, but not necessarily within the same clause for *persuade*-type verbs (Examples (9a–b) from Li, 1990, pp. 20–21):

(6) a. *Wo *meiyou* gaosu guo ta   [ni   zuo *renhe* shiqing]
      I not-have tell   ASP him [you do any   thing]
      'I have not told him you did anything.'

    b. Wo *meiyou* quan   guo ta   [qu zuo *renhe* shiqing]
      I not-have persuade ASP him [go do any   thing]
      'I have not persuaded him to do anything.'

Next, consider the possibility of overt DPs occurring as the subject of finite, but not infinitival, clauses; as observed earlier by Koptjevskaja-Tamm (1993, 1994), and as we have seen for child language acquisition, this is one of the cross-linguistic hallmarks of a finiteness distinction. Li observes that, although lexical subjects may be allowed in the subject position of tensed complements of *tell*-type verbs, they are never allowed in the infinitive *persuade*-type verb complements (Li's examples (14b and d), p. 23)[11]:

(7) a. Wo quan   ta   [(*ta) jie   yan]
      I   persuade him [he   stop smoking]
      'I persuaded him (*he) to stop smoking.'

    b. Wo gaosu ta   [(ta) yiding hui de jiang][12]
      I   tell   him [he certainly will get prize]
      'I told him that he will certainly get the prize.'

Similarly, Li notes that empty categories in the subject position of *persuade*-type complements cannot be interpreted as a variable bound by a

---

[11] This argument was also made by Huang (1987), who lists several such obligatory object control verbs for Chinese (e.g., *shefa* 'try,' *bi* 'force,' *yaoqiu* 'request,' *mingling* 'order,' *qing* 'request,' among others), noting that the embedded subject of the complements of these verbs is obligatorily null and therefore has "the precise properties of PRO" rather than of pro (p. 326).

[12] Adding an adverbial adpositional phrase to the subordinate clause in (7b) apparently sharpens the contrast with (7a) even more; in the sentence in (7c) below, the overt expression of the subordinate clause subject pronoun *ta* 'he' is not only possible, but strongly preferred. My thanks to Joaquim Kuong for this observation and example.

    7c. Wo gaosu ta [*zai zheci bisai zhong* ta yiding   hui de jiang]
         I   tell   him [*in this competition*   he certainly will get prize]
         'I told him that *in this competition* he will certainly get the prize.'

topic, contrary to those of finite *tell*-type complements (Li's examples (15a and d), p. 23:

(8) a. *Zhangsan$_i$, wo jiao Lisi [e$_i$ chi fan]
        Zhangsan I   ask Lisi [eat meal]
        'Zhangsan, I requested Lisi e to eat.' (i.e. 'that Zhangsan eat')

    b. Zhangsan$_i$, wo gaosu Lisi [e$_i$ yiding hui de jiang]
        Zhangsan I   tell Lisi [certainly will get prize]
        'Zhangsan, I told Lisi that (Zhangsan) would certainly get the prize.'

Finally, Li, citing Tsang (1981), points out that the modal verb denoting ability (*hui* 'will, can') has become a grammaticized future-tense marker in Chinese, similar to *will* in English; as such, it can occur in finite *tell*-type, but not in infinitive *persuade*-type, complements (Li's examples (12a–b), p. 22):

(9) a. *Wo quan/bi   ta [hui lai]
        I   persuade/force him [will come]

    b. Wo gaosu ta [huoche hui kai]
       I   tell him [train will leave]

In sum, if these examples and intuitions turn out to be correct, it looks as if Chinese does indeed have a nonfinite as well as finite clause type.[13]

---

[13] Li (1990) also provides an additional piece of evidence to support her argument for a finite/nonfinite distinction in Chinese—namely, a kind of co-occurrence restriction between certain temporal adverbs such as *congqian* 'before' and the completive/experiential aspect marker *guo*, such that these must co-occur and be interpreted within the same clause, as shown in (i)–(iii) below:

i. Wo congqian gaosu guo ta [ni lai zher]
   I before   tell ASP him [you come here]
   'I told him before that you came here.'

ii. Wo gaosu ta [ni congqian lai guo zher]
    I tell him [you before come ASP here]
    'I told him that you have been here before.'

iii. *Wo congqian gaosu ta [ni lai guo zher]
     I before   tell him [you come ASP here]
     'I told him that you have been here before.'

(Continued)

Consider, now, what morphological evidence for a finite/nonfinite distinction exists in the primary language data available to a child acquiring Chinese: apparently none—no verbal inflections for tense or agreement, no difference in the verb form in matrix versus subordinate clauses, and no overt distinctive case marking of any sort. Moreover, in Chinese, as a non-raising language, the position of the verb does not vary in clauses according to finiteness, as in German or French (or for *be* in English). Exacerbating the learnability problem even further, Chinese is a null-subject language, which therefore requires children to distinguish between something like *pro* and PRO or, namely, between exactly those circumstances under which overt subjects are possible but dropped versus those in which an overt subject is completely impossible, as in Examples (7a–b) above.

The existence of a +/– finite distinction in Chinese is thus quite severely underdetermined by the input data, creating a true poverty of the stimulus problem for its acquisition. Nonetheless, the fact that native Chinese speakers end up with knowledge of the *ungrammaticality* of sentences such as those starred above, especially considering that superficially similar constructions are indeed present in the input, strongly suggests that finiteness and its role in licensing case on subjects is a primitive feature of the grammar—somehow part of UG—regardless of language-specific differences in expressing it morphologically.

Summary

In sum, we are led to the conclusion that the morphology of finiteness, to the extent it exists in a particular language, may be only a partial and cross-linguistically arbitrary reflex of this feature rather than a determinant

---

Li argues, however, that this within-clause co-occurrence restriction is relaxed for *persuade*-type verb complements, which are presumably nonfinite, thus allowing the aspectual marker *guo* in the lower clause to be interpreted across the infinitive clause boundary (i.e., as part of the matrix clause), as in (iv):

    iv. Wo congqian qing   ta   [chi guo fan].
        I   before   invite him [eat ASP meal]
        'I invited him to eat before.'

Li's interpretation was not readily accepted by my Chinese informants, who saw no difference in grammaticality between (iv) and (iii); that is, both were considered okay if *guo* applied to the lower verb, and both were ungrammatical if *guo* applied to the matrix verb. However, Li's judgments as presented in Examples (6)–(9) above in the text were indeed confirmed.

or trigger for its acquisition; in fact, this must be so, if speakers of a language without *any* morphological evidence for finiteness nonetheless still end up with knowledge of its syntactic effects. That, in turn, suggests that young children acquire knowledge of finiteness quite independently of, and prior to, their acquisition of the particular morphological forms associated with it. They must then obviously figure out how to map the feature to whatever morphological means exist for spelling it out in the target language.

The ease of this particular mapping process is likely to depend on how regular and reliable the morphological correlates of finiteness are for the language in question. In Chinese, there are no morphological correlates; hence, the child is conveniently "done" with this process as soon as knowledge of finiteness is available (although the acquisition of this knowledge itself may be contingent on subtle semantic features of the class of verbs in question). For acquirers of a verb-raising language, such as German or French, for example, the position of verbs appears to be a more reliable correlate than verbal morphology. Moreover, because non-thematic verbs such as copular and auxiliary elements almost always appear in raised positions in the clause (because typically one of the very reasons for their presence in a clause is to indicate finiteness), we might expect the child to place these correctly as soon as they are acquired. This is not necessarily the case for thematic verbs, however, whose position in the sentence is more likely to vary (i.e., either raised or unraised depending on the presence of auxiliaries or negators, etc.) in the input. As we saw earlier, this is indeed what the acquisition research shows (e.g., Verrips & Weissenborn, 1992; see also Lardiere, 1999, for additional discussion).

For English, we have seen that pronominal case is a more reliable correlate of finiteness than (thematic) verbal inflection, and therefore we would expect the productive mapping for nominative case forms to be acquired more robustly at an earlier stage than that for the relevant verbal morphology (3SG nonpast agreement, past tense); again, the L1 acquisition data do seem to show this. Vainikka (1993/1994), for example, notes that for two of the four children she studied, Eve and Sarah, nominative case marking appeared from the earliest stages observed; for a third child, Nina, nominative case forms (for 1SG) show up in connection with the appearance of modals and auxiliaries. Valian (1991) observed that even the lowest-MLU group (mean MLU of 1.77) among the 21 American children whose acquisition of subjects she investigated "show uniform use of nominatively cased NPs in subject position" (p. 52).

The overall point to be made here is that the verbal morphology associated with finiteness is absolutely not the same thing as finiteness itself, and in some cases may not even constitute reliable evidence for it. The fact that there is not a simple one-to-one correspondence between features and forms (as demonstrated in the sentences in (1)–(3), for example), is evidence in itself for a dissociation between them and for the necessity of one (or more) mapping interfaces or sets of correspondence rules between feature and form (see, e.g., Aronoff, 1994; Beard, 1995; Jackendoff, 1997; Smith & Tsimpli, 1995). This also means that, until this mapping is acquired, it may not be possible for the acquisition researcher to definitively infer knowledge or, more to the point, *lack* of knowledge of the abstract categories and features based on only the presence or absence of morphological form. In our particular case here, that would be (lack of) knowledge of finiteness—and its associated phrase structure functional category—based on non-targetlike inflection for tense and/or agreement on verbs. Most especially, the omission of such inflection in production data may not constitute reliable evidence for the absence of finiteness, as we see quite clearly in the data from acquirers of K'iche' Maya reported by Pye (2001).[14]

In addition to verbal inflection, there exist other manifestations of finiteness such as the placement of verbs, the licensing of null subjects under constrained conditions, and the assignment or checking of case on subjects. Moreover, it appears that the child has knowledge of these other syntactic operations even in advance of working out the inflectional paradigms of thematic verbs. Of course, in native language acquisition, we know that the inflectional paradigms of verbs uniformly end up getting successfully acquired. That is to say, children manage to negotiate successfully the mapping between some grammatical feature —in this case, finiteness, to a morphological form or set of forms.

With these points in mind, then, let us now turn to second language acquisition, where we do not find such uniform success.

---

[14] Although a great deal of debate has focused on how to interpret morphological *omission* in both first and second language acquisition data, it is also important to note that the interpretational problem may cut both ways—namely, in correctly interpreting the presence of forms in learner production data that may not be mapped to exactly the same feature as in the mature native speaker grammar, for example, the (Primacy of) Aspect Hypothesis, which I return to in the following chapter (see Bardovi-Harlig, 2000, for a general overview and references). However, the focus on omission, especially in L1 acquisition, is motivated by the observation that children's morphological errors are largely ones of omission rather than commission; that is, in the acquisition of agreement morphology (perhaps the most widely studied morphological domain), children only rarely produce affixal mismatches for grammatical person agreement.

III. Knowledge of Finiteness in SLA

On the face of it, we might expect at least the earlier stages of second language acquisition to resemble those of first language acquisition with respect to deficits and variability in the production of the verbal morphology associated with finiteness. Most studies that have addressed this issue have done so within the context of examining the L2 initial state (or near-initial stages) and have reported that this is indeed typically the case (see for example, Dulay & Burt, 1974; Eubank, 1993/1994; Gavruseva & Lardiere, 1996; Grondin & White, 1996; Haznedar, 2001; Haznedar & Schwartz, 1997; Klein & Perdue, 1997; Müller, 1998; Prévost, 1997, 2001; Prévost & White, 1999, 2000; Vainikka & Young-Scholten, 1994, 1996a, 1996b; Zobl & Liceras, 1994; see also Hawkins, 2001a, and White, 1996, 2000, 2003b, for an overview of recent initial-state research). In this section, let us briefly turn to a few hypotheses regarding the learner's initial grammatical representation that have become prominent in recent SLA literature. Because this book is mainly concerned with the end state of second language acquisition, I summarize and address only those particular aspects that can be informed by data from an end-state grammar. It is important to keep in mind, moreover, that the explanatory goals of initial-state studies may be quite different from those investigating the L2 end state. For much greater in-depth discussion of the L2 initial state, see Schwartz and Eubank (1996) and White (2003b).

Given the similarity in morphological variability to first language acquisition, is L2 acquisition of finiteness really like L1 acquisition? In L2 studies, as in L1 acquisition, morphological deficits in learner production data have often been taken to indicate an underlying deficit in the syntactic feature or functional category associated with that particular type of inflection. In this case, the abstract formal feature in question is [± finite], presumably associated with an inflectional functional category such as IP/TP or (for German and other V2 languages) possibly CP. Simply put, if learners do not produce the morphological affixes of finiteness, does that mean they do not have this distinction in their L2 grammatical representation? Or that they fail to project the associated functional categories that host this feature in the syntactic phrase structure? Let us take a look at some studies that have directly addressed these questions.

The Truncation Hypothesis

One way in which the comparison between L1 and L2 acquisition of finiteness has been specifically addressed can be found in a recent series of studies by Prévost (1997, 2001) and Prévost and White (1999, 2000) conducted within the framework of the so-called Truncation Hypothesis (following Rizzi, 1993/1994).

Recall that young children's variable omission of finiteness morphology (or production of so-called root infinitives—RIs) appears to be correlated statistically with syntactic properties such as the failure to raise verbs in verb-raising languages,[15] as well as with the non-targetlike omission of subjects in non-null-subject languages. According to the Truncation Hypothesis, the child who is in this RI stage of acquisition has not yet fixed the functional projection CP as obligatorily projected in main clauses (as required by the Root Principle of Rizzi, 1993/1994). That is, the child in some sense does not "know" that main clauses must be CPs, and she or he may optionally "truncate" the clausal phrase structure at any category below CP, such as IP or VP. Because functional categories are associated with IP and CP, then within this model the presence or absence of finiteness morphology gives an indication of the underlying syntactic representation: Projections truncated below IP should exhibit nonfinite morphology, no modals or auxiliaries, no verb raising, and either no overt subjects or, alternatively, subjects that bear some sort of default case marking. On the other hand, clauses that do project an IP and/or a CP should contain targetlike raising, correct subject case marking, and correct finite morphological form.

For second language acquisition, Prévost (1997) and Prévost and White (1999) looked at spontaneous production data collected from four children and four adults learning either French or German as a second language, in order to investigate whether L2 learners also project different types of root clauses (CP, IP, VP) in early stages of acquisition. Although the Truncation Hypothesis was not confirmed for the adult learners, Prévost and White argue that the children's L2 data were mostly consistent with the hypothesis, especially for the two child L2 French learners (who were only 5 years old when recording started, compared with age 8 for the two child L2 German learners): Neither null subjects nor nonfinite verb forms were found in CPs (for three out of the four children), subject clitics occurred

---

[15] With the notable exception of Pye (2001) mentioned earlier, possibly suggesting that this correlation is neither causally necessary nor universal.

statistically more frequently with finite-marked verbs, and negators systematically preceded nonfinite verbs and followed finite-marked ones. This conclusion was further supported by Prévost (2001) in another similar study looking at data collected from a 3-year-old anglophone child, Cindy, learning German as a second language. As the authors point out, these findings suggest that the omission of finiteness morphology by children (but not adults) directly mirrors an underlying syntactic representation that is similarly nonfinite. That is, similar to many findings for L1 acquisition (especially of German and French), the authors claim that children at this stage of L2 acquisition apparently have not yet learned that main clauses in the language they are acquiring must be finite.[16]

It should nonetheless be pointed out that, just as in the L1 data, the data for child English L2 acquisition do not clearly exhibit the hypothesized correlations that form the basis of the Truncation Hypothesis. Two case studies have been reported: one by Gavruseva and Lardiere (1996) of an 8-year-old Russian child learning English, whose CP clauses included a high percentage of forms not marked for finiteness in obligatory finite contexts; and the second by Haznedar and Schwartz (1997) of a 4-year-old Turkish child learning English whose data showed no developmental relation between the drop-off in null subjects (which happened abruptly) and the consistent production of verbal finite inflectional morphology (which increased only very gradually). Neither of these results is predicted by the Truncation Hypothesis.[17]

---

[16] In a similar type of study, Belletti and Hamann (2000) investigated the L2 acquisition of French by two children: one German-speaking and the other Italian-speaking. They found that neither child produced root infinitives or null subjects, and they concluded that neither went through an RI/null subject phase (p. 125). However, given that each of the children already had over a year of "systematic exposure" to French, from the ages of 2;8 and 2;4, prior to data collection (p. 117), it is quite possible that such a stage was missed by the investigators. Prévost (2001) reports that the length of time of Cindy's RI phase lasted only 4 months, compared with 18 months for Kenny and Greg, the L2 French children he examined. He suggests that this might be a function of Cindy's younger age at exposure, and notes that the children in Belletti and Hamann's study were even younger still.

[17] Yet another study, by Ionin & Wexler (2000), examined the L2 acquisition of English by 20 Russian-speaking children ranging in age from 3;9 to 13;10, with a similarly wide range of age at exposure as well as extent of classroom instruction in English. The authors also found no evidence for an optional or root infinitive stage, although they are careful to point out that they were not looking at children whose L2 grammars were in an initial stage. (Additionally, the relatively advanced ages of many of the informants would presumably rule out an OI stage if, as suggested by Wexler, 1994, 1998, this stage is maturationally constrained.)

As mentioned above, second language acquisition data on morphological marking of finiteness collected from adult learners have never supported the Truncation Hypothesis. Prévost and White (1999, 2000) report that, for the adult French and German L2 data they looked at, both finite- and non-finite-marked forms were present from the earliest recordings, suggesting that there was no point at which learners used only nonfinite forms and then developmentally replaced them with (only) finite ones in obligatory finite contexts. (Müller, 1998, reports a similar finding.) Moreover, both finite and nonfinite forms were used in similar finite contexts, such as in CPs, preceding negation, or with subject clitics. Interestingly, although both finite- and nonfinite-marked verbs were common in finite contexts, finite-marked forms were rarely found in nonfinite contexts—an asymmetry the authors suggest is due to learners' knowledge of the syntactic effects of finiteness. In other words, they found that finiteness marking on verbs, although often omitted, is nevertheless not random.[18]

In sum, there appears to be some evidence for age-related effects that distinguish child from adult second language acquirers within a theoretical model that makes use of the same interesting correlations as those found in L1 acquisition—namely, between the morphological marking of finiteness and syntactic phenomena such as verb placement and the presence and case marking of overt subjects. Whereas such correlations are apparently strong for young children acquiring both first and second languages (at least for French and German), it appears that this effect may diminish with the increasing age of children, and it disappears entirely within adult second language acquisition. The data from Patty, an adult acquirer of English, turn out to be clearly compatible with this latter finding (as we will see), but obviously cannot speak to the more interesting question of whether the Truncation Hypothesis properly accounts for both child L1 and L2 acquisition. Our interest in these studies with respect to Patty, rather, lies in their support for the view that the omission of finiteness morphology is not a reliable reflection of the learner's (lack of) knowledge of finiteness.

---

[18] Müller (1998) did find certain (ambiguously) finite forms occurring in both finite and nonfinite contexts in the L2 data she examined from Bruno, a 16-year-old Italian-speaking acquirer of L2 German. However, she considered these particular forms to be underspecified and apparently not instances of productive finiteness marking. She also argues that "real" finiteness marking in her data (for the second- and third-person -*st* and -*t* present-tense verb forms, respectively) is not random.

Transfer Hypotheses

Among the various proposals that have been made regarding the status of L1 influence in the L2 learners' initial grammatical representation, let us look at three of them here, all of which in some manner involve the nature and extent of transfer of functional categories and features from the L1.

Full Transfer/Full Access

The Full Transfer/Full Access (FT/FA) Hypothesis of Schwartz and Sprouse (1994, 1996) proposes that the abstract properties of the L1 grammar in its entirety constitute the initial grammar of the L2. In other words, learners will initially adopt the clausal phrase structure (with concomitant head direction and word order effects), functional projections (e.g., TP, CP, DP), and associated formal feature specifications (e.g., for tense, aspect, person, number, gender/noun class, case, etc., or, more abstractly, of formal specifications such as "weak" or "strong") of their native language.

Grammar restructuring under FT/FA is input-driven, occurring in case of a mismatch between this initial representation and what is needed to parse or accommodate the L2 input. Precisely because of the possibility of such restructuring, we could hypothesize following FT/FA that acquired properties of an end-state L2 grammar such as Patty's which are also present in the L1 (such as knowledge that thematic verbs do not raise in English—also true for Chinese) are likely to have transferred from the L1, but we could never test this conclusively. That is, from the perspective of the end state, we have no way of determining the precise source of this knowledge in a way that could test the Full Transfer part of the hypothesis, because of the possibility of having acquired the property in question via the Full Access part. Thus, Full Transfer is truly interesting with respect to the initial state only and must be tested with initial-state data (as in fact it has been), and I will have little more to say about it here.

Full Access, on the other hand, is quite a different matter. One might question whether or not Full Access in the FT/FA model ever permits the (eventual) resetting of a parameter or feature specification for which there is no positive evidence in the input. Schwartz and Sprouse (1996) suggest not; that is, if the feature in question has already been set to a different value in the L1 than that required by the L2, and there is no positive evidence to force restructuring of the grammar, they propose that fossilization will result:

> [C]onvergence on the TL grammar is not guaranteed. ... In
> brief, given that the starting point is not simply open (or set to
> learning-theoretically delearnable 'defaults'), it may be that
> the L2 acquirer (L2er) will never be able to arrive at the TL
> grammar: either the data needed to force restructuring simply
> do not exist ... or the positive data needed are highly obscure,
> being very complex and/or rare. This view can then account for
> (aspects of) fossilization in L2 acquisition... . (p. 42)

However, in this case, it is not clear then exactly what "Full Access"
actually means. If there were positive evidence available in the input, there
might be no reason to invoke UG at all, anyway. One need invoke (full)
access to UG only in the absence (or rarity, obscurity, etc.) of positive evidence (as Schwartz & Sprouse, 2000, rightly emphasize)—exactly the circumstances, however, under which they suggest in the quote above that
fossilization will occur.

Moreover, given the model's sole reliance on properties of the L1 in
determining whether there will be (relevant types of) fossilization in the L2,
there would be no way to account for the observation—common throughout
the literature (see e.g., Birdsong, 1999; Birdsong & Molis, 2001; Long,
1990)—that, in general, nativelike ultimate L2 attainment is possible, but
is typically inversely correlated with age of acquisition. That is, the model
seems to predict that there should be no differences (of the relevant sort)
between the L2 attainment of child versus adult speakers of the same L1
acquiring the same L2 with respect to fossilization.[19] I put aside these questions for now, but return to the issue of full access in chapter 7.

Partial Transfer Hypotheses[20]

Two other initial-state hypotheses are particularly relevant for our purposes
here for their perspective on the relation between morphological inflection
for finiteness and properties of the L2 clausal phrase structure. In both of

---

[19] In connection with this point, Schwartz and Sprouse (1996) note: "This approach to fossilization strikes us as much more promising than the notion of a 'critical period'. The problem with an explanation of fossilization based on a critical period is that it does not offer a
sufficiently articulated theory of precisely which aspects of the TL can be acquired and
which cannot" (p. 49). At present, I think this rather bleak assessment is essentially correct.

[20] I am following White's (1996, 2000) classification scheme here.

these models, morphological deficiency in learner production data has led their proponents to conclude that learner knowledge of the abstract categories and/or features associated with the corresponding inflectional forms is also somehow defective.

The first of these—the Minimal Trees Hypothesis proposed by Vainikka and Young-Scholten (1994, 1996a, 1996b, 1998)—has argued (following similar models for L1 acquisition) that only lexical categories (e.g., VP, NP, AP) are initially available to the learner; in second language acquisition, the phrase structure configuration (e.g., SOV or SVO word order) for these categories is transferred from the L1 into the L2. However, the functional categories of the L1 (T/AgrP, CP, DP, and knowledge of associated features, including finiteness) do not transfer. These must be acquired instead on the basis of the input—specifically as a result of learning the morphological items associated with them.[21]

How is this relevant to the L2 end state? Following Vainikka (1993/1994) and other so-called Weak Continuity models for L1 acquisition,[22] Vainikka and Young-Scholten propose that the subsequent developmental path with regard to the acquisition of functional categories is hierarchically *implicational*; that is, functional categories are gradually acquired in successive stages in a bottom-up kind of learning process (which is nonetheless argued to be UG-constrained), and the projection of higher functional categories (e.g., CP) in the grammatical representation is necessarily contingent on the projection of lower ones, including those categories associated with IP, such as T/AgrP and NegP; see (10):

---

[21] Vainikka and Young-Scholten (1998) propose that the input triggers for the representation of functional categories differ for children and adults. Specifically, they claim that bound morphemes such as affixes trigger the projection of related functional categories for children but not for adults, whereas adults make use of free morphemes instead. I return to a discussion of this bound versus free morpheme proposal later.

[22] See for example, Clahsen et al. (1993/1994), Clahsen and Penke (1992), and Radford (1990, 1995, 1996).

(10)

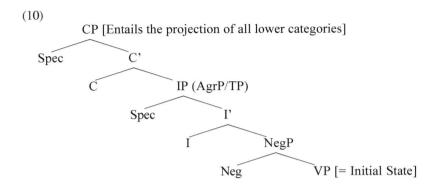

This implicational order of the acquisition of the L2 phrase structure, as well as the reliance on inflectional morphology to generate it, set up fairly clear predictions for the order of acquisition of various morpholexical elements associated with each functional category. Ultimately, we would expect an end-state grammar to instantiate the features associated with *all* the categories for which there is morphological evidence in the input. Note, in fact, that if all categories are indeed present in the L2 end-state grammar, we cannot be sure of the developmental order in which they were acquired. However, we should not expect to find that morpholexical elements (such as complementizers) associated with outer categories have been acquired if obligatory elements (such as verbal inflectional morphology) associated with more inner ones have not. Specifically, in the case of finiteness marking in English, we should not expect to find CPs lacking the inflectional features associated with finiteness. I return to this prediction and further discussion below.

The second partial transfer hypothesis is the Valueless Features (or Weak Transfer) Hypothesis of Eubank (1993/1994, 1994, 1996), who proposed that L2 acquirers transfer all the categorial projections from their L1 into the L2, including functional projections, but that features associated with these projections are unspecified or "inert" until the learner acquires the inflectional morphology associated with them. The specification of finiteness features in particular is viewed under this model as a prerequisite for learner knowledge of verb raising (or non-raising), and the acquisition of the morphological paradigm is in turn viewed as a prerequisite for specifying the abstract formal features correctly. The developmental prediction thus generated for the L2 grammar is that learners will not acquire knowledge of verb raising until they have acquired the verbal morphological paradigm, and until then should demonstrate variable or optional verb raising.

In a somewhat later series of papers (Eubank & Grace, 1998; Eubank et al., 1997; Eubank et al., 1998), the Valueless Features Hypothesis was modified to incorporate Vainikka and Young-Scholten's (1994) claim that early projections do not include functional categories, as well as Beck's (1998) Local Impairment Hypothesis, according to which certain abstract features might be permanently unacquirable (i.e., "impaired"). Thus, even if finiteness inflectional morphology is eventually acquired, learners may still not be able to specify the feature relevant to verb raising. This failure is thought to be driven by maturational factors, such as L2 acquisition beyond a critical period during which the relevant feature must be specified. Optional verb raising, then, according to the revised hypothesis, may be expected to persist into the L2 end-state grammar.

We return to the predictions made by both the original and revised versions of the Valueless Features Hypothesis, as well as more in-depth discussion of associated verb-raising studies, in chapter 5.

IV. Finiteness in an End-State L2 Grammar: Patty

As mentioned earlier, children acquiring their native language eventually manage to successfully implement the mapping between a given abstract formal feature of their language and the corresponding morphological form or set of forms. Initial-state SLA studies are not designed to address whether second language acquirers also eventually succeed at this task, although some of these studies, as we have seen, do suggest possible eventual outcomes. We know that nativelike attainment in all respects is not necessarily (or even typically) the case in second language acquisition, particularly in the case of acquisition by adults. The data from Patty highlight one of the sharpest differences between first and (adult) second language acquisition—namely, in ultimate attainment outcomes—but what is the actual nature of this difference?

One of the most obvious features of Patty's English production is the frequent omission of finiteness morphology on verbs. Similar to the observations made by Prévost (1997) and Prévost and White (1999, 2000) for the adults in their studies, we can definitely rule out any sort of truncation analysis for Patty. That is, the morphological variability evident in her grammar does not exhibit the same correspondences with other grammatical characteristics as those observed for children that were mentioned earlier.

First, there is no correlation of morphological omission with the presence of null subjects. In fact, Patty clearly knows that subjects are required in English, often produces expletive subjects, and only rarely produces null subjects. Null subjects occur overall in fewer than 2% of the nearly 1,500 obligatory finite contexts requiring overt subjects, and these are quite evenly distributed between clauses both marked and unmarked for finiteness. (It is not even clear that all of what I have classified as null subject utterances are actually missing subjects, since they might admit alternative analyses.) More precise numbers are provided in Table 3.1, with some of the clearer examples following in (11).

TABLE 3.1. Patty's Overt vs. Null Subjects in Obligatory Finite Contexts.

Recording	Overt	%	Null	%
1	362	99.45	2	00.55
2	788	97.89	17	02.11
3	329	97.92	7	02.08
Total	1479	98.27	26	01.73

(11) a. well at that time maybe mix in a little English
      b. they always say that think I'm Shanghainese
      c. so then for the first time met his parents
      d. was in China
      e. I have friends from Indonesia also speak Hokkien

It is also the case that Patty often produces CPs with missing verbal inflection for finiteness, contrary to Truncation Hypothesis predictions. Several examples of these are also provided in (12):

(12) a. that my cousin ask me to come
      b. that's how he interact people
      c. you would amaze, how he know so many thing
      d. when he interview me, and then he say "well, I think you have some accent"
      e. I do remember that the manager say that I have to speak up when I doing my customer
      f. well, if he want to interpret, he can't do it
      g. I don't think that God give us problem
      h. because he give us sad, you mean?
      i. maybe we are the one who chosen
      j. he have the inspiration to say what he want to say

It is also the case, of course, as the examples in (12) show, that Patty has clearly acquired a CP projection, despite the fact that her verbal inflection for tense and agreement marking remains seriously deficient. This fact constitutes a problem for the implicational structure-building approach taken in the Minimal Trees Hypothesis, since it looks as if CP has certainly been projected before the inflectional properties of lower categories such as AgrP or TP have been fully acquired. (However, this is only a problem depending on what sort of criteria we adopt for "acquisition" and which morphological elements associated with these categories we allow to "count" in enabling projection of the next higher category. I return to this issue directly below.)

In the case of knowledge of finiteness, as I have argued elsewhere (Lardiere, 1998a) and further elaborate on here, we observe in Patty a distinct split between her apparent knowledge of the abstract formal feature itself, which seems to be perfectly acquired, and her knowledge (or use) of appropriate verbal inflectional forms, which is clearly non-nativelike in many respects. (By nativelike or non-nativelike, I mean in relation to the particular variety/(ies) of native-speaker input she is actually and constantly exposed to.) Let us turn to evidence for this claim.

Tense Marking and Pronominal Case

Lardiere (1998a) reported the rates of past-tense marking in obligatory finite past contexts (see that article for a more detailed account of how these contexts were determined and for a list of excluded types of data). In general, unclear or ambiguous contexts were excluded, with the overall effect of erring on the side of possibly slightly overestimating Patty's rate of suppliance.[23] Past-tense marking was considered supplied if the copula or auxiliary (if present) or thematic main verb (if no auxiliary was present) was marked for past tense (as in the examples in (13a) below), even if agreement was wrong (as in the examples in (13b)) or if other elements of the VP were

---

[23] This is because much of the excluded data tended to be (apparently) unmarked for past tense, thus possibly depressing the overall percentage of the "unmarked" category, which would have been higher had (some of) these items been included. For further information and justification, see Lardiere (1998a). On the other hand, there is additional evidence, which I discuss below and in the next chapter, that Patty's suppliance of past-tense marking is actually much better (although still obviously non-nativelike) when written data are also taken into consideration. (Lardiere, 1998a, reported on spontaneous oral production data only.)

improperly inflected (as in the examples in (13c)). Examples of non-suppliance of past-tense marking are provided in (13d).

(13) a.   since my mom *was* a teacher
         my grandfather never *spoke* it
         she *didn't* tell me that
         and then he *gained* his sight
         she # he *would* look at my journal

    b.   so two of us *was* living in Chinatown
         her son and future daughter-in-law *was* in my training

    c.   so we *were* dance for, like, couple dance, right?
         I *was* graduate in 1980
         my heart *would* bounding

    d.   Jesus *is* raise after three days
         yesterday they *open* until five
         and then I *start* taking TOEFL, you know?
         I *change* my major on my first year to accounting
         but then after awhile, he just *give up*

The results showed that Patty produced past-tense marking in only about 35% of obligatory contexts—a rate that remained stable over the nearly 9-year recording period. Thus, it is obvious that Patty's past-tense marking is clearly non-nativelike. The precise numbers are given in Table 3.2 below (based on Lardiere, 1998a, p. 16).

TABLE 3.2. Past Marking in Finite Past Obligatory Contexts.

Recording	Suppliance/Contexts	%
1	24/69	34.78
2	191/548	34.85
3	46/136	33.82
Total	261/753	34.66

One of the points made in Lardiere (1998a) in reference to Patty's past-tense marking was methodological: Does this percentage (34.66%) constitute "acquisition"? According to criteria cited among the relevant literature, this figure falls far short of what some Partial Transfer Hypothesis advocates have considered sufficient evidence for the projection of the associated functional category (TP, in this case).[24] Eubank (1993/1994), for example, appears to have considered a 25% suppliance rate of tense marking in the case-study data he examined to be insufficient for positing acquisition of tense (no positive criterion was provided, however), and Eubank and Grace (1998) employed a 70% criterion of 3SG agreement marking on an oral translation task as indicating acquisition of agreement. Similarly, Vainikka and Young-Scholten (1994) employed a criterion for acquisition of agreement as the production of a correct agreement affix in at least 60% of raised thematic verbs (i.e., excluding modals, auxiliaries, and the copula) and at least two correct instances of at least four different affixes of the (regular, thematic) verb agreement paradigm. More to the point, the production of agreement and tense under these criteria in these studies was treated as evidence for the projection of the appropriate syntactic phrase structure (i.e., AgrP and TP), and *their omission equated with a corresponding absence of these functional categories in the learner's grammatical representation.*

Under this view, it appears that Patty's rate of past-tense marking would be considered insufficient to meet these criteria for acquisition and specifically for her projecting those functional categories for which the associated overt morphology is taken to be a sign of knowledge of finiteness. However, we also have good reason to believe that this conclusion would be inaccurate, at least in Patty's case.

Despite Patty's low suppliance rates of past-tense marking (and even lower rates of inflectional agreement marking, to be discussed shortly), I have argued that she has perfectly acquired the finiteness distinction in English. Recall that for English, we observed earlier that it is the distinctive form of pronominal subjects—that is, the presence of subject or nominative case marking on subject pronouns—that can serve as a more reliable correlate of clausal finiteness in the input than verbal morphology. Patty has definitely learned this. Examining the same finite contexts as those used to determine her rate of past-tense marking, we find that her suppliance of nominative case marking on subjects in finite clauses is perfect, at 100%, as shown in Table 3.3 (from Lardiere, 1998a, p. 18).[25]

---

[24] Moreover, this percentage plummets if we were to exclude from consideration copular and auxiliary forms, which are often excluded from consideration in other studies. I return to this point below.

[25] Although only past contexts were used for this study, I should point out that there are no errors in choice of case for any pronoun in any context in the entire corpus. There are (very infrequent) instances of null subjects, which I discuss shortly.

TABLE 3.3. Pronominal Subject Case Marking in
Finite Past Contexts.

Recording	Suppliance/Contexts	%
1	49 / 49	100
2	378 / 378	100
3	76 / 76	100
Total	503 / 503	100

These figures suggest that Patty has acquired a functional projection above the verb, presumably TP, specified for finiteness, which (following Chomsky, 1995) checks the case of a subject DP—in this case, a pronoun—which has raised into its domain. This case checking is clearly not optional or variable in Patty's English grammar, occurring 100% of the time.

How do we know that Patty has not simply learned that pronominal subjects are associated with one special kind of spell-out, and objects another? If we compare Patty's pronominal case marking on the subjects of finite versus nonfinite clauses, it becomes clear that it is indeed finiteness rather than "subjecthood" that is determining case. Taking a look at the nonfinite contexts, we observe similarly perfect choice of non-nominative case marking on those subjects, as shown in the examples in (14):

(14) a. why do you want *me* to go?
      b. that doesn't have anything to do with *me* leaving home
      c. it's the best for *me* to stay in Shanghai
      d. maybe they don't want *us* to use it after office hour
      e. so for *them* to learn English, you know ...
      f. so he make *me* spending money

In sum, despite a very low rate of past-tense marking, Patty's pronominal case marking is perfectly distributed throughout the data, strongly implicating the presence of TP in her grammar, specified for finiteness. Here we have compelling evidence that verbal finiteness inflection is distinct from knowledge of the formal syntactic feature of finiteness itself.

Agreement Marking

What about Patty's agreement marking? Lardiere (1998b, 1999) reported on suppliance of agreement in nonpast obligatory finite contexts. Agreement rates were calculated in these contexts for thematic (lexical) verbs, auxiliaries *do* and *have*, and the entire paradigm for copular/auxiliary *be*. The results are shown below in Table 3.4, based on Lardiere (1998b, p. 366):

TABLE 3.4. Patty's Agreement Marking in All Nonpast
Obligatory Finite Contexts.

Recording	Suppliance/Contexts	%
1	61 / 125	48.80
2	51 / 59	86.44
3	62 / 87	71.26
Total	174 / 271	64.21

At first glance, the overall total of 64% looks pretty good—meeting Vainikka and Young-Scholten's (1994) 60% criterion, approaching the 70% minimum standard set by Eubank and Grace (1998), and exceeding both studies' standards if we look at only the later two recordings. However, this comparison is misleading. Vainikka and Young-Scholten (1994, 1996b) explicitly excluded auxiliary and copular forms from their calculations of their data. Likewise, although Eubank and Grace included copular and auxiliary forms among their oral translation task items, they counted those items as distracters and also excluded them from their calculations, reporting only the results for 3SG -*s* marking on main lexical verbs. The same procedure when applied to Patty's data reveals that an overwhelming proportion of her agreement marking (as well as obligatory contexts) comes from precisely those items that were excluded in the above-mentioned studies—primarily copular and auxiliary *be*. Table 3.5 provides the results of Patty's agreement marking (i.e., 3SG -*s*) on lexical main verbs.

TABLE 3.5. Patty's Agreement Marking on Lexical Main Verbs in Nonpast Obligatory Finite Contexts.[26]

Recording	Suppliance/Contexts	%
1	2 / 42	04.76
2	0 / 4	00.00
3	1 / 22	04.54
Total	3 / 68	04.41

As is apparent from Table 3.5, Patty's agreement marking on lexical main verbs is virtually nonexistent, at an overall suppliance rate of only about 4% to 5%—low enough, perhaps, to qualify as noise or performance error, perhaps a misplaced contracted *be* form (i.e., -'s). If, however, we examine the rate of agreement marking for just those nonpast contexts involving auxiliary/copular *be* in Patty's data, as shown in Table 3.6 below, we find rates of suppliance ranging from about 83% to 94%, with well over 90% suppliance in the later two recordings.

TABLE 3.6. Patty's Agreement Marking on Auxiliary/Copular *Be* in Nonpast Obligatory Finite Contexts.

Recording	Suppliance/Contexts	%
1	57 / 69	82.61
2	50 / 53	94.34
3	59 / 63	93.65
Total	166 / 185	89.73

What accounts for this enormous difference in lexical verb (i.e., 3SG -*s* affixation) versus copular/auxiliary *be* agreement marking, and what (if anything) does it indicate? One obvious factor in accounting for the difference is the effect of input frequency of these respective kinds of contexts—roughly mirrored in Patty's own production.[27] Another is a com-

---

[26] Recall that obligatory contexts for 3SG -*s* affixation are actually quite limited—primarily to stative verbs or verbs denoting a habitual action.

[27] A breakdown of types and tokens of the finite element in all finite contexts has been calculated for the two native speaker interlocutors (one of which is Patty's husband) in Patty's third recording, as a rough indicator of ongoing NS input. That breakdown shows that copu-
(Continued)

parative lack of distributional complexity. The nonpast *be* agreement paradigm is not uniform (i.e., the form varies across person distinctions in the singular), but, as mentioned earlier in the chapter, it consistently appears in a given form (depending on the subject) in a raised position associated with finiteness. Recall our observation from earlier in the chapter that the finite/nonfinite distinction in English may simply not be easily inducible from the morphological form of lexical thematic verbs in the input. Instead, elements such as modals, auxiliaries, and the copula, to the extent they are present in a clause, are likely to be more reliable indicators of finiteness.

In my view, the data from Patty clearly show that it is not the case, as Eubank (1994) suggests, that until the 3SG -*s* affix is productively acquired learners are "speaking in nonfinite clauses" (p. 91). At the same time that learners are omitting 3SG affixation in English—persisting into the L2 end state in Patty's case—they are nonetheless producing morphological reflexes of finiteness elsewhere. Having (correctly) determined that finiteness is associated with one or more Infl categories in English, Patty in fact rather consistently locates it there, in her choice of pronominal subject case and use of the *be* paradigm. Let us turn to some additional data next.

More on Patty's Finiteness Marking (All 3SG Contexts)

Whereas Lardiere (1998a, 1998b) reported figures for Patty's past-tense marking and nonpast agreement marking, respectively, there is another category we ought to consider, representing a fairly sizable group of Patty's utterances—namely, those past contexts that are not marked for past tense but that nonetheless are marked in some way for finiteness (e.g., use of nonpast copular or auxiliary forms, incorrect modal usage of *will* vs. *would*, etc.).[28] Additionally, as I discuss in more detail in the next chapter, reliably determining obligatory contexts for use of past-tense marking is not entirely unproblematic, given native speakers' own occasional use of

---

lar/auxiliary *be* alone accounts for over 37% of all contexts—more than all lexical verb types combined (31%). Non-lexical types, including copular/auxiliary *be*, other auxiliaries, and modals, make up about 69% of all finite contexts in the NS production data for Recording 3. (See also Tincoff et al. (2000) for the frequency of *be* counts in mothers' input to children for L1 acquisition.)

[28] Herschensohn (2000) reports a similar preponderance of this type of error in her case study of the L2 acquisition of French by two anglophone adults, Emma and Chloe. She notes that Emma, in particular, was unable to sustain past-tense marking in extended discourse and frequently reverted to present-tense marking in obligatory past contexts.

so-called "historical present" and nonpast marking in subordinate clauses in some "sequence of tense" constructions.

For yet another, supplemental, way of looking at the data, therefore, I calculated Patty's rate of morphological marking for every finite context with a 3SG subject, regardless of tense—that is, her suppliance of either past-tense marking or agreement marking, whether on thematic verbs or via copula/auxiliary use. Additionally, her use of a modal in correct position was construed as an instance of finite marking, even though modals are generally uninflected. These results offer a composite view complementary to the obligatory past contexts (which, of course, included all person/number categories) previously reported in Lardiere (1998a). Examples from the 3SG contexts are given in (15):

(15) Lexical verb marked: he *followed* the instruction
    it *means* different, you know?
    he *came* to United State two years before me

    Lexical verb unmarked: the maid *pick up* a lot of Hokkien from us
    but then after awhile he just *give up*
    but he *love* opera

    Copula marked: since my mom *was* a teacher
    who *is* the tax accountant
    but *it's* very very slow

    Copula omitted: this one better than the other one
    he around adult a lot
    front tooth a little bit black

    Copula unmarked: supposed *to be* everybody *be* able to do nine
    you know how this going to *be* sound[29]

---

[29] This type of error, involving the use of infinitive *be*, is rare; that is, I view it as a probable lexicalized or performance error. There are only four instances in the entire corpus, three of which involve the phrase *be able to*. Although there are too few instances to make any generalizations about, it is interesting that, in the examples shown here in the text, the infinitive *to be* is in an unraised position (cf. the intended meanings: 'you know how this is going to sound' and in the preceding example: 'everybody is supposed to be able to do nine' or 'it's supposed to be that everybody is able to do nine' with either a raised or expletive subject). In this latter utterance by Patty, the subject is unraised, and both the matrix and embedded verb forms are nonfinite.

Auxiliary *be* marked:	she *was* chosen from forty people
	she *'s* not moving away
	his family *'s* coming up, too
Auxiliary *be* omitted:	he just feeling bad, you know?
	and then the answering service answering
	she just hanging around
Other auxiliaries marked:	time *has* pass
	it *doesn't* stick anymore
	she *got* stuck on the first piece
Other auxiliaries unmarked:	so he *don't* even come up here?
	she *don't* speak very fluently[30]
Modal provided:	she *should* be able to
	this place that *will* do the catering
	how *can* she memorize so much
Modal not provided:	(he said) he call me last night[31]

---

[30] The only type appearing with 3SG subjects in this unmarked auxiliary category is *don't*. Although not a common error, there are a few instances of missing *do/have* auxiliaries from other non-3SG contexts, such as: *we go over for an hour now* (intended meaning: 'we've gone/been going for over an hour now'); *since then, because of the training, I be able to overcome that*; *but how you get into my voicemail?*; *why you have to go back?*

Note that, although I did not count them this way, in examples such as *she don't speak very fluently* it may certainly be possible to interpret Patty's use of *don't* as formally similar to a modal on a par with *can't* or *won't*, and therefore a morphological indicator of finiteness despite lack of agreement or tense marking. Otherwise we might expect something like *she not speak very fluently*, which she virtually never produces. (There is a single example in these data—*it's not hurt* (intended meaning, referring to a pair of new shoes: 'it doesn't hurt' or 'they don't hurt'), which though incorrect is still marked for finiteness.) The reason I did not treat *don't* this way, however, is because Patty does exhibit a distinction among *don't*, *didn't*, and *doesn't*; that is, all these forms are present in her production data.

[31] The intended meaning is 'he said he *would* call me last night'. In this particular case, clarification was requested from both native speaker interlocutors to interpret Patty's potentially ambiguous utterance, as evident in the transcript of the recording excerpt shown here:

PAT: You know, I call B. this morning and nobody answer. And I start to worry.
NS1:   Do you have his phone number where he is?
PAT: Well, he either stay in Eliotville, because *he said he call me last night*, and he never did.
NS2:   He said he *'d* call you?

(Continued)

Out of a total of 578 finite contexts with 3SG subjects, two-thirds (66.78%) were marked somehow for finiteness (even if not for past tense in an obligatory past context), whereas one-third (33.22%) were not. These results are shown in Table 3.7:

TABLE 3.7. Total 3SG Finite Marking (Including All Lexical Verbs, Auxiliaries, Modals, Copula).

Recording	Yes	(%)	No	(%)	Total #
1	94	(52.22)	86	(47.78)	180
2	182	(77.12)	54	(22.88)	236
3	110	(67.90)	52	(32.10)	162
Total	386	**(66.78)**	192	(33.22)	578

Similar to the earlier findings (Lardiere, 1998b, 1999) I reported for nonpast agreement, the overwhelming majority (approximately 78%) of all finite-marked forms with 3SG subjects comprise non-lexical categories, consisting of auxiliaries, modals and the copula. On the other hand, the overwhelming majority (about 82%) of all non-marked forms in obligatory contexts with 3SG subjects are lexical verbs; that is, finiteness inflection is much more likely to be omitted on lexical thematic verbs than on non-thematic elements. Across all the data, the most frequent finite-marked form (fully three-quarters of all finite-marked forms) is of copular/auxiliary *be* (i.e., *is*, *was*, *-'s*).

Extracting only thematic verbs from among the total items in Table 3.7 above (as is typical in studies on finite inflection, as noted earlier), yields the results presented in Table 3.8:

NS1:   He said he *would?*

PAT: Yeah, he would. In the morning I talk to him from Eliotville, and then even if he stay over Eliotville, he will give me a call, you know?

NS1:   Yeah.

PAT: And then I call her house and nobody answer.

Again, although not a common error, there are a few instances of missing modals from other (non-3SG) contexts, such as: *oh gosh, I wish I remember it* (probable intended meaning in context: 'I wish I could remember it'); *I notice it next time*; *maybe I go back today*.

TABLE 3.8. Lexical Verb Finite Marking Only (3SG Excluding All
Auxiliaries, Modals, Copulas).

Recording	Yes	(%)	No	(%)	Total #
1	12	(15.19)	67	(84.81)	79
2	20	(30.77)	45	(69.23)	65
3	15	(24.19)	47	(75.81)	62
Total	47	**(22.82)**	159	(77.18)	206

Table 3.8 shows that fewer than 23% of lexical verbs with 3SG subjects bear some sort of finiteness marking on the verb itself. The overwhelming majority of these (83%) are irregular past forms. Regular affixal
past and affixal 3SG -s are both scarce, each making up only about 8.5% of
finite-marked verbs in these data (i.e., the Yes column in Table 3.8), and
only about 2% of the total lexical verbs represented in Table 3.8. Patty
clearly disprefers affixal marking of finiteness on the main verb. I provide
more in-depth discussion of Patty's past-tense marking in the following
chapter; for now, let us consider one possible explanation for the data on
agreement.

Revisiting the Position versus Form of Finiteness Marking

As mentioned earlier (in Footnote 21), one proposal for accounting for an
observed disparity in the acquisition of bound versus free morphemes in
adult SLA comes from Vainikka and Young-Scholten (1996a, 1998), who
argue that the input triggers for functional categories differ for children and
adults. Specifically, they claim that children acquire regular verbal para-
digmatic affixes associated with a particular functional head before the free
morphemes associated with the same head, whereas the opposite is true for
adults. That is, bound morphemes are claimed to serve as more salient triggers for functional category projections for children than they do for adults,
who instead depend on the acquisition of free morphemes to trigger new
structure. Leaving aside for the time being the (controversial) question of
whether the acquisition of any sort of morpheme is necessary to "trigger"
phrase structure, let us look at their claim that child acquisition differs from
adult acquisition of morphological agreement, and that this difference de-
rives from some type of a sensitive period for language development related
to the availability of bound morphology (1998, pp. 98–99).

Vainikka and Young-Scholten (1998) observe in their data that (German) affixal agreement forms, even after they have been acquired by adults,
are nonetheless produced much less consistently than by L1 children at

comparable stages of development. The English L2 data from Patty are certainly compatible with the general observation that the consistent target-like production of affixal forms seems to pose problems for a much longer period of time (possibly into the end state) for adults than for children. But I am much more skeptical that this holds as a result of different "triggering" preferences between children and adults—specifically, an initial preference by children for bound morphology and/or the lesser perceptual salience of bound versus free morphemes for adults.[32]

In support of their triggering claim, Vainikka and Young-Scholten (1998) cite findings from the English morpheme order studies carried out in the 1970s for both first and (adult and child) second language acquisition. They write:

> In one of the original studies, Bailey, Madden and Krashen (1974) noted that the order of acquisition for adult L2 learners was similar to that of L2 children, but dissimilar to that of L1 children. If we look at these morpheme orders in terms of order within specific functional projections ... we can see that L1 children tend first to acquire affixes—that is, bound morphemes—related to the specific projections whereas L2 learners initially acquire free morphemes and subsequently the corresponding affixes. (p. 98)

The very first observation to make is that, if L2 children's morpheme orders are more like those of L2 adults rather than those of L1 children, we are probably not looking at a critical or sensitive period phenomenon with respect to triggering phrase structure, contrary to Vainikka and Young-Scholten's claim. Vainikka and Young-Scholten themselves cite a German-English L1 bilingual acquisition study (Döpke, 1998) suggesting that "the treatment of bound morphemes differs from what has been observed for monolingual German acquisition" (p. 109). Additional evidence against critical period-related triggering differences for bound versus free morphemes can be provided: Haznedar (2001) has reported that the 4-year-old Turkish-speaking child she observed acquired the English copular and aux-

---

[32] Heather Goad (personal communication, April 21, 2004) has helpfully pointed out to me that some bound morphology (e.g., the late-acquired English 3SG nonpast agreement affix and [+strident] segments in general), is highly salient and perceptible, the latter involving a concentration of energy in higher frequencies which enables it to appear adjacent to any type of segment, including stops. A reviewer informs me as well that perceptual salience has been "convincingly discounted" in the context of SLI deficits in regular inflectional morphology. I return to a brief discussion of salience in chapter 7.

iliary *be* considerably earlier than affixal 3SG *-s*. Eubank (1993/1994) like-wise examined data from Muriel, a French-speaking child learning English who was only 4;6 at the beginning of recording (see Gerbault, 1978), and reported that Muriel did not fully acquire regular agreement and tense in-flection during the entire 11-month course of data collection, although aux-iliary *do* and modals were more "widely productive" from fairly early sam-ples (Sample 7).

Second, as evidence for their claim, Vainikka and Young-Scholten cite the English morpheme order ranking (for IP) as: past and 3SG followed by auxiliary, in L1 acquisition, versus the exact opposite order—auxiliary, followed by past and 3SG, for L2 acquisition. First of all, as Zobl and Liceras (1994) point out, both 3SG *-s* and regular past cluster "at the bot-tom of the hierarchy" for both L2 and L1 acquisition. Although Vainikka and Young-Scholten correctly list the order of these affixes with respect to "auxiliary," it is not quite correct with respect to "copula." Brown's (1973) study reported that L1 children acquired the uncontractible copula *be* prior to regular past or 3SG *-s* affixation; the L1 order in deVilliers and deVilliers (1973) ranks the contractible copula *be* higher than either regular past or 3SG *-s*.[33] Both Brown's and the deVilliers' L1 studies also rank (non-affixal, free morpheme) *irregular* past much higher than either regular past or 3SG *-s*; under minimalist assumptions, we presume that the relevant feature checking is occurring regardless of whether tense marking is regular or irregular, again implicating the presence of the appropriate functional category for hosting such feature checking.[34]

Another consideration is the acquisition of modals. The morpheme order studies did not include modals due to the difficulty in establishing reliable obligatory contexts for them. However, Brown (1973) suggests that the modals *can* and *will*, as well as semi-auxiliaries *gonna*, *wanna*, and *hafta* are productive at his learners' Stage II, at least as early as regular past

---

[33] In addition, we may observe that the uncontractible copula is often associated with I-to-C movement (e.g., *What is it?*; *Are you hungry?*), implicating the presence of a CP at this (early) point in learners' grammars.

[34] The minimalist assumptions in question here refer to the hypothesis that lexical items are inflected (possibly only featurally) in the lexicon or on entering the numeration prior to in-sertion into the syntactic structure. (See Chomsky 1995, pp. 238–239.) Of course, the as-sumption of uniform feature checking of past tense across both regular and irregular forms is presumably contingent on a uniform LF interpretation being assigned to both; in this regard, Brown (1973), while acknowledging that regular versus irregular forms "constitute partially distinct learning problems" (p. 260), indicates that the calculation of obligatory contexts for both regular and irregular past was determined by contextual information that the action the child named had occurred in the past.

and 3SG -*s* affixation (which did not reach Brown's 90% criterion until Stages IV–V). Valian's (1991) study on the acquisition of subjects showed that "children uniformly produced a subject if their utterance had a modal" (p. 77), and, as mentioned earlier, that their (pronominal) subjects were correctly marked for nominative case, suggesting that modals can support the kind of triggering role in child L1 acquisition attributed to bound affixes by Vainikka and Young-Scholten.

Vainikka's own (1993/1994) study shows that several modals appear in the very first file for Adam, well ahead of regular past-tense or agreement affixation, and at least concurrently with past-tense marking (regular vs. irregular not specified) for Eve and Sarah. Vainikka indicates that Sarah's earliest files (1–6) contain five instances of copular *is*, one instance of copular *are*, five instances of 1SG contractible *am* (i.e., *I'm*), the semi-auxiliary *wanna* (e.g., *I wanna ride my horse*) and at least two instances of *don't*, but no instances of regular past or agreement affixes. For Nina, 1SG nominative case marking on pronominal subjects (which I have argued is a more reliable indicator of finiteness) occurred consistently with modals and auxiliaries. Eve's earliest files (1–4) contain one instance of *are* and the utterances *I don't want to*, *I did it*, and *I can*, but no instances of 3SG -*s* or the past tense suffix -*ed*. In terms of emergence, therefore, there is apparently little basis for the bound affix claim.

Next, consider the -*ing* affix, which is by all accounts among the first English morphemes acquired in both first and second language acquisition. Vainikka and Young-Scholten argue that this affix is associated in (both L1 and L2) learners' grammars only with VP or possibly with a "low functional projection" such as Aspect, which accounts for its early emergence. For L2 acquisition, Zobl and Liceras (1994) point out that auxiliary *be*, although ordered after copular *be*, nonetheless clusters with the latter and also with -*ing* at the top of the rank order, and this is true for both L2 children and adults. This contrasts with L1 acquisition, in which -*ing* and auxiliary *be* are "at opposite ends of the hierarchy" (p. 169).

However, in a recent study of young children's early knowledge of discontinuous dependencies, Santelmann and Jusczyk (1998) report that 18-month-old children are already sensitive to the dependent relation between auxiliary *be* and -*ing*, across up to three intervening syllables (e.g., *the archeologist is always digging*). (Interestingly, Golinkoff et al., 2001, cited by Santelmann and Jusczyk for performing a similar experiment "in reverse," found that when the auxiliary *is* was paired in experimental conditions with -*ing* versus -*ly* versus -*lu*, the children preferred -*ing*.) Santelmann and Jusczyk conclude that such findings show that "even infants who do not regularly produce function morphemes such as *is* or *the*, are nonetheless sensitive to [their] presence. ... Moreover, ... not only are they sensitive to the presence of these functor morphemes, but 18-month-olds can track relationships between them" (p. 127). It is not clear how or even whether we should attempt to interpret this finding in regard to early phrase structure (Santelmann & Jusczyk certainly do not make any claims about this), but it does suggest that if particular input items were indeed acting as designated triggers for phrase structure, then *is* would certainly be an available if not the preferred candidate to trigger IP in English L1 acquisition, well in advance of its reliable appearance in production data. (Indeed, Santelmann & Jusczyk found that this preference for *is* was very strong among those children who were "already" into the two-word stage.)

Finally, in connection with the L2 morpheme order finding that copular/auxiliary *be* is high on the list for both adult and child L2 acquirers, note that the 3SG form of contractible *be* (i.e., -*'s*) at least behaves like a bound affix—phonetically and allomorphically identical, in fact, to plural and possessive -*s*, and yet is acquired early. In sum, I think there is more than enough counterevidence from the morpheme order studies to call into question Vainikka and Young-Scholten's claims about the primacy of bound versus free morphemes for children versus adults.

Turning away now from the morpheme order studies, recall what has been found for the L1 acquisition of other languages discussed earlier in this chapter: Raised, non-affixal copular and/or auxiliary forms are acquired early and correctly. Verrips and Weissenborn (1992) report the following for French L1 acquisition:

> In the case of the finite verbs which precede negation, we assume that the child has figured out that they are marked for agreement. ... The verbs that precede negation, namely *être*, *avoir* and *aller*, morphologically mark person (i.e. 1st person vs. 2nd/3rd person), by suppletion, as opposed to the verbs following negation, which mark by 0-inflection. ... We suggest that the child analyzes the suppletive forms as being marked for person prior to the analysis of the verbs with 0-inflection. (pp. 311–312)

For German, recall similar findings—for example, Clahsen and Penke's (1992) observation that "[b]efore the acquisition of subject verb agreement, modal verbs, forms of *sein* ('to be') and verbs inflected with -*t* appear in V2 patterns, i.e., in the position in which the finiteness feature [+F] occurs..." (p. 210). Clahsen, Penke, and Parodi (1993/1994) likewise report that in their data, "in Stages I and II, auxiliaries, modals and copulas are always finite in terms of their morphological form ... [N]early all modal verbs, auxiliaries and copulas appeared in the V2/V1 position in Stages I and II" (p. 414). Vainikka and Young-Scholten's L2 model in fact follows Clahsen (1990/1991) in positing for German L1 acquisition an underspecified functional projection for finiteness (FP) at a developmental point where modals and copular *sein* are being produced, but the regular verb agreement paradigm has not yet been acquired. This projection is in fact required in order to accommodate raised finite free morphemes.

The overall point here is not to deny that adults have some sort of difficulty with (some) bound affixal morphology (Patty clearly does), or even that this difficulty is correlated with age (as independently suggested by other researchers as well, such as Johnson & Newport, 1989,[35] Newport 1990, etc.). Rather, the data suggest that neither adults *nor children* start out projecting functional categories on the basis of bound affix triggers on verbs. It appears, as discussed earlier, that finiteness is initially associated with (one or more elements in) IP, rather than with the verb, and that this is where its morphological correlates are most reliably located, both in the input to the learner and in the learner's own grammatical representation, as reflected in their experimental and spontaneous production data. Both children and adults must then work out the relation between affixal morphology on verbs and finiteness, and children appear ultimately to succeed at this much more quickly than adults.

There is one more piece of evidence that we can add to support this overall picture—namely, the overextension of copular/auxiliary *be* to contexts where either the verb itself should be marked and is not, or where the verb is in fact marked, resulting in double-marking.

In the English L1 acquisition context, Brown (1973) observes for Adam that at the point "when *it's* became frequent in appropriate contexts (*It's hot*; *It's dog*; *It's here*) it promptly overgeneralized to certain inappropriate contexts. The following are representative: *It's fell … It's has wheels … There it's goes …*" (p. 392).[36] This incidence of overgeneralization prompted Brown to conclude that *it's* for Adam was monomorphemic; however, Brown emphasizes that, although *it's* was morphophonologically unsegmented, it was not grammatically unanalyzed:

---

[35] In fact, Johnson and Newport (1989) reported that determiners—a non-affixal morpheme—incurred the highest error rate among their study participants.

[36] Although the contractible copula was the next-to-last morpheme to be acquired (late in Stage V) of Adam's morpheme-order ranking), Brown (1973) notes that *it's* was exceptional from early stages: "The form *it's*, which seems to contain the contracted copula or auxiliary *'s*, was heard between [Stages] II and III in 89 percent of all obligatory copula contexts and in 100 percent of all obligatory progressive contexts. … This is to say that the development of *it's* was discontinuous with and much more rapid than all other pronoun + copula combinations" (pp. 391–392).

A[nother] item of evidence suggests that *it's*, though monomorphemic, was not simply a pronunciational variant of the word *it*. When
it was in the grammatical role of verb object, as it was hundreds of
times, the overgeneralization of *it's* never occurred. This is, in the first
place, striking evidence that Adam had knowledge of grammatical relations. As such it confirms our judgment that these relations are
known from Stage I on. In the second place the failure to overgeneral-
ize *it's* to the object role indicates that the form was an allomorph of
it, conditioned by a grammatical role. *In effect the nominative form of
'it' and not just a free variant in the pronunciation of a word.* (p.
392; italics added)

For second language acquisition, *be*-overgeneralization errors have been
observed and discussed in recent work by Ionin and Wexler (2001, 2002)
on the acquisition of English by native Russian-speaking children. Ionin
and Wexler found this to be a widespread error in their data, constituting
25% of all utterances with an overt, finite *be* auxiliary. Although it was
possible for some of these errors to be construed in the progressive (and
therefore as simply missing the verbal -*ing* affix), most of them could not,
such as in cases with a generic, stative, or clearly past meaning within the
situational context. Some examples are given in (16), from Ionin and Wexler's (6b–6e):[37]

(16) they *are* help people when people in trouble
     he *is* want go up then
     he *is* run away, I stayed there
     in one episode he *is* said to Bart, "I kill you"

In Ionin and Wexler's data, these *be* forms usually occurred with otherwise uninflected verbs, leading the authors to conjecture that the *be* form
was substituting for verbal affixation (which could not be easily accessed
by these learners) as a kind of default form for checking Tense features (in
my account here, finiteness). Note that these forms always appear as auxiliaries, presumably associated with some IP category, which, I have argued,
is initially the preferred locus for morphologically indicating finiteness
even when the thematic verb itself is required to be so marked. As Ionin
and Wexler point out, the children in their study were at various stages of

---

[37] Haznedar (2001) provides a similar example from Erdem's data (p. 31, Example 31b):

Investigator: OK # good # where did you learn this? Did you do it in the nursery?
Erdem: No # I *am* do it in Turkey.

L2 acquisition and presumably are more likely to eventually come to acquire correct verb affixation; they note that their most advanced participant almost never omitted either past or 3SG -*s* affixes. We have seen, on the other hand, that in adult second language acquisition this result may never be attained.

What about Patty? She also overgenerates *be*, although perhaps not as often as some of the subjects in Ionin and Wexler's study; nor are the majority of these cases clear-cut as to whether they could be construed as simple -*ing* omissions in progressive aspectual contexts. We also find occasional double-marking of finiteness. A few examples of *be*-overgeneration are shown in (17):

(17) a.   that *is* make a difference
    b.   I *was* have a breakthrough
    c.   so I *was* stay by myself in the dormitory when I was in China
    d.   a child without discipline *is* only do harm to her or him
    e.   I'm still # I *was* still wrote to my friend
    f.   I *was* suddenly have to write # try English
    g.   this *is* all depends on the doctor's recommendation
    h.   I'*m* start to have a lot of friends

Perhaps the most informative example involves the self-"correction" shown in (18), suggesting that Patty somehow caught herself failing to mark finiteness, involving a verb she occasionally has trouble accessing the correct form for (as we will see in the next chapter):

(18)   he also # he'*s* also speak in tongue that day

Thus, even in the L2 end state, *be*-overgeneration can still be a productive device for indicating finiteness and, in my view, also indicates a more widespread inclination to tie morphological finiteness directly to its associated functional position in the clause if possible, rather than on the (unraised) verb itself.[38] In other words, I think it likely that the initial primary expression of finiteness as a morphophonological reflex associated with the same functional category (IP), which actually hosts the abstract feature in

---

[38] Such an inclination would follow in the overall spirit of Zobl and Liceras (1994), although of course not in the technical details of their analysis, which relied on the markedness of affix lowering to account for the L2 morpheme orders in English. The more general idea, though, is that learners know where the [±finite] feature is located in the phrase structure; the morphological expression of this feature, although untargetlike at PF (in the *be*-overgeneration instances), nevertheless reflects that knowledge.

question, is shared by all learners of English, not just adults, and reflects their early knowledge of that feature. We know that L1 acquirers of English (and probably child L2 acquirers) eventually converge on the correct PF exponence of finiteness. The data from Patty, however, show that this non-targetlike but rather utilitarian way of expressing finiteness may persist into the adult L2 acquirer's grammatical steady state.

The fact that regular past and 3SG affixation cluster at the bottom of the morpheme-order hierarchy for both L1 and L2 acquisition may well reflect the additional fact that the use of these affixes also happens to re-quire knowledge of additional semantic and grammatical functions; they are (I repeat) not the same thing as finiteness itself. Children of course do even-tually work out the association of these affixes with the semantic/functional intricacies of past tense (discussed in the following chapter) and nonpast (habitual, generic, stative, etc.) 3SG agreement, whereas adult L2 acquirers seem to take longer to do this and might never do so fully. This failure may involve any or all of functional, maturational, L1-related (either syn-tactic or phonological) processing, or other possibly idiosyncratic reasons. (In fact, Patty completely accepts native speakers' use of 3SG -s but thinks it feels a bit "strange" when she produces it in her own conversational speech, undoubtedly in part because its omission has become so entrenched in her output over the past 25 years. The effect, I imagine, might be some-what similar to my listening to a lot of BBC and then attempting to speak temporarily with a British English accent instead of my own American English one.)

Returning to Vainikka and Young-Scholten's claim that bound versus free morphemes differ in their role of triggering phrase structure for children versus adults, we can agree that (some) bound affixes do indeed appear to pose more of a learning problem for adults than children. However, I think the effects of this learning problem lie not in triggering phrase structure at the initial state, but rather in some difference—probably maturationally constrained in some way—between adults and children in the process of working out the correspondences between abstract features and phonological forms, as reflected in their respective states of eventual ultimate conver-gence with the input. At least in Patty's case, however, this difference is apparently unrelated to her knowledge of clausal phrase structure or the fun-damental formal property of clausal finiteness.

4

The Acquisition of Past Tense

In the preceding chapter, we observed in Patty's data a perfect correlation between clausal finiteness and the form of pronominal case marking, which I have argued demonstrates that she has nativelike knowledge of the finite/nonfinite distinction in English. At the same time, as we have seen, the morphological correlates of finiteness (particularly thematic verb inflection) are clearly non-nativelike in her grammar. Returning to Patty's incidence of past-tense marking, we observed that it was fairly low—less than 35% overall in obligatory past contexts over an approximately 9-year period of data collection.

In this chapter, I consider this low rate of past-tense marking. I present a more detailed breakdown of Patty's past-tense marking by verb type, introduce additional data from written (e-mail) samples, and discuss various factors that have been argued in the second language acquisition literature to play a role in the production and distribution of past-tense marking. I will not argue that Patty's grammatical representation of past tense in English is completely identical to that of native speakers, because I have no evidence that could show that it is. However, I would additionally like to reconsider what it actually means to acquire "past tense" in English, how the nature of this feature contrasts with that of finiteness, and whether the morphosyntactic status of [± past] as a unitary interpretable feature and a "parameterized option" in UG (following Hawkins, 2000) can be maintained.

Let us first turn to a look at Patty's past-tense marking by verb type, to see whether we can extract any generalizations from the data.

What Does Patty Typically Mark for Past Tense?

At first glance, we appear to encounter in Patty's data the type of variability in past-tense marking that has often been reported in the SLA literature, in which even within closely proximate utterances (adjacent or nearly adjacent) we see both the presence and absence of inflection on the same verb type, or presence and omission of the auxiliary *be*:

(1) a. and also my mom also *speak* Mandarin
        yeah, they *spoke* uh, Mandarin also

 b. I *was applying* to college
        and uh, I *applying* mostly to junior college

 c. they *born* the same year
        because she *was born* in # in February
        and the other *was* in December

 d. and then he # he *gained* his sight
        yeah, Saul *gain* his sight

 e. and then I *said* "Oh, so you're Jewish, huh?"
        and then I *say*, "Well I have a girlfriend that I can introduce you to."

We also find variability in past-tense marking in coordinated VPs within the same sentence, as shown in (2):

(2) a. so I *wrote* and *speak* fluently
 b. even if I *buy* it and *left* it there until next year
 c. I *met* him and *go* out and ...
 d. *went* to school and *learn* English

However, on closer examination, past-tense marking in Patty's spoken production data turns out to be somewhat less variable than one might expect from looking at the above examples or at her overall rate of suppliance in obligatory past contexts. That is, the majority of verb types requiring past-tense marking occur rather consistently either marked or unmarked for past tense, rather than sometimes marked and sometimes not.

First, let us take a look at the non-lexical types (i.e., modals, auxiliaries, and the copula), which in fact account for a sizable chunk—approximately 43%—of all obligatory past contexts. In the spoken production data, past-tense marking for copular and auxiliary *be* in fact is indeed highly variable; the same is true for auxiliary *do*. It is important to keep in mind, however, as pointed out in the preceding chapter, that just because copular/auxiliary *be* is not marked for past tense does not mean it is not marked at all—many of its occurrences in obligatory past contexts appear in nonpast finite form (e.g., *is* instead of *was*).[1] However, the modal *would* is usually produced where required (vs. *will*), whereas the modal *could* is not (i.e., it is rather consistently produced as *can*) and the required semi-modal form *had to* is always produced as *have to*. Table 4.1 lists each non-lexical verb type followed by the number of obligatory past contexts in which each type was past-marked or not (or omitted altogether).

TABLE 4.1. Past-Tense Marking in Past Contexts for Non-Lexical Types.

Verb Type	Past	Nonpast	Omitted	Total
BE (aux)	28	10	10	48
BE (cop)	63	113	9	185
DO (aux)	16	23	2	41
HAVE (aux)	**	**	1	1
CAN/COULD	2	18	**	20
HAVE/HAD TO	0	16	**	16
WILL/WOULD	10	0	1	11

** Indicates lack of context (see Footnote 3 below).

Excluding the non-lexical types, we are left with 91 remaining verb types, comprising 431 tokens.[2] Of these 91 types, 70 are used in only one

---

[1] One interesting source of the apparent variability in past marking of *be* is Patty's occasional use of the contracted form *-'s* in obligatory past contexts. These are likely viewed as errors by her native speaker interlocutors (and were coded as such), but it is certainly possible that, in her English idiolect, Patty uses the contracted form *-'s* for both *is* and *was*. Consider the following example from the transcript of her second recording (in which the *she* in question (her cousin) is no longer in China and had not been for decades at the interview time):

NS: And where was she, in China?
PAT: She*'s* in Peking and she was a dancer in a Peking Opera.

[2] Of course, these represent only those lexical verbs requiring past-tense marking on the verb itself, not the entire list of lexical verbs that occur (in any given grammatical context) throughout the spoken data, of which there are well over 100 additional types.

form, although in more than half of these there is only one occurrence (i.e., one token) in a past-tense context in the data, which would seemingly make it impossible to provide evidence for true within-verb variability. However, even those verb types for which there is only one token each appear to conform to a few general predictions we can make about whether any given verb is likely to be marked or not. Of the remaining 21 lexical verb types, 12 of these reach or exceed 75% consistency in past-tense marking. Only nine lexical verb types appear truly variable, falling below a 75% consistency rate. We can derive the following generalizations:

(a) Although not all irregular verb types are typically past-marked where required (some never are), those verbs that are consistently past-marked are overwhelmingly irregular. This feature of the data could have a few different explanations, one of which is phonological, especially considering the following observation:

(b) Past-tense marking that would result in a final consonant cluster (i.e., much of regular affixal past-tense marking) is typically omitted. I return to a more detailed examination of this aspect of Patty's grammar in the next section.

The two generalizations (a–b) above mirror similar observations previously reported in the SLA literature for English acquirers whose native languages were Chinese or Vietnamese (e.g., Bayley, 1991, 1996; Sato, 1984, 1990; Wolfram, 1985; Wolfram & Hatfield, 1984).

(c) The most frequent lexical main verb type, by far, is *have*. (Interestingly, this is also true for a sample of production data from her native English-speaking interlocutors analyzed for verb type frequency.) In Patty's data, however, it is never marked for past, nor is it marked when used in its semi-modal form *have to*.

(d) Phrasal verbs are typically not marked for past, even when they are irregular (e.g., *come across*, *fall asleep*, *find out*, *give up*, *hang out*, *look at*, *move in/move out*, *pick up*, *turn out*).

Table 4.2 provides the breakdown of past-tense marking for lexical verbs by verb type, indicating how many tokens of each were marked or not marked for past tense.

TABLE 4.2. Past-Tense Marking on Lexical Main Verbs in Past Contexts.

Verb Type	Past	Nonpast	Verb Type	Past	Nonpast
ACCEPT	1	0	LAUGH	0	1
ANSWER	0	3	LEARN	0	8
APPEAR	0	1	LEAVE	9	1
ARRIVE	0	1	LIKE	0	2
ASK	1	5	LIVE	0	5
BECOME	0	1	LOOK AT	0	3
BELIEVE	0	1	LOSE	1	0
BUY	2	0	LOVE	0	2
CALL	0	3	MAKE	0	1
CHANGE	0	1	MEET	15	1
CHOOSE	1	1	MEMORIZE	0	1
CLEAN	0	2	MIX	0	2
COME	11	2	MOVE	0	8
COMPLETE	0	1	NEED	0	7
CONNECT	0	1	PASS	0	1
COPY	0	1	PERFORM	0	1
DECIDE	2	0	PICK UP	0	3
DIVORCE	0	1	PLAY	0	5
DO (main verb)	5	1	READ	1	5
DRIVE	1	0	REFUSE	0	1
FALL ASLEEP	0	1	REPEAT	0	1
FEEL	0	1	SAY	7	23
FIND	1	2	SEE	3	4
FIND OUT	0	1	SEND	0	2
FINISH	0	1	SIT	0	4
FLUNK	0	1	SHOW	0	1
FOLLOW	1	0	SPEAK	22	14
FORGET	3	0	SPEND	0	6
GAIN	1	1	START	0	15
GET	6	6	STAY	0	2
GIVE	0	2	STOP	1	0
GIVE UP	0	3	TAKE	3	5
GO	19	2	TALK	0	2
GRADUATE	0	1	TEACH	0	3

(Continued on next page)

Table 4.2 (Continued from previous page)

Verb Type	Past	Nonpast	Verb Type	Past	Nonpast
HANG OUT	0	2	TELL	4	2
HAVE (main vb) [3]	0	54	TEND	0	1
HEAR	1	3	THINK	3	2
HELP	0	1	TRAVEL	0	1
IMPROVE	0	1	TRY	1	9
INTERVIEW	0	1	TURN OUT	0	1
INVITE	0	1	USE	0	1
JUMP	0	1	UNDERSTAND	1	1
KEEP	0	1	WANT	0	9
KICK	0	1	WRITE	8	0
KILL	0	1	WORK	0	5
KNOW	8	1	**Total**	**143**	**288**

The following table, Table 4.3, provides a summary of the individual consistency rates for verb types from Patty's spoken production data for

---

[3] Regarding auxiliary *have*, I did not include present perfect utterances in the past-tense marking data (for which there are relatively few contexts anyway). These may have been ambiguous between past and nonpast interpretations (e.g., *we haven't look at it carefully*, which in context could also have been felicitously interpreted as 'we didn't look at it carefully'), but were more likely to include or be relevant to present time (e.g., *I haven't talk to D. yet*; *we go over for an hour now*; *but I haven't been writing as much*). However, I did include one unambiguously past (temporal) context requiring perfective marking, in which Patty's omission of the perfective auxiliary *have* rendered the utterance incorrectly as nonpast where a past context had been clearly established: *I may apply to N.* [name of university] (cf. 'I may have applied to N.', recalling which colleges she had applied to). There were also a few arguably past perfect contexts, five of them noted here:

(i)   *(so when I knew A.) I already stop working at B.* [name of restaurant] (cf. 'I'd already stopped working');
(ii) *(so by the time A. and I arrive there) he left already* (cf. 'he'd left already');
(iii) *(I was dating a man) that I met in a club previous week* (cf. 'that I'd met...');
(iv) *the first year in junior college I already took, uh, eight credit* (cf. 'had already taken');
(v)   *M. was # was left even before that* (cf. 'had left'?).

These were included in the data, but counted simply as past contexts rather than past perfect contexts; that is, in these cases, I looked at whether the lexical verbs *stop*, *leave*, *meet*, and *take* were past-tense marked rather than coding for whether perfective auxiliary *have* was provided and past-tense marked. There is no indication that Patty has acquired the past perfect construction. I return to these examples later in this chapter.

which there were two or more tokens in the data. These are presented in a continuum from consistently unmarked to marked for past tense, with the total number of tokens given in parentheses following the verb.

TABLE 4.3. Continuum of Past Marking % Rates
(for Verbs with Two or More Tokens) in Past Contexts.

Never past marked:

(0%)	ANSWER (3)	LIVE (5)	SIT (4)
	CALL (3)	LOOK AT (3)	SPEND (6)
	CLEAN (2)	LOVE (2)	START (15)
	GIVE (2)	MIX (2)	STOP (2)
	GIVE UP (2)	MOVE (8)	TALK (2)
	HANG OUT (2)	NEED (7)	TEACH (3)
	HAVE (54)	PICK UP (3)	WANT (9)
	LEARN (8)	PLAY (5)	WORK (5)
	LIKE (2)	SEND (2)	

Usually not past marked:

(10%)	TRY (10)	
(17%)	ASK (6)	READ (6)
(23%)	SAY (30)	
(25%)	FIND (4)	HEAR (4)

Sometimes past marked:

(37%)	TAKE (8)			
(43%)	SEE (7)			
(50%)	CHOOSE (2)	GAIN (2)	GET (12)	UNDERSTAND (2)
(60%)	THINK (5)			
(61%)	SPEAK (36)			
(67%)	TELL (6)			

Usually past marked:

(83%)	DO (6)
(85%)	COME (13)
(89%)	KNOW (9)
(90%)	LEAVE (10)
(91%)	GO (21)
(94%)	MEET (16)

Always past marked:

(100%)	BUY (2)	DECIDE (2)	FORGET (3)	WRITE (8)

Of the remaining 40 verb types for which only one token each occurs in the data, 35 of these are unmarked for past. These are listed in Table 4.4.

TABLE 4.4. Past-Tense Marking for Single-Occurrence Verb
Types in Past Contexts.

Unmarked for Past Tense:				
APPEAR	COPY	GRADUATE	KICK	REFUSE
ARRIVE	DIVORCE	HELP	KILL	REPEAT
BECOME	FALL ASLEEP	IMPROVE	LAUGH	SHOW
BELIEVE	FEEL	INTERVIEW	MAKE	TEND
CHANGE	FIND OUT	INVITE	MEMORIZE	TRAVEL
COMPLETE	FINISH	JUMP	PASS	TURN OUT
CONNECT	FLUNK	KEEP	PERFORM	USE

Marked for Past Tense:				
ACCEPT	DRIVE	FOLLOW	LOSE	STAY

As is evident from the data, regular past-tense suffixation is relatively rare, produced on only eight tokens (about 6%) of regular verbs in past-tense marking contexts. This very low percentage is comparable to that for 3SG -*s* affixation discussed in the previous chapter. It appears that finite verbal affixal morphology is highly problematic for Patty.

Some Methodological Concerns

Having presented the data, let me also now present a couple of caveats regarding data analysis. Whereas the temporal context is usually clear (and those that were unclear are not included in the analysis or the tables above), the precise grammatical context is often ambiguous. This makes it possible to determine whether or not an utterance is past-tense marked in a past context overall (e.g., as reported in Lardiere, 1998a), but not exactly how it should be coded in terms of which element should bear the morphological past-tense marking. For example, as pointed out by Brown (1973) for English L1 acquisition, it is not always possible to establish obligatory contexts for modals. Thus, Patty's utterance *so she perform and always send me the picture*, in a past temporal context, would be appropriate in the context in which it was uttered with either past-tense marking on both verbs (and was coded this way), but also with the habitual-past modal *would*, in which case neither verb itself would need to be marked.

A similar problem holds in trying to determine whether an utterance should be in the past progressive form or the simple past, in cases where either is possible, thereby affecting whether one counts an auxiliary as missing or the main verb as unmarked (or incorrectly marked), as in the examples: *good that I # I live with, uh, friends of my father; then the answering service answering.* (This type of problem will also obviously affect the determining of likely aspectual contexts (e.g., perfective vs. imperfective, telic vs. atelic, etc.) in relation to what has come to be known as the Aspect Hypothesis. This hypothesis essentially makes predictions about what types of verbs are developmentally likely to be past-tense marked, usually based on the inherent lexical aspect of a given verb or predicate, and I discuss it in more detail in the next section.) In sum, any breakdown of past-tense marking by verb type, with its appearance of quantitative precision, can in fact be viewed as only "more or less" precise, but in any case at least precise enough to allow us to observe the more robust patterns that occur in the data.

Finally, it should be pointed out that even in cases where past temporal contexts can be clearly established in conversational or narrative discourse, even native speakers do not always use the past tense, but instead may switch back and forth between past tense and what is known as the *historical present* tense. This type of tense alternation has been linked to ways in which a speaker organizes a narrative—for example, in changing a scene (Wolfson, 1979) or allowing the narrator "to present events as if they were occurring at that moment" (Schiffrin, 1981, p. 59). Therefore it is not clear to what extent many contexts for past-tense marking can even be considered truly obligatory. I return to this point later in the chapter.

Some Possible Factors Affecting Past-Tense Marking

Phonological Reduction

As mentioned earlier, Patty's past-tense marking data suggest that she is much less likely to produce regular past-tense inflectional affixes on verbs than irregular past forms in obligatory contexts, at least in her spoken production. Although there are several possible sources of this outcome, the one in particular that I would like to focus on in this subsection is phonological. We can identify two phonological factors likely to play a significant role in Patty's regular past-tense marking: The first is phonological transfer from the L1, and the second is the variable nature of the input with respect to -*t/d* deletion among native speakers of (American) English. I should emphasize here that I am not suggesting that phonology is the *only* source of Patty's difficulties with past-tense marking, but rather that it is one of possibly several interacting factors, and undoubtedly a major one.

L1 influence

Let us first consider the possibility of phonological influence from Patty's native languages, Hokkien and Mandarin. Although Hokkien (as well as Cantonese, another Chinese language in which Patty is fluent) does allow syllable-final voiceless stops -*p*, -*t*, and -*k*, no Chinese language permits final consonant clusters. (Mandarin does not permit *any* consonants in final position except the nasals -*n* and -*ŋ*.)[4,5] In the event of L1 phonological transfer—surely a highly plausible assumption for an adult second language acquirer—the implications for an affixation process that causes words to add [d] or [t] are obvious, in particular if such affixation results in a final ((C)VCC) cluster (e.g., *talked, laughed, moved*). Thus, even if Patty's

---

[4] The Beijing regional variety (not Patty's) also allows final -*r*.

[5] Ramsey (1987) notes that in another Chinese language, Shanghainese, a glottal stop is "all that remains of what was once a series of stop distinctions in final position (i.e., -*p*, -*t*, and -*k*)" (p. 93), placing this language on a diachronic continuum represented on one end by Cantonese (as well as Min dialects such as Hokkien), which have preserved -*p*, -*t*, and -*k* as final stops, and Mandarin, which has lost them completely. He also notes that another Chinese variety, the Gan dialects of Jianxi province (southwest of Shanghai) is important as a "transition between North and South," where in some areas the distinction between final -*p* and -*t* has been lost; furthermore, the "younger generation of the city confuse -*k* and -*t* as well" (p. 96). I mention this because, interestingly, Patty's frequent substitution of a glottal stop coda following vowels in CVC syllables in place of English -*d* or -*t* (and sometimes -*k*) is a fairly prominent characteristic of her English pronunciation (e.g., *maid* = [meʔ]; *hardly* = [haʔli]; *about* = [əbauʔ]; *get out* = [gɛʔauʔ]; *brought up* = [brɔʔʌp]; *pick* = [pɪʔ]; *like* = [laiʔ]). Although I discuss -*t*/*d* deletion in the next section (following a large literature in the variationist tradition), it should be observed that -*t*/*d* deletion may actually be too crude a measure if the possible replacement of -*t*/*d* by other segments such as glottal stops is taken into consideration, and thus finer-grained acoustic analyses may be required.

In addition, Patty's pronunciation of both English and Mandarin is clearly influenced by phonological features of southern Chinese language varieties (e.g., Hokkien and Cantonese) in some respects; for example, the distinctions among dental, palatal, and retroflex sibilants required in Mandarin are typically neutralized in Patty's Mandarin, uniformly produced as a dental (e.g., *chi*→*ci*, *zhi*→*zi*, *shi*→*si*, following standard Pinyin orthography); that is, she pronounces Mandarin with a Chinese southern accent. In Patty's English, this shows up as a similar tendency to de-palatalize initial sibilants (e.g., producing *shower* as *sour*).

knowledge of English past-tense marking were perfectly nativelike (a claim I am not making) such an affixation process would invariably clash with a powerful native language constraint that prohibits the formation of such clusters.[6]

Variable final -t/d deletion

In addition to native language influence, let us consider another conspiring phonological factor, namely, the possibility of variable *-t/d* deletion, common among native English speakers for monomorphemic words (Guy, 1980; Labov, 1989), and thus almost certainly present in the input. For second language acquisition, Bayley (1991, 1996) in particular has investigated *-t/d* deletion in connection with variability in past-tense marking by native Chinese speakers acquiring English. Bayley (1991) found that even advanced Chinese learners of English variably inflected anywhere from 26% to 80% of verbs for past tense depending on the following factors:

• *Verb salience*: This indicates the extent to which the past-tense form differs from the present along a saliency hierarchy, with suppletive (e.g., *go/went*) and ablaut irregular (e.g., *come/came*) forms being the most distinct and the most likely to be past-tense marked. Note that this factor would provide an additional explanation for the wildly uneven distribution of regular versus irregular past-tense marking we have already observed in Patty's data. I return to this issue (and a different sort of account) at the end of this section.

• *Preceding and following phonological segment*: Deletion is sensitive to the phonological environment; for example, final *-t/d* deletion is more likely to occur following an obstruent or nasal than a liquid or a vowel.

• *Verbal aspectual type (perfective vs. imperfective):* Perfective events were more likely to be marked than imperfective ones, generally following the Aspect Hypothesis. I return to the issue of lexical aspect in the next subsection.

---

[6] There is a very large literature on the role of L1 transfer in the second language acquisition of phonology; for major works or collections of papers, see Archibald (1993), Hannahs and Young-Scholten (1997), Ioup and Weinberger (1987), Major (2001), Strange (1995) and many others, including a special thematic issue of *Second Language Research* on L2 phonology edited by Archibald and Young-Scholten (2003). Recent relevant work by Goad & White (2004a, 2004b, 2005) and Goad, White, and Steele (2003) will be touched on in chapter 7.

• *Type of speech style* (e.g., reading a prepared passage vs. conversation, with the latter resulting in greater deletion).

• *Social network affiliation*: Speakers in mixed Chinese/English social networks have a higher likelihood of -*t/d* deletion than those in predominantly Chinese social networks.

Bayley found that, whereas English native speakers were much more likely to preserve final -*t/d* in affixal past-tense marking contexts (e.g., *packed*) than in monomorphemic contexts (e.g., *pact)*, Chinese-speaking English learners overall were somewhat more likely to delete -*t/d* in past-tense marking contexts compared with monomorphemic ones. However, as Bayley points out, this tendency apparently shrank with greater exposure to input from native English speakers; that is, the picture becomes more complicated when the factor of social network affiliation is taken into consideration. For those Chinese speakers whose social networks were primarily Chinese—that is, whose opportunity for acquisition was presumably quite limited due to lack of interaction with English native speakers, past-tense marking was actually *better* than for those Chinese speakers in mixed Chinese and English social networks.

At first glance, of course, this finding is puzzling, since we would expect the opposite result—that those participants whose exposure to English input was greater would perform better on past-tense marking than those whose exposure was less. Bayley found that the rate of -*t/d* deletion among speakers in both types of social networks was roughly the same for past participles versus monomorphemic contexts, and concluded that deletion in past participles was therefore the result of a phonological process rather than underlyingly grammatical. The speakers in mainly Chinese networks exhibited a much sharper difference in -*t/d* deletion in past-tense marking versus in participles and monomorphemic words, whereas this distinction appeared to be much less pronounced among the speakers in mixed networks. In other words, native Chinese speakers in the group having greater interaction with native English speakers were more likely to reduce *all* final clusters regardless of grammatical function, thus suggesting, according to Bayley (1996), a "combination of nearly categorical inflectional marking followed by variable -t/d deletion" (p. 116). Deletion in this case is primarily phonological in nature. He further concludes:

> The greater likelihood of -t/d deletion by speakers with mixed networks results in the appearance of a greater number of surface errors, even though these speakers mark more regular past tense verbs underlyingly than speakers who belong to Chinese net-

works. Speakers with more opportunities for acquisition have indeed acquired more. Their partial acquisition of native speaker patterns of variation, however, has obscured their acquisition of a morphological affixation rule. (pp. 113–114)

What has *not* been acquired, Bayley proposes, are the morphophonological constraints that would limit the application of a variable phonological process across morpheme boundaries, which native English speakers apparently are constrained by (because they tend not to delete affixal -*t/d* past-tense marking). In other words, Bayley suggests that when the morphological rule ("add a past-tense suffix") and the phonological rule ("delete final -*t/d*") clash, the morphological rule wins out among native English speakers, whereas the phonological rule prevails for the native Chinese speakers.

Among those Chinese speakers studied by Bayley whose social networks were mixed, none had been in the United States for more than 4.5 years (the range was 3–54 months, with a mean of 21.5 months). Let us compare this overall modest length of residence in the United States with that of Patty, who had lived in the United States from 10 to 18 years when her speech was recorded, and whose social network was not only mixed, but in fact overwhelmingly English-speaking.

Following Bayley's argument that greater exposure to native speaker input results in greater -*t/d* deletion while at the same time increasingly neutralizing the difference in final -*t/d* production rates among monomorphemic, past-tense-marked, and past-participle-marked words, we should expect that Patty will exhibit robust -*t/d* deletion across the board. That is, we should find high rates of final -*t/d* deletion and even less of a difference in applying it within monomorphemic words and past-participle forms as opposed to past-tense forms than Bayley found. If we also assume L1 influence, then this deletion should be especially pronounced within final consonant clusters. In general, this is indeed what we do find.

Finally, if lack of past-tense marking is largely due to phonological factors, then we should expect Patty's written English to exhibit much higher rates of past-tense marking than her spoken English (although this may also be influenced by the nature of the production type, i.e., written vs. spoken). In the following section, I introduce written (e-mail) data showing that this is also the case.

First, with respect to across-the-board deletion, final -*t/d* following a vowel is often either dropped or glottalized. The latter possibility suggests the representation of some consonant in this syllable-final position (although not necessarily -*t* or -*d*—see Footnote 5); this is especially noticeable when followed by a word containing an initial vowel, a context in which flapping would typically occur in the variety of American English Patty is exposed to (e.g., *brought up, get out, make it up, get into*). In final clusters, however, *-t/d* is overwhelmingly dropped regardless of the grammatical context. These characteristics suggest strong L1 phonological influence.

Comparing past-tense marking with *-t/d* deletion in monomorphemic words containing final consonant clusters, we observe deletion in nearly all cases in Patty's spoken data, strongly implicating the operation of a robust phonological constraint. Table 4.5 provides a comprehensive list of monomorphemic word types and tokens (including irregular verbs ending in *-t* or *-d*, such as *left, told*), taken from the longest of Patty's recordings (Recording 2). In this recording, we can see that the deletion rate for such word types is overwhelmingly high—at $205/211 = 97.16\%$.[7]

Turning to past participles, there are relatively few of these in the data—only about 45 across all three recordings, and some of these contexts should arguably be excluded from analysis—for example, *born again* (in a religious context, probably formulaic); *you would amaze* (not clear how the argument structure of this psych verb is represented in Patty's English idiolect); *all taught in English* (direct repetition of interlocutor's previous utterance); *M. was # was left even before that* (= 'had left'? 'was gone'? cf. *be*-overgeneralization errors in the previous chapter).

---

[7] This percentage is even higher ($247/253 = 97.63\%$) if we include contracted negative auxiliaries (*-n't*) and superlative adjectives ending in affixal *-est*. Following Bayley, the word *and* was excluded from analysis; final *-d* is categorically deleted in this highly frequent word. These deletion percentages contrast starkly with similar spontaneous speech data provided by Hawkins (2000) for SX, an advanced learner of English whose L1 is also Chinese. Whereas Patty virtually always omits *-t/d* in final clusters in monomorphemic contexts, SX apparently *never* does. (The same discrepancy also holds for participial inflection, to be discussed below.) Perhaps the difference stems from the variety of English that each informant has been exposed to in the input environment, or the manner in which that variety was acquired. Because all of Patty's previously-acquired languages (Hokkien, Mandarin, Indonesian, and Cantonese) disallow final consonant clusters, there may be a more pronounced cumulative transfer effect. In any case, it looks as if phonological factors do not play much of a role in SX's past-tense marking in English. Interestingly, the rate of past-tense marking in SX's speech is nearly identical to that of Patty's *written* production—at around 77% suppliance (although of course this could be purely coincidental).

TABLE 4.5. Word-Final Consonant Clusters with *-t/d* Deleted or Retained.

TYPE (# of Tokens)

Final *t/d* Deletion:

ACCEN[T] (4)	FRIEN[D] (3)	REQUIREMEN[T] (3)
ACCOUNTAN[T] (2)	FRIEN[D]s (9)	SECON[D] (10)
ALMOS[T] (2)	FRON[T] (5)	SEN[D] (5)
APARTMEN[T] (1)	GOVERNMEN[T] (2)	SOUN[D] (2)
AROUN[D] (5)	GROUN[D] (1)	SPEN[D] (3)
BACKGROUN[D] (1)	HOL[D] (2)	STAN[D] (1)
BES[T] (1)	HOUSEHOL[D] (2)	STUDEN[T] (1)
COL[D] (1)	JUS[T] (29)	TES[T] (1)
CORREC[T] (2)	KIN[D] (3)	TOL[D] (2)
DIALEC[T] (2)	LAS[T] (5)	TRANSCRIP[T] (1)
DIFFEREN[T] (11)	LEAS[T] (2)	TURBULEN[T] (1)
DILIGEN[T] (1)	LEF[T] (11)	UNDERSTAN[D] (5)
EN[D] (3)	MIN[D] (1)	WAN[T][8] (4)
EXCEP[T] (2)	MOS[T] (4)	WEEKEN[D] (1)
FAS[T] (2)	NEX[T] (2)	WEN[T] (17)
FIRS[T] (8)	PERCEN[T] (6)	WORL[D] (2)
FLUEN[T] (1)	POIN[T] (10)	

Final *t/d* Retention:

DIFFICULT (1)
FIRST (3)
LAST (1)
PARENTS (1)

With respect to *-t/d* deletion, however, it is worth pointing out that nearly all (regular) verb types for which past-participle marking would result in a final cluster follow our prediction; that is, they are produced by Patty without affixal inflection, with only one exception—one token of *called*. These types are as follows, with the number of tokens in parentheses: *close* (4), *engage* (2), *look at* (1), *mix* (1), *pass* (1), *pass away* (1),

---

[8] Excludes *want*+infinitive V and *wanna*.

raise (2), *surprise* (1), and *transfer* (1). In addition, the following participles are also unmarked: *buy* (1), *marry* (4), *worry* (1). Sample utterances are
provided in (3):

(3) yeah but we haven't *look* at it carefully
     I was so *worry* about it last week
     I should have *buy* the other, too
     we were *engage* before I left home
     now that my mom is *pass* away

In general, except for the single instance of *buy* noted above, all irregular verbs are produced in their participial form; these types are as follows:
been (1), *born* (4), *brought up* (2), *chosen* (2), *gone* (1), *left* (1), *stuck* (1).[9]
More examples are given in (4).

(4) tomorrow I think it will be *gone*
     where I was *brought* up
     maybe we are the one who *chosen*
     they *born* the same year
     well, she got *stuck* on the first piece

We do find one interesting difference, however, between Patty's past-
tense marking and past-participle marking with respect to regular extra-
syllabic (epenthetic) marking (i.e., for regular verbs already ending in a -*t* or
-*d*, such as *accept*). These are typically inflected if they are past participles,
whereas the deletion rate for such verbs is higher for past-tense marking.
Past-participle examples are given in (5):

(5) you were *treated* like uh[/a?] animal
     I was *accepted*
     if you *interested* to hear it
     which, like, *connected* or something

Because there are so few of this type of verb overall (only 10 tokens in
past-participle contexts and 40 in past-tense-marking contexts), it is difficult to compare them directly; yet the few instances there are nonetheless

---

[9] Note, however, that for the irregular forms ending in -*t*, final -*t* is pronounced as indicated
above in the text: always dropped in a cluster (e.g., *left* = [lɛf]) or sometimes glottalized after
a vowel (e.g., *taught* = [tɔʔ]; *brought up* = [brɔʔʌp]).

suggest a possible grammatical as well as phonological component to the omission of past-tense marking in Patty's English. Whereas fewer than 8% of these verbs are marked in obligatory past-tense-marking contexts (3/40), 9 out of the 10 past participles are inflected, and the tenth could arguably be more correctly analyzed as a *be*-overgeneration error rather than a true past-participle context (*I was graduate in 1980*).[10] I return shortly to possible non-phonological sources of Patty's failure to mark past tense.

In the meantime, however, let us turn to one more piece of evidence which additionally demonstrates that phonological factors appear to play a considerable role in Patty's past-tense marking—namely, evidence from written production data.

Spoken versus written (electronic) production

In addition to the spoken data discussed above, 21 e-mail samples collected over a nearly 6-year period (1997–2002) were also analyzed for past-tense marking. With respect to inflectional omissions, one should of course be quite wary of a format in which typos could and often do occur, even among native speakers who are fairly good typists. In Patty's case, as with other second language learners, one cannot determine with certainty whether an inflectional omission is representative of her language knowledge or merely typographical. Where correct forms are appropriately provided, however, I have assumed that we can take these to indicate genuine morphological exponence—that is, a somewhat idealized portrait of what Patty's spoken English would be like if phonological factors did not intervene.

In contrast to Patty's spoken data, her overall rate of past-tense marking in the e-mail data is at least *twice as high*—at about 78% suppliance in obligatory contexts. Table 4.6 illustrates this difference.

Among the differences between the spoken and written data, we find the relative (in)variability of copular/auxiliary *be*—there are 34 obligatory past contexts for *be* in the written data, and, unlike in the spoken data, all but one of them are supplied and appropriately past-marked. On the other hand, one striking similarity with the spoken data is the verb *have* used as a lexical main verb—again, it is the most frequent lexical verb type and again, it is never marked for past.

---

[10] This utterance immediately followed in reply to an interlocutor's utterance *OK, were you graduated already?*, which may have set up a past-participle context for Patty's reply.

TABLE 4.6. Spoken versus Written (E-mail) Past-Tense Marking
in Past Contexts.

Recording[11]	Suppliance / Contexts	%
1	24 / 69	34.78
2	191 / 548	34.85
3	46 / 136	33.82
4	38 / 93	40.86
E-mail	120 / 154	**77.92**

Table 4.7 provides a more complete breakdown of past-tense marking by verb type of Patty's e-mail data.

In sum, it looks as if phonology unquestionably play a crucial role in the low rates of past-tense marking we observe in Patty's spoken production data. Furthermore, it appears that both learner-internal (L1 phonological transfer) and learner-external (variable -*t/d* deletion in the target language environment) factors could conspire to exert considerable pressure on Patty to omit regular past-tense marking in particular.

---

[11] As mentioned earlier in chapter 1, because nearly all of Patty's written data were collected after the spoken Recordings 1–3 were made, I decided to examine additional spoken data from a more recently recorded interview (Recording 4) that was made near the end of the 5-year range of e-mail data reported here, in spring 2002. This was to ensure that the higher percentage of past-tense marking in Patty's written data was not due to some rather phenomenal developmental spurt that might have occurred after Recording 3, but in fact reflected a genuine performance gap between her spoken and written production. This recording, which is fairly short, was made during a visit to her home and was slanted toward eliciting additional past tense contexts by asking her questions about a weekend trip she had just taken.

In Recording 4, past-tense marking was appropriately supplied in 38/93 = 40.86% of obligatory contexts, a rate that does not significantly differ from that of her previous Recordings 1–3. Moreover, because of the particular conversational topic of this recording, approximately *half* of all instances of past-tense marking supplied (18/38 = 47.37%) are accounted for by a single verb type: *went*. We have already seen that this verb is nearly always past-tense marked in obligatory contexts in Patty's previous recordings. The overrepresentation of *went* in the data in Recording 4 is likely inflating Patty's overall rate of past-tense marking; were it to be removed, that rate would actually appear to drop (to about 27% overall suppliance). Thus, there is clearly a large gap between her written and spoken production rates of past-tense marking at about the same point in time.

TABLE 4.7. Past-Tense Marking of Patty's E-mail Data.

Verb Type	Past	Nonpast	Verb Type	Past	Nonpast
BE (Aux)[12]	6	1	MISS	0	1
BE (Cop)	27	0	NEED	1	1
CAN/COULD	1	0	OFFER	1	0
DO (Aux)	12	1	PLAY	1	0
GET (Passive aux)	1	0	PUBLISH	1	0
WILL/WOULD[13]	0	5	REFUSE	1	0
ASK	2	0	REQUEST	0	1
BUY	3	0	SAY	3	0
CALL	1	0	SEE	2	0
CHANGE	1	0	SEND	0	1
CODE[14]	1	0	SHARE	1	0
COME	1	0	SPEND	1	0
CRY	1	0	START	2	0
DECIDE	1	1	STAY	0	1
DESCRIBE	0	1	STRIKE	1	0
DO (main verb)	1	0	SURVIVE	1	0
END UP	1	0	TAKE	1	0
FALL IN LOVE	0	1	TALK	0	1
FEEL	4	0	TELL	2	0
FORGET	1	0	THINK	6	0
GET	4	3	TREAT	1	0
GIVE	2	0	TRY	4	0
GO	5	0	USE	1	0
HAVE (main verb)	0	13	VALUE	1	0
IMPLANT	1	0	VISIT	2	1
INCLUDE	1	0	VOLUNTEER	0	1
KNOW	1	0	WALK	1	0
LEAVE	1	0	WANT	1	0
LOSE	1	0	WIN	1	0
MAKE	2	0	**Total**	**120**	**34**

---

[12] The Nonpast total consists of one omission of auxiliary *be*.

[13] The Nonpast total includes one omission.

[14] The written phrase was: *...for 1/2 of what they coded us* [sic = 'quoted'].

In the following sections, I consider some additional, non-phonological explanations for variable past-tense marking in SLA that have been proposed in the literature. The first of these—the role of aspect—was also reported by Bayley to interact significantly with past-tense marking of L2 English by the native Chinese speakers in his study. Let us turn to the question of whether we find any relation between aspect and past-tense marking in Patty's data.

The Role of Aspect in Past-Tense Marking

Several second language acquisition studies, following related work in L1 acquisition, have investigated whether past-tense marking is initially used by learners to encode aspectual distinctions, such as perfectivity or telicity, rather than tense—a proposal that has come to be known as the Aspect Hypothesis (see e.g., Andersen, 1991; Andersen & Shirai, 1996; Bardovi-Harlig & Reynolds, 1995; Robison, 1990, 1995). Within these studies, a distinction is usually drawn, following e.g., Comrie (1976) and Smith (1990), between grammatical and lexical aspect. The former, typically realized as a perfective versus imperfective opposition, grammatically encodes completion versus ongoingness of an action or event, whereas the latter refers to inherent semantic features of verbal predicates that denote punctuality, duration, telicity, and stativity. I return later to some complications in the interactions among tense, grammatical aspect, and lexical aspect, but in the meantime an example from Robison (1990, p. 316) succinctly illustrates the differences between them:

(6) a. I was making a pair of pants.
     b. I made a pair of pants.
     c. I am making a pair of pants.

Sentences (a) and (b) are both marked for past tense, whereas sentence (c) is nonpast; both (a) and (c) are grammatically aspectually imperfective, whereas (b) is perfective; and the predicate of all three sentences (a–c) MAKE A PAIR OF PANTS shares the same lexical aspect, that of a telic "accomplishment" within the Vendler (1967) classification system usually adopted in most L2 acquisition studies investigating the acquisition of past-tense morphology and its relation to aspect. One specific claim supported in the studies cited above is that when past-tense marking first emerges in second language acquisition, it is initially used to mark telic (achievement and accomplishment) verbs, whereas non-telic (stative and activity) verbs are significantly less likely to be past-marked.

It is important to point out that the Aspect Hypothesis was formulated as a *developmental* hypothesis about emerging verbal tense morphology for learners in early stages of acquisition. Therefore, we should not necessarily expect it to be applicable to an end-state English acquirer like Patty. In cases like Patty's, however, where her production of past-tense morphology has apparently fossilized, one might ask whether her usage pattern possibly reflects an earlier "arrested" developmental stage in which tense morphology, where present, is really being used mainly to mark aspect. (At least I am sometimes asked this question at conference presentations!) This is especially possible in Patty's case given that her native language is Chinese, which is claimed to grammatically mark aspect rather than tense (Li & Thompson, 1981). In this sense, a developmental tendency claimed to be universal would be bolstered by the likelihood of transfer from the native language. I therefore analyzed both the spoken and written data (separately) to investigate whether, for Patty, aspectual telicity correlates with past-tense marking.

For the spoken data, the same database of past contexts used earlier to report on Patty's past-tense marking (Lardiere, 1998a) was coded for telicity. For the written data, the same set of past contexts from the 21 e-mail samples used to report the results shown in Table 4.6 in this chapter was also coded for telicity. Modal and hypothetical predicates (e.g., *[our social worker] could not tell us*; *[didn't he know that it] will get back to me?*) and unclear or ambiguous utterances were excluded. Some examples (all from the written data) are provided in (7):

(7) Telic, past-marked:

I called a week ago
since it got demolished
A.'s company just bought a new computer

Atelic, past-marked:

which included four weeks severance pay
M. needed a companion to go to Symphony
I felt terrific

Telic, not past-marked:

we fall in love with her
we finally get a call
I request five

Atelic, not past-marked:

they have problem with my attendance
he still seeing you at the time
we miss you on the New Year

The results for both the spoken and written data (as we might expect for an end-state L2 speaker) do not exhibit Aspect Hypothesis effects; that is, they reveal no significant contingency between telicity and past marking. These findings are summarized in Tables 4.8 and 4.9, for the spoken and written data, respectively:

TABLE 4.8. Past-Tense Marking (Spoken) as a Function of Aspectual Telicity.

Telicity	% Past-Marked		% Not Past-Marked	
Telic	40.43	(112/277)	59.57	(165/277)
Atelic	35.04	(130/371)	64.96	(241/371)

(χ^2 (1) = 1.97, p = .16, n.s.)

TABLE 4.9. Past-Tense Marking (Written) as a Function of Aspectual Telicity.

Telicity	% Past-Marked		% Not Past-Marked	
Telic	83.33	(55/66)	16.67	(11/66)
Atelic	78.75	(63/80)	21.25	(17/80)

(χ^2 (1) = 0.49, p = .48, n.s.)

In sum, the results indicate that, even though Patty's past-tense marking remains in some way clearly non-targetlike, it has nonetheless advanced to the point of being extended to atelic predicates in roughly the same proportions as for telic predicates, well beyond the developmental scope of the Aspect Hypothesis.

Another methodological caveat

In addition to the various methodological concerns mentioned earlier in this chapter, we can add another interesting and important one that emerges in rather striking fashion from the aspect data. In analyzing the lexical semantics of verbs even in advanced stages of second language acquisition, we are particularly susceptible to falling prey to Bley-Vroman's (1983) Comparative Fallacy. Specifically, it becomes clear in context that Patty's representation of the lexical semantics of certain verbs, while certainly overlapping with that of native speakers to a considerable extent, also subtly diverges in some ways, in some cases bearing distinct traces of L1 influence. In other words, we cannot be sure whether for Patty the lexical semantics of English verbs match those of English native speakers. In my opinion (at least with respect to my own data), the discrepancies may be serious enough to cast some doubt on analyses of lexical aspect that are (necessarily) based on native speaker intuitions about which aspectual or other semantic features are associated with particular verbs occurring in particular grammatical and extra-grammatical contexts. Some examples are provided in (8) to illustrate the point. The first line in each pair is Patty's actual utterance, and the second is the approximate intended meaning (either clear from the context or confirmed with her in subsequent queries).

(8) a.   even I just *wear* it, it's not hurt
   a'. [speaking about new shoes:] 'even though I've just put them on/am wearing them for the first time, they don't hurt'

   b.   a year after I # I *wrote* my journal
   b'. 'a year after I started writing in/keeping my journal'

   c.   and then suddenly, on the third hour, I think, they all *speak* in tongue
   c'. 'they all began to speak in tongues'

   d.   no, you just # you just *laugh* around
   d'. 'no, you were just joking around'

   e.   and I *hear* it so many time
   e'. 'and I listened to it so many times'

   f.   because I cannot *hear* anything they say
   f'. 'because I couldn't understand anything they said'

   g.   which *struck* me more than a week now
   g'. 'which struck more than a week ago and has continued to affect me since then'

In Examples (a–c) above, the intended meanings include an aspectually punctual inchoative or inceptive sense that is likely absent from native speakers' semantic representations of the verbs in question, and that clashes with adverbial modification elsewhere in the sentence (although that modification provides important clues to the intended meaning). Another adverbial clash occurs in example (g) between the expected punctuality of *struck* and the adverb phrase *more than a week now*. In example (a), Patty's usage of *wear* suggests that, for her, its representation in English bears some resemblance to its Chinese lexical counterpart, which is ambiguous between 'to wear' and 'to put on'. The same is also true for her use of *hear* in examples (e) and (f), whose Chinese equivalent can mean 'to hear', 'to listen' and 'to understand from what one hears'.

It would be difficult to estimate the extent to which such semantic discrepancies pervade Patty's L2 lexical representations, since these differences are likely to go undetected by interlocutors, for example, in cases where no obvious adverbial mismatch arises or where the conversational context can accommodate possible underspecification or ambiguity. In addition to the interesting implications for L1 transfer, there is also a bit of a cautionary tale here (and see Lardiere, 2003b for some additional discussion). The data suggest that even the most stringent criteria available for coding lexical aspect among second language learners may occasionally fail if they are based solely on native speaker intuitions and target language diagnostic constructions (e.g., compatibility with the addition of phrases such as "for an hour" vs. "in an hour," etc.). This is even more likely to be so if, unlike Patty, the learners in question are still in the early stages of acquisition, with more limited lexical resources at their disposal.

The Discourse (Narrative) Hypothesis

Yet another account of the distribution of past-tense marking, known as the Discourse Hypothesis, proposes that second language learners use emerging verbal (past-tense) morphology to distinguish foreground from background in narrative discourse (Bardovi-Harlig, 1995, 1998). Again, this is a developmental hypothesis that is tied to proficiency level; Bardovi-Harlig (1995) points out that "very low level learners show no systematic use of tense (Schumann, 1978) and that advanced learners must eventually use past in both foreground and background to reach a targetlike use of tense in English narratives" (p. 264). Bardovi-Harlig's own studies found among intermediate learners a tendency to use more past marking in the foreground rather than background, although she notes that other studies have found different patterns.

The data from Patty, an end-state acquirer, show that even though she has not achieved the targetlike use of tense, she nevertheless uses past marking with roughly equal consistency in both foreground and background in spontaneous narration. Five narratives were excerpted from her spoken production data, three from the first recording and two from the final recording.[15] Within each narrative, every utterance that constituted an obligatory past context was coded twice: once for foregrounding (sequentially ordered events that make up and advance the story line) versus backgrounding (scene-setting, elaboration, or evaluation of the foregrounded events), and once again for past-tense marking. An example from one of these narratives, Patty's retelling in her own words of the biblical story of the conversion of Saul, is shown below; following Bardovi-Harlig (1995), foregrounded utterances are notated by numbers in square brackets; coded verbs are italicized[16]:

(9)

Foreground	Background
	Yeah. And then # and then they have #
[1] and then Jew[s] *see* it too,	
	that they *speak* in tongue,
[2] and then they *say* that, you know, that "this is the wonderful work of God," or something.	
	But # and then they *have* another #another # another guy who # who # her # his name *is* Saul, I think. He # he *is* a killer, OK? Every time he # he *saw* someone um, that *talk* against, OK? he just *want* to kill them.
[3] And then one day Christ *appear* in him, you know? telling him # telling him, um, to go # to go back somewhere, you know? Away. Um, something like that. [4] And he *was* so scared [5] he lost his # he *lost* his sight.	

---

[15] The written e-mail data contained insufficient narrative data to analyze.

[16] Many thanks to Debby Schiffrin for her helpful advice and assistance with the coding of foregrounded versus backgrounded utterances. (Of course, any errors are mine alone.)

Again, as we might expect from an end-state learner, the data show no contingency between narrative grounding and past marking. The results are shown in Table 4.10.

TABLE 4.10. Past-Tense Marking (Spoken) as a Function of Narrative Grounding.

	% Past-Marked		% Not Past-Marked	
Foreground	31.71	(13/41)	68.29	(28/41)
Background	29.95	(11/38)	71.05	(27/38)

(χ^2 (1) = .07, p = .79, n.s.)

Despite the low rate of past marking overall, Patty's management of temporal devices can be quite sophisticated in complex narratives, including her use of adverbial modification. Additionally, although there are not enough contexts to generalize from, she does appear to use past tense to indicate relative temporal anteriority in some past-perfect contexts, even when these are narratively ordered in reverse of the sequence in which the events actually occurred. The following examples illustrate this:

(10) a. so I *invite* Adam to # to the party
        and then meanwhile there's # I *was dating* uh, a man
        that I *met* in a club previous week,
        so he *was waiting* for me all this night ...
        so by the time Adam and I uh, *arrive*
        he *left* already

      b. the first year in junior college I already *took*, uh, eight credit

      c. M. was # *was left* even before that

There is one past-perfect context in which the anterior event is unmarked for past. However, because marking the verb would result in a word-final obstruent cluster (*stopped*), we can already predict on independent phonological grounds that Patty would be unlikely to mark it; on the other hand the irregular verb (*knew*) of the later event is marked:[17]

(11)   so when I *knew* Adam
        I already *stop* working at B. [name of restaurant]

---

[17] The intended meaning of *knew* here is something like 'met' or 'started to get to know'.

It appears from everything we've seen so far that whether a verb is regular or irregular is a pretty good probabilistic indicator of whether or not it will be marked for past tense in Patty's spoken data. As mentioned earlier, the tendency to mark irregular verbs has been argued within the variationist tradition to follow from a principle of saliency—that is, that the past is most likely to be marked when the form of the past tense is least like the nonpast base form. However, a different sort of explanation for second language learners' preference for past-marking irregular versus regular verbs has recently been proposed. Let us turn next to a look at that proposal.

The Declarative/Procedural Model

The Declarative/Procedural model (Ullman, 2001a, 2001b) is a revised descendant of the Dual-Mechanism model of Pinker and Prince (1988), which posits two distinct systems for the learning and processing of language. The first is an associative memory component that underlies stored knowledge about memorized words and associations between them, such as the pairing between a so-called strong verb and its associated irregular past form. The second is a computational component associated with sequential grammar, motor, and cognitive skills that subserves the implicit learning and use of a symbol-manipulating grammar, such as the "procedure" used to compute the past tense for regular verbs. That is, in short, for *native* language speakers, regular inflection is considered procedural and irregular declarative.

Ullman (2001b) extends the model's predictions to second language acquisition by later learners exposed to the L2 after late childhood or puberty. He hypothesizes that morphologically complex forms presumed to be compositionally computed by the procedural system in L1 acquisition are instead largely dependent on the declarative/lexical memory system (i.e., are simply memorized in their entirety in L2 acquisition) or perhaps constructed by explicit rules learned in declarative memory in a pedagogic environment, the nature of which "could in principle differ radically from the implicitly learned grammatical rules of L1" (p. 109). Reliance on the declarative system is predicted to be especially likely for high-frequency items because "higher levels of exposure should increase the likelihood of memorization" (p. 109). This shift to a greater reliance on declarative memory is posited to increase with increasing age of exposure to the L2. There is a kind of escape clause, however, that is certainly relevant in Patty's case: Greater experience and practice with the L2 is predicted to improve *procedural* computation.

In Patty's case, these two hypotheses—relatively late age of exposure to the L2 leading to reliance on declarative memory versus high amount of exposure and practice leading to reliance on procedural computation—potentially cancel each other out in a way that makes predictions difficult to generate. (We do not have any idea how much exposure and practice is enough to effect a shift "back" to procedural computation, but it is probably a safe bet that Patty more than meets the criterion.) It is also not clear why, if reliance on procedural memory is subject to a critical period as suggested by Ullman (based on the results of rodent studies—see pp. 108–109), it should be recoverable in later life as a function of exposure. However, let us take a more detailed look at the data in terms of the model to see whether we can apply any aspects of it to Patty's knowledge of English past-tense marking.

One prediction we might derive is that if the procedural computational system is in some sense impaired or atrophied relative to the declarative memory system, we might expect to find an overall lower rate of regular past-tense marking than irregular, since most regular verb types are less frequent than most irregular types. A stronger test would be to see whether there are any frequency effects such that the most frequent (among both regular and irregular) verb types are more likely to be past tense marked.

The findings for Patty's spoken data analyzed for past-tense marking with respect to verb regularity are shown in Tables 4.11a and 4.11b. There is indeed a huge effect for verb regularity for the spoken data, with irregular verbs marked significantly more often for past tense in obligatory contexts than regular verbs:

TABLE 4.11a. Rate of Past-Tense Marking on Regular vs. Irregular Verbs, Spoken Data (Lexical Main Verbs Only).

Verb Type	% Past-Marked		% Not Past-Marked	
Regular	5.80	(8/138)	94.20	(130/138)
Irregular	46.08	(135/293)	53.92	(158/293)

(χ^2 (1) = 68.648, $p < .001$)

TABLE 4.11b. Rate of Past-Tense Marking on Regular vs. Irregular Verbs, Spoken Data (*All* Verbs Including Copula/Auxiliaries/Modals).

Verb Type	% Past-Marked		% Not Past-Marked	
Regular	5.80	(8/138)	94.20	(130/138)
Irregular	41.30	(254/615)	58.70	(361/615)

$(\chi^2(1) = 62.62, p < .001)$

As can be seen from the above tables, Patty is far more likely to produce past-tense marking for irregular rather than regular verbs. We observed earlier, however, that phonological factors could account for some of this result. However, contrary to what we would expect if Patty were relying primarily on declarative memory, there do not appear to be frequency effects for the regular verb forms; that is, the most frequent regular verbs are not more likely to be inflected than infrequent ones in Patty's spoken data. From all the regular verbs produced by Patty in her spoken data, the top 10 with respect to frequency are listed in (12) below (based on frequency data from Francis and Kučera (1982). These are the regular verbs we would expect to be more consistently past-tense marked under the Declarative/Procedural model. However, the data show that only 2 out of 48, or about 4%, are inflected. This rate is similar to or even slightly less than her overall past-tense-marking rate for all regular verbs regardless of frequency.

(12)   look   (0/3)
             ask   (1/5)
             want   (0/9)
             call   (0/3)
             start   (0/15)
             move   (0/8)
             show   (0/1)
             use   (0/1)
             try   (1/2)
             appear   (0/1)

             Total   (2/48) = **4.17%**

Moreover, we have already seen that the most highly frequent lexical verb produced both by Patty and her interlocutors is the irregular verb *have*, which she never marks for past. Thus, it appears that the Declarative/Procedural model fails to accurately capture Patty's past-tense marking production. On the one hand, high-frequency regular verbs appear no more likely to be tense-marked than lower-frequency ones, and at least one very highly frequent irregular verb is also never marked.[18] On the other hand, Patty's previous lengthy exposure to and extensive practice in her L2 have not led to any noticeable improvement over the 8-year course of the recordings in the application of regular past-tense marking by a procedural grammar rule.

Turning now to Patty's written data, we see quite a different picture emerge regarding regular versus irregular past-tense marking: The advantage for past-tense marking on irregular verbs is essentially wiped out, with very little difference between regular and irregular:

TABLE 4.12a. Rate of Past-Tense Marking on Regular vs. Irregular Verbs, Written E-mail Data (Lexical Main Verbs Only).

Verb Type	% Past-Marked		% Not Past-Marked	
Regular	76.92	(30/39)	23.08	(9/39)
Irregular	70.49	(43/61)	29.51	(18/61)

($\chi^2(1) = .4992, p = 48$, n.s.)

TABLE 4.12b. Rate of Past-Tense Marking on Regular vs. Irregular Verbs, Written E-mail Data (*All* Verbs Including Copula/Auxiliaries/Modals).

Verb Type	% Past-Marked		% Not Past-Marked	
Regular	76.92	(30/39)	23.08	(9/39)
Irregular	78.26	(90/115)	21.74	(25/115)

($\chi^2(1) = .0303, p = .86$ n.s.)

In the written data, moreover, even relatively infrequent regular verbs are inflected, such as *implanted, published, coded* [= 'quoted'], *survived,* and *valued.* (However, the highly frequent irregular verb *have* is still never past-marked, even in the written data.)

---

[18] The same holds for irregular verbs *can, give, hear, make, read, say,* and *sit,* which are also all highly frequent.

To summarize, Patty's spoken data do not appear to support the Declarative/Procedural model. For the written data, given the higher rate of past-tense marking we find across the board, including on low-frequency regular verbs, we might conclude that she is able to procedurally compute past-tense marking (except for *have*). In that case, however, one might well ask what prevents the procedure from applying more categorically—say in the 90% to 98% rather than the 70% to 78% range of consistent application. Given the model's vague appeal to an unspecified but large amount of exposure and practice to account for improved past-tense marking, the written data are not incompatible with this weaker claim. However, until the model is further developed and more tightly constrained for SLA, it is not really clear what would count as a good test of it, or especially why Patty's data appear to fail to conform to its predictions.

So What is [± Past] in English, Anyway, and What Does Past-Tense Marking Mark?

The conventional or core semantic notion of past tense is that it grammatically indicates that an event or state occurred at a point prior to speech time. In morphosyntactic terms, [± past] is typically viewed as a formal feature of a functional category T[ense]; in more recent versions of a minimalist-type framework, we might descriptively represent it within a phrase marker as follows:[19]

---

[19] I have no particular commitment to the exact internal structure of the left-periphery (CP) categories at this point, although as I will show, I think it is possible (following Ludlow, 1999) that past-tense marking is a reflex of some of the features generally thought to be located within CP that I have listed in the tree in (13) below. As for Aspect, some researchers view it as comprising multiple categories—e.g., "outer" ASP and "inner" ASP—located above and within the scope of VP, respectively (e.g., Rice, 2000; Slabakova, 2001; Travis, 2003, 2005). Nothing in what follows hinges on these distinctions aside from the much more general point to be discussed below that past-tense marking may also double as a morphological reflex of other functions in English, such as perfective aspect in English for events, as I discuss next.

(13)   CP (ForceP, FocP, TopP, etc.)

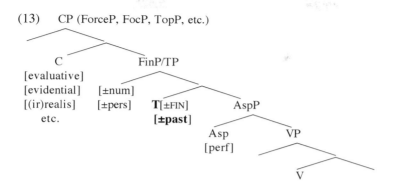

As a point of departure, let us turn to one characterization of [± past], that of Hawkins (2000) and Hawkins and Liszka (2000, 2003):

> One view of [±past] is that it is not an intrinsic feature of T, as [±finite] might be, but is parametrised, with some languages selecting it and some not. ... Chinese, in contrast to English, appears not to have selected [±past], although it does have syntactic reflexes of a [±finite] feature (Li, 1990: 18) ... [and]

> The [±past] contrast of English is an interpretable feature of T. ... *In the absence of this feature, there is no requirement for an inflected verb form.* (Hawkins 2000, p. 6, italics added)

In viewing the presence or absence of the [± past] feature itself as the selection of a binary parameter value, the excerpt quoted above provides us with one possible answer to the question of what it would take to acquire past tense in English by a native speaker of Chinese: *parameter resetting*. Hawkins' formulation, moreover, ties the selection of the positive value (i.e. presence) of the [± past] feature to a requirement that the feature be morphophonologically realized, in the form of past-tense marking.[20]

The basis for this argument comes from data showing that native speakers of Chinese, a language arguably lacking the feature [± past], do not attain as high a percentage of past-tense marking in obligatory contexts in

---

[20] Note that this requirement also has the effect of potentially conflating two distinct objects—the positive value of the parameter (i.e., the (external) selection vs. non-selection of the feature [± past] by a given language), with the actual feature-internal value of the setting [+ past] versus [− past].

their L2 English as do native speakers of languages that do have [± past], such as Japanese and German. Hawkins argues that this result is predicted by the Failed Formal Features Hypothesis (FFH; Hawkins & Chan, 1997), according to which parameterized features not selected in early childhood language acquisition subsequently become unavailable in later language acquisition. The relevant data comparing past-tense marking for high-proficiency speakers from different L1s are shown in Table 4.13 (based on combined data from Hawkins, 2000; Hawkins & Liszka, 2000), with the relevant cell for SX, a native Chinese speaker, highlighted in bold.

TABLE 4.13. Proportion of Inflected Simple Past Tense Verb Forms out of Tokens of Verbs Used in Past Tense Contexts in Spontaneous Speech, Compared with Final Consonant Cluster Retention in Monomorphemes and Inflected Participles (from Hawkins, 2000 and Hawkins & Liszka, 2000, combined Tables 2).

Informant	L1	Proficiency	Inflected Past Tense	Monomorphemic Cluster Retention	Inflected Participles
Bayley (1996)	CHI	High & low (combined)	44%	65%	74%
SX	**CHI**	**high**	**77.1% (74/96)**	**100% (27/27)**	**100% (8/8)**
HF	JAP	high	89% (137/154)	100% (29/29)	100% (10/10)
KK	JAP	high	98.6 (72/73)	100% (13/13)	100% (3/3)
MK	GER	high	94.5% (103/109)	100% (20/20)	100% (26/26)

Table 4.13 shows that, in accordance with the FFH, SX provides a significantly lower proportion of past-tense marking than the Japanese and German native speakers in this study. Note, however, that the FFH cannot easily account for why SX's past-tense marking is as high as it is—at around 77% suppliance, presumably significantly higher than chance.[21]

---

[21] In fact, the rate of past-tense marking for SX ranged from around 82% to 100% on another task in a study by Liszka (2000), in which participants were asked to use both real and novel verbs in controlled contexts, some of which unambiguously required a simple past tense form (Hawkins, 2000, p. 12). In the nonce word condition, both native Chinese speakers (SX and LL) appear to have significantly outperformed MO, one of the Japanese speakers, in past tense inflection (p. 16). In the absence of further discussion concerning the relation of task type to the theoretical claims of the FFH, it looks as if these data do not convincingly support the model.

According to Hawkins, there is a form-function pairing for the Chinese speakers between past-tense marking and "conceptual awareness" that a proposition refers to a past event, somehow bypassing the morphosyntactic feature [± past] that would "syntactically mandate" past-tense marking (p. 20).

This is actually an interesting claim, insofar as it hints at the autonomy of representational levels, such as an autonomous (morpho)syntactic level (following, say, Jackendoff, 1997 or Aronoff, 1994), although Hawkins does not really follow up on it. It implies that both the syntax and the conceptual system have independent access to the (morpho)phonological component (PF), although Hawkins obviously conceives of the form-function mapping as somehow more automatic or iconic for one correspondence relation (syntax–PF) than the other (conceptual system–PF). Based on the available data, however, and in the absence of a more detailed account for this claim, I see no obvious way to tease apart whether it is an occasional failure of the mapping between conceptual awareness and past-tense marking, or that between a morphosyntactic feature [+ past] and past-tense marking, that is responsible for the inconsistent application of past-tense marking observed for SX (or for Patty). Within a minimalist-syntax framework, Hawkins characterizes [± past] as an interpretable feature, which means its associated semantic features must be checked in LF. However, it is not at all clear how these features differ from the type of conceptual awareness Hawkins has in mind.

What are some of the semantic or functional features associated with past-tense marking? In this part of the chapter I would like to examine more closely the main theoretical premise underlying Hawkins' study—namely, that [± past] is a parameterized morphosyntactic feature selected by some languages but not others, the parametric status of which is reflected in direct fashion by (obligatory) past-tense marking in the data. To do this, let us look briefly at some of the functions associated with *past-tense marking* (henceforth, PTM), that illustrate that in fact there is a many-to-one[22] func-

---

[22] Given the different forms of past marking among the class of all verbs (e.g., irregular verbs), this function is actually many-to-many. But I would like to retain the intuition that for any given verb (with rare exceptions mainly involving a transitive vs. intransitive contrast), the very same morphological form that we refer to as "past" can be used to express several different functions—what Aronoff (1994) refers to as a "morphomic function." Also see Halle and Marantz (1993) for detailed discussion involving past-participle formal identity with past-tense marking (of the verb stem itself), which I do not go into here.

tion-form pairing in English that complicates the acquisition picture considerably.

PTM as an Expression of Eventive Perfect Aspect

In English, there is near-identity between the morphological expression of the completion or culmination (i.e., perfectivity) of events (as opposed to states) and the temporal situating of an event prior to the time of speech. In a recent work on the semantics of tense (from which I quote liberally in what follows), Ludlow (1999) writes:

> In most non-IE languages the so-called past is generally just some form of aspectual marker. Is the same true for IE languages? The case is certainly good for English, in which our so-called past tense morphemes are dead ringers for perfect aspectual markers. (A prime example is the '-ed' morpheme, which is taken to show that the event in question has culminated.) (p. 160)

Therefore, in eventive sentences like *Paul walked the dog* or *We ate lunch in the cafeteria* the input with respect to past-tense marking is ambiguous between past tense and perfective aspect. Another way to put this is that PTM would be morphologically compatible with both of these functions. Assuming these are distinct functions, we might well ask which one Patty is representing when she produces PTM on verbs. An even more interesting question raised above by Ludlow, however, is which function(s)—past tense, perfective aspect, or both—are actually being represented by native *English* speakers when they produce PTM in eventive contexts.

PTM as an Expression of Counterfactuality or Hypotheticality

The particular morphological form used to indicate past tense for any given verb is identical to that used to set up an irrealis context. Again, to quote Ludlow (1999):

> It is a notorious fact that past tense does not behave like past tense in counterfactuals (e.g. if I had a million dollars...) ... there is a sense that some deeper third element underlies both tense and counterfactual modality—that tense can't simply be a primitive element that refers to the past. (p. 161)

There is some evidence from Patty's data that this particular function poses morphological difficulty for her, whose hypothetical utterances include ones like the following:

(14) even if he *stay* over Eliotville, he will give me a call
       even if I *buy* it and *left* it there until next year...

PTM as an Expression of Topic Time Included Within the Time of a State (Klein, 1994, 2000)

Klein (1994, 2000) observes that PTM can be used to indicate "the time for which an assertion is made"—that is, *topic time* rather than speech time. In stative sentences like *Patty's first husband was Vietnamese*, the use of *was* does not mean that the individual-level predication of her first husband—in this case, BE VIETNAMESE—held (only) prior to speech time. Rather, it means that the past topic time is included within the state of his being Vietnamese. It also implies that he is no longer her husband at speech time. In case he is still alive, he is still Vietnamese.

PTM as an Expression of Politeness and/or Distance

A non-past temporal example of the use of PTM to convey politeness is *I was wondering if I could borrow your Chomsky 1999* ('and still am').

PTM as an Expression of an Uninterpretable Feature (in T?) of Stative Subordinate Clauses—"Sequence of Tense"

In sentences like *Roger said that he disagreed with her analysis*, one interpretation is that 'he still does'; that is, his disagreement is ongoing. Although morphologically marked for past tense, this instance of PTM is in fact "tenseless" or "not semantically active" (Kuhn & Portner, 2002).

Almost all of these types of subordinate clauses in Patty's data are unmarked for past. Some examples are given in (15):

(15) we did not expect it *will* be so fast
       I thought we *have* a special deal
       they did not know whether or not she *will* be back
       they thought that *I'm* from north
[but] he took me to lunch the other day and told me he *valued* me very
       much

PTM as a Possible Expression of Evidentiality?

We do not normally consider English to be a language with grammaticalized contrastive evidentiality markers (as are present in, say, Turkish or Korean). As pointed out by Papafragou and Li (2002), however, failure to evaluate the sources of evidence in attempting to assess its reliability "could have dire consequences" (pp. 510–511). We might therefore expect evidentiality to be a good candidate for a primitive feature of language whatever form it takes in any given language. In English this can of course be accomplished via lexical means (*know, hear, allegedly, presumably,* etc.) and also via the use of epistemic modality, which indicates "the degree of speaker commitment to the truth of the proposition embedded under the modal" (Papafragou, 1998, p. 610).

An utterance such as *John was thinking of starting up a dot-com company* is ambiguous between a past interpretation in which we believe that John was thinking about it and then stopped thinking about it (e.g., because maybe the dot-com economy crashed), and one in which maybe he is still thinking about it but that is the latest information about him the speaker can vouch for. Ludlow (1999) writes:

> Ideally, what we would like to say about so-called past tense morphology is that it is really telling us something about the kind of evidence that we currently have for our claims ... what we are taking to be tense morphemes or aspectual markers might actually be evidentials. There is a real grammatical phenomenon (or class of phenomena) that we sloppily call tense and which we suppose to be connected to temporal reference. What we really have on our hands is most likely not a single phenomenon but a mixture of modality and evidentiality. (pp. 161–163)

Note that if anything like what Ludlow suggests is true, the morphosyntactic feature [± past] in English is possibly somewhat of an artifact of linguistic description (as he points out)—an amalgam of more primitive features clumped together and realized in a particular morphological way for a particular language. Klein makes a similar point for the German Perfekt (which in fact functionally overlaps considerably, although not completely, with the English Past):

> Traditional categories such as Perfekt or Passiv are not primitive notions of linguistic theory; they turn out to be nothing but *gross ways of clustering semantic and syntactic properties of their components.* [...]

These components are: "temporal relations, temporal intervals, the characterization of these intervals by the lexical content of simple and complex expressions, the distinction between finite and nonfinite expressions, and finally, the notion of assertion (in the case of declarative clauses)." (p. 381; italics added)

To summarize, unless the same features or properties are always clustered in exactly the same way cross-linguistically, such that they are uniformly realized by the same (PTM) morphological means in each language—which surely does not appear to be the case—it is doubtful we can speak of that amalgamated feature as being parameterized in the sense intended by Hawkins, such that some languages have it and some don't. In other words, given the range of application of PTM in English (i.e., a many-to-one mapping between function and form), it is not clear what sort of coherent argument can be made that an interpretable feature F [± past] is parametrically not selected by Chinese just because there isn't a single overt morphological reflex that encodes or divides up exactly the same bunch of stuff—some interpretable, some not—in exactly the same way English does.

There is probably some degree of overlap, for example, between the aspectual properties of English past (at least for events) and the well-known aspectual markers *le* and *guo* in Chinese. (The latter, denoting experientiality, entails a past temporal feature and in some ways resembles English present perfect.) To whatever extent there is overlap among the features encoded by different kinds of morphological exponence (e.g., tense or aspect or evidentiality) across languages, it would be difficult to characterize those associated features as parameterized in a binary ("all or nothing") way for an individual language.

The acquisition situation for any given language seems far more complex. For English, working "backward" from decoding PTM in the input, the array of functions it expresses appears to range over the entire extended functional phrase structure, from CP down through AspP. Moreover, given the semantic, pragmatic, and (in the case of sequence of tense agreement) grammatical complexity of what we consider [± past], it is understandable why it would be more difficult to acquire than [± finite], since the latter seems to be a more fundamental formal grammatical distinction, with greater consequences in the syntax (e.g., affecting verb raising, determination of case, possibility of licensing null subjects, etc.).

Alternative Kinds of L1 Influence in Acquiring
Past-Tense Marking

Is there any way we can account for the apparent discrepancy Hawkins observed between Chinese speakers, on the one hand, and German and Japanese speakers on the other, with respect to the former's higher rate of omission of past-tense marking? Recall that his explanation was that German and Japanese, like English but unlike Chinese, were parameterized to select a feature [±past]. Because the ability to acquire such parameterized features was presumed to be lost beyond a certain critical period, native Chinese speakers would be unable to reset the parameter selecting [± past] for their L2 English. Let us assume now, for the sake of argument, that native Chinese speakers acquiring L2 English have noticed that past-tense marking in English, especially for eventive predicates, appears to bear some resemblance (i.e. exhibits at least some degree of overlapping) to perfective *le*-marking in their native L1 (similar, say, to the correlation that a native German or French speaker might be expected to draw between English past-tense marking and the German *Perfekt* or French *passé composé*).[23] An example from Chinese (taken from Li &Thompson 1981, p. 196) is shown in (16):

(16)   wo   wang-*le*   ta-de   dizhi
       I   forget-PERF 3SG-GEN   address
       'I forgot his/her address.'[24]

---

[23] See Carroll (2001) for arguments regarding the plausibility of this assumption. She writes, for example: "[W]e have good reason to suppose, given the existence of equivalence classification as a general phenomenon of L2 learning, that category creation will take place in an extremely conservative fashion, learners mapping L2 stimuli onto L1 categories wherever they can" (p. 196). Note that this recategorization should be analyzed in terms of component properties or features, rather than "morphemes," (as also proposed by C. Brown, 2000, for phonological transfer in terms of features rather than phonemes). It is clearly not the case that Patty has simply replaced Chinese *le* with English PTM. One kind of evidence for this comes from the frequent co-occurrence of [past] + [neg] in Patty's English, which would be disallowed in Chinese (i.e., *le*, as an indicator of perfectivity, cannot occur in negative contexts). Patty's robust use of PTM for stative verbs, which would not be *le*-marked in Chinese, provides additional evidence.

[24] There is another interesting complication here, related to our earlier discussion of cross-linguistic aspectual differences for equivalent verbs and remarked on by Li and Thompson (1981) for this particular example. They point out that although the verb *forget* can be atelic in English (e.g., *S/he is forgetting her/his French*), this reading is impossible in Chinese, where only a telic interpretation for the corresponding verb *wang* is allowed (p. 196). The
(Continued)

We should at least consider the possibility that the differential tendencies among learners' L1s to omit elements that are recoverable from the discourse context (or elsewhere in an utterance) might distinguish Chinese learners from, say, German learners of English. Li and Thompson (1981), for example, point out that in Chinese, "Often the conditions for the use of perfective *le* would appear to be satisfied, and yet no *le* appears" (p. 205). They observe that *le* is not required if an event already contains another "perfectivizing expression" (p. 206), or might be required on only the first event in a sequence of events (p. 198).

Li and Thompson also note that individual native speaker judgments may vary regarding the obligatoriness of *le*—depending on the extent to which the event is judged by the individual speaker to be bounded. For example, in (17) (their example (27), p. 191),

(17) ta   jia   yang-*le*   yi-ge   hen ke ai   de   xiao mao
     3SG home raise-PERF one-CL very can love REL small cat
     'His/her family had a very lovable little cat.'

they write that "some native speakers feel that -*le* is not necessary," because they "don't feel strongly" that the quantified direct object is bounded; others feel that the *le* indicates that this utterance represents the beginning of a sequence of utterances about the cat, and other native speakers feel it is fine as it is because they feel the direct object *is* bounded (p. 191). The overall point I would like to make here is that the degree of obligatoriness in expressing the morphological reflexes of certain features depends on conditions that may be rather more flexible and underspecified among the speakers of one language than for those of another. This needs to be recognized as a type of L1 influence.

Now consider the input available to the Chinese-speaking learner of English, such as Patty. Even among native English speakers, there are commonly occurring conversational conditions under which the selection of [+ past] is warranted but not truly obligatory, as in the use of politeness marking, sequence of tense agreement, and most strikingly, the so-called

---

complication is that lexical semantic differences of this type, if they transfer, might partially obscure the input data that would enable Chinese learners of English to differentiate tense versus aspect in English (i.e., to learn that PTM applies equally to English stative as well as eventive verbs, since, for a Chinese speaker, verbs like *forget* will not have a stative reading). Of course, the same problem confronts the English learner of Chinese trying to figure out the conditions for applying or withholding *le* aspectual marking.

historical present. The widespread optional use of historical present by native English speakers ("in novels and plays, travelogs and book reviews, as well as in accounts of sporting events, in jokes, and in conversational narrative" (Wolfson, 1979, p. 168), all of which Patty would certainly be exposed to), presents language data to the learner that even native English speakers' use of past-tense marking may be variable and not always obligatory. It may be difficult for the ESL learner to determine precisely those conditions under which it is obligatory, especially for speakers whose L1 apparently provides considerable latitude with respect to omitting recoverable or redundant elements. (Note that I am not suggesting here that Patty's variable omission of past-tense marking is the same as native English speakers' use of historical present.)

This difficulty, however, should not be taken as evidence that some kind of [past] feature is not in principle acquirable or representable by Patty or the Chinese participants in Hawkins' study. The latter's requirement of near-nativelike production of past-tense marking as evidence for knowledge of [past] is unrealistic given the (presumably constrained) optionality of past-tense marking available even to native English speakers in relating events that occurred prior to the moment of speech. Indeed, rather than the complete absence of the relevant corresponding syntactic category, as Hawkins proposes, a more likely source of past omission is the potential difficulty in determining the pragmatic or discourse conditions under which past-tense marking is required or omissible in English. We saw, for example, that there is no apparent correlation between Patty's past-tense marking and discourse foregrounding versus backgrounding, whereas the use of historical present among native English speakers is thought to be related to this narrative distinction.[25] Positing a more indirect type of L1 influence based on assuming that past-tense marking is often morphophonologically redundant and may be omitted, bolstered by a fair amount of evidence to this effect from the input, would better account for the data than a parametric explanation, since the latter incorrectly predicts either random or no past-tense marking—not what we find. (I address this non-randomness in the next section.)

---

[25] For attempts to characterize the distribution of use of historical present among native English speakers, see Schiffrin (1981), Wolfson (1979), and references cited therein.

Incorrect Past-Tense Marking

We have so far considered Patty's rate of past-tense marking as a percentage of suppliance in obligatory past contexts. As mentioned above, determining obligatory contexts is not always easy, because of the possibility of ambiguously interpreting the grammatical context (e.g., in the case of possibly missing auxiliaries) or optional use of historical present even by native speakers of English. Another way to look at the data is to examine those utterances for which past-tense marking was actually produced, to see whether or not it was supplied in an appropriate temporal and grammatical context. This allows us to catch instances of incorrect overuse as well as appropriate usage.

The data for this section include the spoken data from Patty's Recordings 1–4 (see Footnote 11) and written data that included e-mail messages covering a period of about 7 years (1997–2004), as well as written answers elicited in response to a small set of written questions. (Thus, there are somewhat more data covered in this section than in previous sections.)

Two primary factors were considered in analyzing the data—whether the use of past-tense marking was felicitous and semantically appropriate given the temporal reference or context, and whether it was formally appropriate given the grammatical context. I did not include those contexts for which the reference time was unclear or ambiguous except in those instances where past-tense marking was formally inappropriate no matter what the temporal context was (e.g., marked on a verb following the infinitive marker *to* as in **to spoke*). I also omitted contexts for past marking on verbs which do not change form in the past tense (e.g., *hit, hurt, let, put*). The net effect of these omissions may be to slightly inflate the percentage of incorrect oversuppliance of past-tense marking; however, this number is nonetheless quite small—roughly only 6% of all instances of past-tense marking. Thus, about 94% of all verbs (or auxiliaries) bearing past-tense marking are appropriately marked.[26]

The overall results are presented in Table 4.14. Errors were classified into two types as noted above: temporal mismatch errors (e.g., past-tense

---

[26] The figure for oversuppliance of past-tense marking may also be slightly inflated due to sentences in which apparently past-marked verbs may have been intended as participles, but an auxiliary is missing (e.g., *if I['ve] left a message to my customer...*; *I['ve] lost two months of missing her*; *he['s] never raised his voice*). There are only a few of these possibly ambiguous sentences in the data, in which the past and past-participle forms of the verb are identical.

marking supplied in a nonpast temporal context) or formal errors (e.g., past-tense marking supplied in an inappropriate grammatical context). Some examples of these errors are shown in the sentences in (18) and (19) below, following Table 4.14.

TABLE 4.14. Appropriateness of Supplied Past-Tense Marking in Patty's Data.

Data Type	**Correctly Supplied** (%)	Temporal Mismatch (%)	Formal Error (%)	**Incorrectly Supplied** (Total %)
Spoken	300/320 (93.75)	4/320 (1.25)	16/320 (5.00)	20/320 (6.25)
Written	249/265 (93.96)	9/265 (3.40)	7/265 (2.64)	16/265 (6.04)
Total	**549/585 (93.85)**	13/585 (2.22)	23/585 (3.93)	**36/585 (6.15)**

In general, when Patty does produce past-tense marking, it is appropriately supplied with only a relatively small percentage of incorrect overuse. There is also no overall difference between her spoken and written data in terms of oversuppliance. Interestingly, half of all oversuppliance is concentrated among only four verb types—namely, *spoke* (6/36 errors), *went* (5/36), *got* (4/36), and *left* (3/36). (Two of the three errors with *left* occur in the expression *left a message*, and the third is a case of formal double-marking of the past in which *left* might actually be intended as a participial form: *M. was # was left* in a context interpreted as 'M. had (already) left'. In this case, the problem might not really be with the lexical verb *left*, but rather with the choice of auxiliary.) Let us look at some of these oversuppliance errors. Examples of temporal mismatch errors are shown in (18) and of formal errors in (19).

(18) a. if people call me and uh, *left* me message [present context]
    b. when you pray what you want, you *got* what you want [present context]
    c. and make sure she *was* not deaf [probably present]
    d. I really hate when your car *got* hit, it will not drive the same [present context]
    e. I hope Sunday *would* be nice [future context]
    f. her father *tried* to spoil her rotten [present (perfect) context]
    g. my Ebay selling *went* very well, at least $500–$600 a month [probably present (perfect)]
    h. Debbie brother *was* very rich now [probably present (perfect, inchoative)]

(19) a. I asked that she *went* to the bathroom to cry
     b. I was very unhappy *lived* with S.
     c. made me *cried* with her, too
     d. he or she have to *spoke* uh, English
     e. they did *went* to school and learn English
     f. we don't *spoke* that much English
     g. so they let me *spoke* it in Mandarin
     h. I'm still # I was still *wrote* to my friend

In addition to these examples, there is another remarkable kind of formal error in which Patty apparently mislinearizes the morpheme -/d/, incorrectly attaching it to the verb rather than the subject, as shown in (20):

(20) a. I decided on Monday that we better *booked* it
         (cf. 'we'd better book it')
     b. otherwise we *ended up* paying high prices
         (cf. 'we'd end up paying...')
     c. I thought I *shared* it with you all
         (cf. 'I thought I'd share it...')

The examples in (20) arguably do not even represent true oversuppliance of past-tense marking, although the verbs in question have the appearance of being past marked.

The spoken production data summarized in Table 4.14 span a period of roughly 16 years, from 1986 to 2002. Patty's percentages of appropriate past-tense marking for all four recorded interviews (Recordings 1–4) over that period of time remain quite consistent, at 95.83%, 92.38%, 95.92% and 97.30%, respectively, and do not differ from her written data. To summarize, where Patty does produce past-tense marking, it typically (although not perfectly) is used in an appropriate temporal context and is grammatically accurate. With respect to past-tense marking, the predominant error in the data thus remains one of omission.

Conclusion

It is important to keep in mind that Patty's written production data suggest that her rate of past-tense marking in English, while obviously not native-like, is still too high, at around 78%, to be simply written off as random behavior or good luck. The fact that it is so much higher than that of her spoken production data indicates that phonology and performance factors play a substantial role in whether she is likely to produce it or not. So do considerations of what function past marking is expressing; for example, we saw that sequence-of-tense agreement is likely not to be marked in subordinate clauses.

We also find difficulty with the actual morphological spell-out of past in some cases, which suggests a breakdown at some point in the correspondence rules or algorithms that guide the mapping from morphosyntactic feature to phonological form. These appear to include basic problems with the production of inflectional affixation per se, such as how and where to spell out what.[27] We can find at least five types of examples suggesting mapping-to-morphophonological-form problems: instances of double-marking as shown in (21), marking in I(nfl) rather than on the verb itself (as noted in the previous chapter) as in (22), marking on the verb itself rather than in I(nfl) (23), marking on the infinitival complement instead of the finite verb or auxiliary (24), and, most curiously, apparent mis-linearization of the morpheme -/d/, in which it is incorrectly attached to the verb rather than to the subject as a contracted auxiliary form (25).

(21) a. they *did went* to school and learn English
     b. I *was* still *wrote* to my friend

(22) a. I *was* have a breakthrough
     b. so we *were* dance for like, couple dance

(23) a. we don't *spoke* that much English
     b. so I can # can, um, *spoke* with uh, people from Taiwan

(24) a. I take uh # I start to uh, *took* it seriously
     b. he or she have to *spoke* uh, English

(25) a. I decided on Monday that *we better booked it* ('we'd better book it')
     b. otherwise *we ended up* paying high prices ('we'd end up paying...')

---

[27] We should keep in mind, following Jackendoff (1997, p. 24) that the interaction of linguistic representations with production is different from that for perception, and we might therefore expect different results from other kinds of data (e.g., perception/parsing data); see also Carroll (2001).

Finally, what kind(s) of L1 knowledge does Patty appear to have transferred? Undoubtedly, there is a strong phonological constraint against final consonant clusters, which at least partially accounts for some of the difference between her spoken and written production. It is clear, however, that phonology cannot account for all of her past-tense omission. The data also suggest the possibility that she is relying on some of the lexical semantic features of equivalent verbs in her L1. Somewhat more speculatively, she may also be assuming greater latitude with respect to optionality of past-tense marking, especially if she represents it as a redundant form of verbal agreement marking for information recoverable from another element in the clause (such as temporal adverbs) or the discourse context.

Actually, I am quite convinced that Patty's own idiolectal representation of at least some of the cluster of properties associated with some internally-complex morphosyntactic feature (or features) that we researchers call "[past]," including how to realize these overtly in English, is indeed non-nativelike. Some of these properties are likely to be influenced by L1 knowledge at various levels of representation, including phonological, lexico-semantic, and discourse-pragmatic. Along with Hawkins' Chinese informants, Patty's representation of [past] is likely to be different in some respects from what is being represented by the German and Japanese speakers in his study as well. What concerns me is an interpretation of these data as support for the view that the morphosyntactic feature [past] is a unitary, parameterized primitive feature that is selected or not in an all-or-nothing fashion by entire individual languages and which in principle cannot be acquired by native Chinese speakers or native speakers of a language with the [no-past] setting. I do not think the data provide evidence for this characterization at all. Instead, we observe that what we call "past-tense marking" serves different grammatical and semantic functions, and that acquiring the form-function mapping is likely to require knowledge of the complementation properties of particular verbs, prosodic knowledge not easily reconcilable with L1 prosodic features in the production (and possibly the parsing) of spoken English, and discourse-level knowledge that may differ in key respects from the L1 with respect to when in fact the overt expression of any of the various functions associated with [past] is obligatory and when it is optional.

5

Clausal Word Order and Movement

In this chapter we examine whether Patty has acquired knowledge of the features that determine whether or not certain sentential elements move in English. Section 5.1 investigates verb raising, which has been connected in both the first and second language acquisition literature to knowledge of finiteness and subject-verb agreement (recall chap. 3 and see Lardiere, 2000, for a review). Sections 5.2 and 5.3 are concerned with the acquisition of *wh*-movement in questions and relative clauses, respectively. Finally, Section 5.4 provides some data on passive sentences.

I. Verb Raising

Some Theoretical Background

As mentioned earlier in chapters 1 and 3, the position of verbs in sentences in relation to negation, adverbs, and inversion with subjects in questions has been linked within linguistic theory over the past decade or so to the complexity (or so-called "strength") of morphological paradigms for subject-verb agreement, although this relation is not universally accepted, and there is still no truly satisfactory explanation for it even among those who do accept it. In this section, I present a brief and necessarily oversimplified overview of the general ideas; for a detailed theoretical critique of the assumed link between rich morphology and feature strength, see recent work by Bobaljik (2001, 2002).

The original (by now well-known) data to be accounted for by the positing of verb raising is exemplified in the comparison of French and English in (1) below, examples from White (1992b, p. 121, following Pollock, 1989):

140

(1) a.   Jean n'aime pas Marie
         *John likes not Mary
         John does not like Mary

    b.   Aime-t-elle Jean?
         *Likes she John?
         Does she like John?

    c.   Jean regarde souvent la télévision
         *John watches often television
         *Marie souvent regarde la télévision
         Mary often watches television

In these French examples, the verb precedes negation in (1a), has inverted with the pronominal subject in (1b) and precedes the adverb, while the adverb itself precedes the direct object in (1c). None of these orders is grammatical in English, which instead relies on *do*-support, as also shown in examples (1a–b). This clustering of distributional properties of the verb in relation to negation and adverbs and in *yes-no* question formation, for both French and English as shown above, has been elegantly accounted for by assuming that finite verbs in French but not English raise from a position inside the verb phrase to a higher position in the clause structure—in this case, IP (or TP), as shown in (2). (Recall from chap. 3 that finite verbs are thought to raise to CP in V2 languages such as German.) This account assumes, of course, that the positions of NEG and of certain manner and frequency adverbs remain relatively fixed (Cinque, 1999; Zanuttini, 1997).

(2) $[_{\text{IP}}$ Jean $[_{\text{I}}$ (n') aime$_i$ pas $[_{\text{VP}}$ t_i Marie$]]]$

In *yes-no* question formation, the finite verb (or auxiliary) in I moves to C; in French (3a), this can be a thematic lexical verb, but not in English (3b), which relies on *do*-support in case there is no other auxiliary:

(3a) $[_{\text{CP}} [_{\text{C}}$ aime$_i$ $[_{\text{IP}}$ elle $[_{\text{I}}$ t_i $[_{\text{VP}}$ t_i Jean$]$

       likes   she   John

(3b) $[_{\text{CP}} [_{\text{C}}$ does$_i$ $[_{\text{IP}}$ she $[_{\text{I}}$ t_i $[_{\text{VP}}$ like John$]$

What is the source of this difference? Pollock (1989), observing that thematically "light" auxiliaries and the copula do appear in IP in English whereas lexical verbs do not, posited a parametric distinction for the raising (or not) of thematic lexical verbs. Because nonfinite verbs in French do not have to raise, the source of verb raising was tied to finiteness, and, as we saw in chapter 3, to the presence of finiteness morphology—specifically, subject-verb agreement inflection. The presence of so-called "rich" agreement in a language (i.e., a more complex subject-verb agreement paradigm) was correlated with verb raising.

Pollock's approach involved splitting IP into distinct functional projections each headed by its own functional category such as AGR(eement) or T(ense); in pre-minimalist theory, the agreement or tense affix was located in its respective projection and the verb raised (in verb-raising languages) to join with it (i.e., in order to get inflected). For English, a language with no verb raising but limited inflection nonetheless (past tense, 3SG nonpast), the morphological inflection of verbs was accomplished by affix-lowering onto the verb, motivated by morphological well-formedness conditions such as the Stray Affix Filter (Baker, 1988; Lasnik, 1981), which prevented the stranding of affixes in functional categories at S-structure.

In more recent minimalist approaches (Chomsky, 1995), the verb is hypothesized to be already inflected in the lexicon prior to entering the syntactic derivation. Movement in this framework is motivated by feature-checking—that is, the need for inflected lexical items to check the feature associated with a particular inflection against the feature in the relevant corresponding syntactic category. Under this approach, all functional features such as tense and agreement are parameterized in a binary "strong/weak" distinction. Strong features attract overt movement for checking in the syntax (resulting in changes or displacement in linear ordering), whereas weak features do not. Thus, going back to our earlier French and English examples, the parametric distinction responsible for the differences in distribution of verb placement could be accounted for in terms of feature strength—whereas French has strong agreement, in English agreement is weak.

SLA Studies in Verb Raising

It is against this theoretical backdrop that studies examining finite verb raising in both first and second language acquisition have been carried out. An early SLA example, following the approach of Pollock (1989), is found in a series of papers by White (1990/1991, 1991, 1992a, 1992b) and colleagues (Trahey & White, 1993), who observed that francophone learners of English, while ordering verbs correctly with respect to negation, nonetheless allow *SVAO (Subject-Verb-Adverb-Object) word orders in which adverbs intervene between the thematic verb and the direct object (following the French word order but ungrammatical in English).[1]

White (1991) compared francophone learners who were explicitly instructed on adverb placement in English with learners who were not. In the Trahey and White (1993) study, learners who were explicitly instructed on adverb placement were compared with learners who received only positive evidence in the form of "input flooding" of clauses containing adverbs in the correct preverbal position. These studies found that the learners who received the explicit adverb instruction significantly improved and outperformed the other groups in rejecting ungrammatical (*SVAO) adverb placement in English, supporting White's hypothesis. However, the instruction group also incorrectly rejected grammatical (SVAP) sentences in which the adverb intervened between a verb and a PP (e.g., *John walks quickly to school*), suggesting that they had developed a kind of overgeneral strategy that simply prohibited adverbs from following verbs. This, plus the fact that a post-test administered a year later found that all groups had reverted to pre-test status (accepting *SVAO sentences), suggested that the instruction employed in the study had not really brought about grammatical restructuring at all.

---

[1] White's earlier (1989) work in adverb placement was originally conceived as involving a potential poverty of the stimulus subset-superset problem: Although different kinds of adverbs could occur in various positions in English, they could not appear in the 'French' position between a verb and its direct object, rendering English a more restrictive language than French with regard to adverb placement (following Stowell, 1981). In that case, what sort of input could inform a native French speaker that the French word order was ruled out in English? Note that the learnability problem is compounded by positive evidence from so-called "heavy NP shift" in which the SVAO linear order *is* possible in English if the object NP contains a relative clause or is otherwise "heavy" enough (e.g., *John enjoyed thoroughly the chicken pot pie that his mother brought over*), and from the occurrence of adverbs post-verbally when the verb is followed by a PP or infinitive clause (e.g., *John waited patiently for his mother to bring over the pie*).

White originally hypothesized that only negative evidence—namely, explicit instruction on adverb placement in English—could force a restructuring of the learners' English grammar to the correct parametric value. With the introduction into the theory of a binary parameter involving verb raising as a way to account for the placement of verbs with respect to adverbs, negation and subject-aux inversion in question formation (thus alleviating the subset problem), White's hypothesis was necessarily modified to whether providing negative evidence was more effective in bringing about grammatical restructuring than positive input alone.

As the theoretical framework evolved such that it was thought that English-type and French-type represented opposite settings of a binary parameter involving whether or not thematic verbs could raise, the learning problem within the parameter-setting model became quite knotty. If learners indeed had knowledge of the parametric properties in question, then they should have been able to deduce from the available evidence—the presence of adverbs in preverbal position, or the existence of *do*-support—that the L2 value of the verb-raising parameter in English was the opposite of their L1-French setting. Due to the presumed clustering effects associated with the parameter in question, learners should also have been able to deduce correct verb placement with respect to adverbs once they had acquired negation or question formation (the latter condition tested in White, 1990/1991), but this was not the case. Because the francophone participants appeared to allow both settings simultaneously in their L2 English, the question that had to be explored was how UG-SLA learning theory could account for this possibility. That question was left temporarily unresolved.[2] I return to the issue of mutually-exclusive parameter settings in chapter 7.

In the meantime, a more recent series of SLA verb-raising papers has appeared within the context of theories of transfer, again taking up the question of apparent optionality within the L2 grammatical representation (with true optionality hypothesized as being disallowed within the minimalist framework and therefore serving as potential evidence for the existence of so-called "rogue grammars" in SLA).

The theoretical relationship thought to hold between agreement morphology and verb raising led to a methodology whereby the presence or absence of agreement morphology in the learner's developing language was taken as evidence for acquisition (or not) of the corresponding functional category projections in the grammatical representation of that language. A series of papers by Eubank and colleagues (Eubank, 1993/1994, 1996; Eubank, Bischoff et al., 1997; Eubank, Cliff et al., 1998; Eubank & Grace, 1998) explored Eubank's proposal that until L2 learners had acquired the agreement paradigm (which in English amounts to acquisition of 3SG non-

---

[2] For an interesting discussion about whether the explicit instruction the instructed group received *could* bring about such parameter resetting, see Schwartz and Gubala-Ryzak (1992) and White's (1992b) reply. The issues raised here, including the possible effects of explicit instruction, whether parameter settings are mutually exclusive, and what sort of evidence (assuming the parameter was correctly formulated and the settings mutually exclusive) would suffice to switch the parameter setting (e.g., *do*-support, preverbal adverbs), foreshadow some of the issues recently examined at length in Carroll (2001).

past -*s* affixation), their setting of the parametric value for strong versus weak agreement would in effect remain unset, or "inert," allowing optional verb raising.

The studies by Eubank & Grace (1998), Eubank, Bischoff et al. (1997), and Eubank, Cliff et al. (1998) empirically tested this prediction with adult native speakers of Chinese (a non-raising language) acquiring English (another non-raising language). The choice of Chinese as the L1 was motivated by a desire to construct the strongest possible test of their claims—even when transfer from the L1 could aid acquisition of the correct feature value in the L2, the feature values nonetheless were hypothesized not to transfer, and the setting of the correct parameter value was contingent on the acquisition of knowledge of agreement to determine feature strength. The prediction was that low-proficiency learners who had not yet acquired nonpast 3SG -*s* agreement marking in English would exhibit optional verb raising (even though neither the L1 nor the L2 has verb raising), whereas more advanced learners who had acquired agreement would not. [3] The studies did not test for verb movement over negation, but only over a limited set of manner adverbs (e.g., only *slowly* and *quietly* in the Eubank, Bischof et al. study).

Contrary to expectations, some of the more advanced learners in these studies—those who appeared to have acquired agreement—did appear to accept English *SVAO sentences, whereas some of the lower-proficiency learners did not. These findings led Eubank to suggest that those beginning learners who did not allow verb raising had in fact not yet even acquired the functional categories in IP, such as AGR, to which verbs could raise (following Vainikka & Young-Scholten, 1994, 1996), whereas even those who had acquired agreement nonetheless suffered from a presumably permanent "local impairment" of knowledge of feature strength (following Beck, 1997, 1998).[4]

None of the studies by Eubank and colleagues looked at naturalistic data, the possibility of verb raising over negation, or a wider array of frequency and manner adverbs. Lardiere (1998b) examined Patty's data for any evidence of optional verb raising. In that study it was hypothesized,

---

[3] Eubank and Grace (1998) adopted a criterion for having acquired agreement (and thus, presumably, AGR) of 70% suppliance in obligatory contexts of 3SG agreement on lexical verbs in an oral translation task.

[4] However, in examining the individual data, we observe that roughly half of the more advanced learners in the Eubank, Bischoff et al. study performed comparably with the native speaker controls, casting some doubt on this conclusion.

following earlier work on Patty's tense and case marking (Lardiere, 1998a, described earlier in chap. 3), that knowledge of formal features is available from the L1, is acquirable in the L2, and is not directly associated with the overt production or lack of inflectional morphology. The fact that Patty's native language is Chinese and that she had reached a steady state in her grammatical representation of English made her a good comparable candidate for testing the proposal that knowledge of feature strength is contingent on the productive acquisition of agreement morphology and/or that adult L2 learners suffer permanent local impairment of knowledge of feature strength.

As noted earlier in chapter 3, Patty's use of 3SG -*s* agreement marking on thematic verbs (the only type of verb considered by Eubank as providing evidence of acquisition of AGR) is exceedingly low, ranging from 0% to 4.76% over the data-collection period.[5] Hence, it is clear that she would have been considered under Eubank's methodological criteria to have not yet acquired agreement, and we can see that at the L2 end state she has in fact *never* acquired it. Yet it is clear from the data that Patty projects extended phrase structure (including CP; see Lardiere, 1998a and above) and handles suppletive elements such as auxiliary and copular *be* and the realization of tense and agreement on these substantially better than on lexical verbs (Lardiere, 1999).

With respect to optional verb raising, Lardiere (1998b) reported that Patty neither raises verbs over NEG nor over adverbs. The data are summarized in Table 5.1, taken from that study (Table 3, p. 369).

TABLE 5.1. Occurrence of Thematic Verb Raising over NEG and Adverbs.

Recording	Raising/NEG Contexts	Raising/ADV Contexts
1	0 / 42	0 / 27
2	0 / 46	1 / 77
3	0 / 24	0 / 18
Total	0 / 112	1 / 122

[5] At the time of writing of the Lardiere (1998b) study, Patty's written data had not yet been compiled, but note that, since the translation test used by Eubank and colleagues was an oral task, the spoken production data from Patty would be more comparable in any case. The rate of *written* nonpast 3SG agreement marking in Patty's data is considerably higher than her spoken production rate—at around 51% suppliance in obligatory contexts. Note, however, that even this higher percentage would fall well below the 70% criterion for acquisition of agreement employed in the Eubank studies.

Some examples involving negation and adverb placement are shown in (4) and (5), respectively:

(4) I do *not* write in Chinese
     I could *not* speak my own language either
     B. *didn't* really say much about his brother
     he did *not* try to do it anymore
     I do *not* like to play in front of people

(5) I *already* took uh # eight credit
     I *just barely* pass the # the minimum
     so she perform and *always* send me the picture
     but S. *immediately* say 'mom, mom, it's not'
     he *always* blame it # blame God

In sum, the production data show that, despite the virtual absence of 3SG -*s* agreement marking, verb raising does not appear to be an option in Patty's English.

More on Verb Raising and Adverb Placement in Patty's English

Clearly, the spontaneous production data reported in Lardiere (1998b) are highly suggestive of a constraint prohibiting verb raising in Patty's grammatical representation of English. However, that study could not conclusively show that Patty knows that verb raising in English is ungrammatical, but rather that she simply does not raise verbs in her production of English. To further test for knowledge of this constraint, Lardiere (2006) elicited acceptability judgments for both grammatical and ungrammatical sentences from Patty as well as from a control group of 25 adult native English speakers.

Two tasks were administered to Patty 18 months apart. The first was a written, binary forced-choice test in which Patty was asked to rate sentences using either Y (yes) for acceptable or N (no) for unacceptable. For those she rated unacceptable, she was asked to provide what she considered to be a more acceptable version. There were 40 sentences, consisting of 10 ungrammatical *SVAO sentences, 10 grammatical SAVO sentences, 10 ungrammatical distracters, and 10 grammatical distracters. Examples of each are provided in (6a–d), respectively:

(6) a. The chef cooked slowly the meat.
     b. The maid carefully ironed the shirt.

    c.   The old guy forgot his umbrella to take.
    d.   The artist painted a very lovely picture.

    The crucial condition for demonstrating knowledge of the ungrammaticality of verb raising was for sentences of type (6a), the ungrammatical *SVAO pattern. Patty correctly rejected all 10 of these, a finding that completely converges with her spoken production data. The results indicate that, for her, there is clearly no thematic verb raising in English.

    However, there is an interesting wrinkle in the results. For the grammatical SAVO sentences, Patty spontaneously created an intermediate category Y/N to express a preference for postposing most of the manner adverbs to the end of the sentence (which of course is also grammatical in English). For example, she rewrote *The kids quickly finished breakfast* to *The kids finished breakfast quickly*. In correcting the ungrammatical *SVAO sentences, she also tended to place the adverb in sentence-final position, so that a sentence like *The chef cooked slowly the meat* was rewritten to *The chef cooked the meat slowly*. At the bottom of the test sheet, she notated the following:

"Y/N = could be either way, prefer to put adverb at the end (conversation) & writing (modify noun) in the front."

    This notation reveals a quite sophisticated sensitivity to adverb placement in English. Even if the formulation of her metalinguistic "rule" is a bit clumsy, Patty's intuition regarding register variation (ultimately regarding a way of highlighting or focusing the relevant information) is one that I as a native speaker of the variety she is exposed to would agree with. Even more striking, she (correctly) did not postpose those adverbs that resist such extraposition, such as *barely* or frequency adverbs like *always* (e.g., *The receptionist always reads magazines* was a straightforward accept (Y) and *The gardener wears always gloves* was marked N and corrected to *The gardener always wears gloves*.) In sum, all grammatical SAVO sentences were judged as either Y (= 'yes, OK') or Y/N; none was rejected outright as all of the *SVAO sentences were.

    Patty took a second written test 18 months later. This time she was asked to judge the items on a scale from 1 (*unacceptable*) to 5 (*acceptable*) and to provide a more acceptable version for any item she ranked 3 or lower. The test consisted of the same 40 items as in the first test, presented in reverse order, with the addition of five grammatical SVAP(reposition Phrase) sentences interspersed among them, such as *The child walked slowly to school*. The latter sentence type was added because earlier research (White, 1991) had shown that francophone learners of English failed to distinguish these from ungrammatical *SVAO items. For this second test, there were 25 adult native English speaker controls, who were also asked to provide more acceptable versions of any sentence they ranked at 3 or lower.

The results of the second test confirmed the findings of the first. For the ungrammatical *SVAO items, Patty again correctly and decisively rejected all 10 of them (on the scale of 1–5, mean = 1). For each one of the 10 ungrammatical sentences, the native speakers' group mean score was < 2, as expected. Their overall mean across all 10 *SVAO sentences was 1.49.

For the grammatical SVAP sentences, Patty correctly judged these to be acceptable (mean = 4.8).[6] Her mean for the grammatical SAVO sentences was 3.7. Once again, Patty assigned the middle point on the scale (3) to nearly the very same SAVO sentences she had 18 months earlier assigned her Y/N rating in the first test, and again rewrote them with the adverb in the (also correct) sentence-final position. For each of the grammatical (SAVO and SVAP) sentences, the NS group mean score was > 4, as expected. Interestingly, some of the NSs also preferred adverb extraposition: 14 out of 16 NS responses rating a grammatical sentence ≤ 3 rewrote the test item postposing the adverb to sentence-final position just as Patty had done. The overall NS means for the SAVO and SVAP sentences were 4.61 and 4.59, respectively.

The results of both of the acceptability tasks converge with the production data and allow us, I think, to conclude with some confidence that there is no optional verb raising in Patty's grammatical representation of English. Moreover, the similarity of the results across both judgment tasks 18 months apart indicates that Patty's knowledge of verb raising (and whatever constrains this in UG) and of adverb placement in English is remarkably stable. Additionally, at least in this case, the results are the same for both types of task—binary forced choice or 5-point scale, keeping in mind, however, that Patty added her own intermediate category for the binary choice task. In this study, eliciting participant correction of perceived ungrammaticality has allowed us to see more clearly what motivated this intermediate category choice.

---

[6] Although this result differs from that of White's, it should not be surprising that Patty judges SVAP sentences correctly, as she freely produces them:

    (i)   so I wrote and speak *fluently* in Indonesia [*sic* = 'Indonesian']
    (ii)   I did *so poorly* in my math
    (iii) Chinese speak *differently* from English
    (iv) and write *simultaneously* with the other party

Another finding of interest to emerge from both the Patty studies and the Eubank studies is that English native speakers themselves seem to be somewhat less categorical in their rejection of some *SVAO sentences than we should perhaps feel comfortable with if the theory were correct. Although the group mean for English NSs' rejection of *SVAO sentences in the Lardiere (2006) study described above was well within expectations (1.49 overall, with means of < 2 for each item on a scale of 1 to 5, compared with a group mean of greater than 4 for the grammatical sentences (*p* < .001 on paired t-tests), certain individual responses indicate equivocal judgments. Whereas it seems possible to dismiss a rating of 5 (perfectly acceptable) on one response to a sentence like *The gardener wears always gloves* as noise in the data probably due to subject error, it is less clear that we should treat intermediate ratings of 3 or 4 that way, especially if the within-subject data also indicate a willingness by the same subject to use the extreme values on the scale. But that is what we do find. Nor does the effect seem to be confined to any particular test item.[7] In the Eubank, Bischof et al. study, which employed a truth-value judgment task, 9% of NS responses indicated a raised-verb interpretation. In Eubank, Cliff et al., the much lower-than-expected rate for NS rejection of ungrammatical *SVAO sentences[8] led to the conclusion that the test instrument itself was at fault. Of course this is possible.

More to the point, Patty's total rejection of *SVAO sentences appears to be even more categorical than that of some native English speakers. Such categorical consistency would be compatible with the possibility that Patty is in fact relying on a representation that has been (and perhaps still is) heavily influenced by Chinese, which does not allow even heavy NP shifting. Is it the case that she is representing a more Chinese-like rather than English-like grammar? As discussed in Lardiere (2006), this is doubtful for the following reasons.

---

[7] The individual ungrammatical item with the highest mean (1.92; i.e., lowest rate of rejection) among the NSs was *The teacher explained clearly the poem*, with grammaticality ratings ranging from 1 to 5, including one 5, two 4s, and two 3s. All other ungrammatical test items except one yielded at least one individual NS rating of ≥ 3 (and not by the same NS rater). Although there was no comparable raising-over-NEG task to confirm my intuition, I suspect that type of test would have yielded more unequivocal results, as was the case in White's studies.

[8] The NS rejection rate ranged from 65% to 100% for individual ungrammatical test items.

First of all, consider the kind of positive evidence available in the input for the properties of English (non-)raising—namely, the presence of *do*-support, which does not exist in Chinese. Patty gives ample indication of having acquired *do*-support, as the examples in (7) suggest:

(7) a. I do not want to spoil her
    b. do not run away from the problems [*imperative*]
    c. did you visit your mom last weekend?
    d. it doesn't stick anymore
    e. didn't he know that it will get back to me?
    f. I did not want to hurt your feeling

Second, Patty has acquired the difference between thematic lexical verbs and forms of *be* with regard to verb raising; that is, she knows that, unlike lexical main verbs, *be* does raise over NEG and adverbs in English:

(8) a. I *was* not bitter or anything
    b. she *'s* not going to eat anyway
    c. *isn't* it generous gift?
    d. human weakness *is* never satisfied [*cf.* he never *raised* his voice]
    e. because it *is* always there [*cf.* and always *send* me the picture]

Again, this distinction is not available in Chinese. Chinese has a copula *shi* 'be' that is generally limited to use in predicate nominal constructions. As shown in (9), there is no difference in placement between *shi* and thematic verbs (such as *zhidao* 'know') with respect to NEG (examples from Li & Thompson 1981, p. 422):

(9) a. women   bu   *zhidao*   ta   zai   nar
        we   not   know   s/he   at   where
        'We don't know where s/he is.'

    b. ta   bu   *shi*   xiaozhang
        s/he   not   be   school.chief
        'S/he is not the principal.'

Finally, as demonstrated in her grammaticality judgment tasks, Patty not only allows adverbs to occur sentence-finally in English, but often *prefers* this position, which is not allowed in Chinese. This is also evident in her naturalistic production data:

(10) a.   I just have to learn it slowly
     b.   which really turned me off completely
     c.   there were some changes in my life recently
     d.   he did not try to do it anymore
     e.   it was nice to hear from you finally

In sum, the data seem to show that Patty has indeed acquired an English-like representation of verb raising and adverb placement.

The status of raising over adverbs as part of the cluster of parameterized properties dependent on the strength of agreement has been viewed by some linguists as somewhat tenuous (see e.g., Chomsky, 1995, Iatridou, 1990; Lightfoot & Hornstein, 1994; Williams, 1994). It seems likely that the position of verbs with respect to NEG rather than to adverbs provides a clearer diagnostic for verb raising, as suggested by Lightfoot and Hornstein (1994). Among those studies that have investigated verb placement with respect to NEG (e.g., Gavruseva & Lardiere, 1996; Haznedar, 1997; White, 1992a), it appears that L2 learners do seem to completely acquire the correct properties of verb placement in much more categorical fashion than they do for adverbs, suggesting that it is possible that adverbs may not participate in the parameter in the same way as originally thought.

Moreover, the hypothesized relation between the robustness of morphological paradigms and verb raising itself has also been called into question (Bobaljik, 2002; Chomsky, 1995; Marantz, 1995; Sprouse, 1998); see Lardiere, 2000, for an overview of three proposals tying morphological paradigms to feature strength). In a more recent revision of minimalist theory, Chomsky (1999) appears to exploit a link between morphological affixation and verb movement, suggesting that verb raising (along with nearly all head movement), being "conditioned by the phonetically affixal character of the inflectional categories" (p. 31), may be relegated to the phonological component.

Pending further theoretical development, the data we have on verb raising with respect to adverbs might be more profitably approached in terms of investigating L2 knowledge of the properties of adverbs themselves (e.g., Alexiadou, 1997; Bobaljik, 1999; Cinque, 1999; Jackendoff, 1972; Laenzlinger, 1996), a fertile and interesting area of study in its own right. At the moment, however, I think it is fair to say there is no clear consensus on how or whether the syntax of adverbs and adverbial phrases should be articulated within the "core" or "narrow syntax" of UG-constrained phenomena. That investigation must be left for future research.

II. Wh-Movement

English Question Formation

In the preceding section, we observed that Patty demonstrates knowledge that verbs do not raise in English. Put in more technical terms, we can surmise that Patty's grammatical representation of English includes a formal feature associated with Infl (or T) that is specified as weak. In this section, we examine Patty's data in relation to an approach that has considerable relevance to end-state grammatical knowledge—Hawkins and Chan's (1997) Failed Functional Features Hypothesis. According to this hypothesis, functional features that are not present in the L1 remain inaccessible to learners acquiring an L2. We consider this issue in greater detail below.

Let us turn now to data from a domain for which, in contrast to verb raising, the feature-strength values are presumed to differ between the L1 and the L2—namely, English question formation (and, in the following section, relative clause formation). This will enable us to examine the question of whether parameterized feature values that are different from those of the L1 can be acquired in the L2—a question that can indeed be addressed by looking at advanced or end-state data.

English *yes/no* questions exhibit subject-auxiliary inversion or, more formally, I-to-C movement, as shown in (11a). In *wh*-type questions there is also clause-initial fronting or movement of the *wh*-feature-bearing element into the [Spec, CP] position (11b).[9] In cases where there is no overt element in I (or T) such as an auxiliary or modal, *do* is inserted and moves to C, as shown in (11c). Of course, because English thematic verbs do not raise to I in the first place, as we observed in the previous sections, they are not eligible to raise to C, as shown in the ungrammatical example in (11d).

(11) a. $[_C$ Are$_i$ $[_{IP}$ the students $[_I$ t_i $[_{VP}$ going to the picnic?]]]]
    b. $[_{CP}$ What$_j$ $[_C$ are$_i$ $[_{IP}$ the students $[_I$ t_i $[_{VP}$ bringing t_j to the picnic?]]]]]
    c. $[_{CP}$ What$_j$ $[_C$ do$_i$ $[_{IP}$ the students $[_I$ t_i $[_{VP}$ plan to bring t_j to the picnic?]]]]]
    d. *$[_C$ Go(ing)$_i$ $[_{IP}$ the students $[_I$ t_i $[_{VP}$ t_i to the picnic?]]]]

---

[9] I am not distinguishing here between movement leaving traces versus (PF-deleted) copies; see Chomsky (1995) and Nunes (1999) for discussion.

In Chinese, on the other hand, *yes/no* questions are formed using question particles (e.g., *ma*) and there is no I-to-C movement (12a);[10] *wh*-expressions are not fronted in the overt syntax but instead remain *in situ*, as shown in (12b–c) (Mandarin examples from Li & Thompson, 1981; Hokkien from Bodman, 1987).

(12) a. ni   xihuan   neiben   shu   *ma*?   (Mandarin)
         you   like   that-CL book   Q
         'Do you like that book?'

     b. women   jintian wanshang chi   *shenme*?   (Mandarin)
         we   today   evening eat   what
         'What are we having for supper tonight?'

     c. ni   qu   *nar*?   (Mandarin)
         li   khi   *toulou/*?   (Hokkien)
         you   go   where
         'Where are you going?'

The difference between question formation in English and Chinese illustrated here has been accounted for formally by positing the presence of a strong versus weak feature in C. In English, this [+wh] (or [+Q]) interrogative feature is strong, inducing movement of the *wh*-expression into the CP to check the Q feature in C (Chomsky, 1995; Freidin, 1999). In Chinese, however, this interrogative feature is weak; thus, no overt raising occurs. Within the Failed Functional Features approach mentioned above, Hawkins and Chan (1997) explicitly claim that the functional features of English C have become inaccessible to native Chinese speakers (p. 219). Their study, which dealt mainly with the acquisition of English relative clauses by native Chinese and French speakers, is discussed in more depth in Section III where we look at Patty's relative clause formation.

For now, however, let us turn to an examination of the data to see whether Patty has managed to acquire the strong feature value in C that has been claimed to trigger overt movement in question formation in English.

---

[10] There is another way of forming *yes/no* questions in Chinese, the so-called "A-not-A" construction, which will not be discussed here. The choice of A-not-A versus question particle constructions is governed by pragmatic factors (see Li & Thompson, 1981, pp. 548ff. for a more extensive discussion).

Patty's Acquisition of English Questions

Developmental stages for the L2 acquisition of English question formation have been described by Pienemann, Johnston, and Brindley (1988) for learners from different L1 backgrounds, adapted and summarized by Lightbown and Spada (1993, p. 63) as follows (using their examples):

Stage 1: Single words or formulae with rising intonation (e.g., *four children?*).

Stage 2: Declarative word order (with rising intonation); no inversion, no fronting (e.g., *it's a monster in the right corner?*; *the boys throw the shoes?*).

Stage 3: *Wh*-fronting, no inversion (e.g., *what's the dog are playing?*; *where the little children are?*) and *do-* (and other) fronting (e.g., *does in this picture there is four astronauts?*; *is the picture has two planets on top?*).[11]

Stage 4: Inversion of the copula *be* in *yes/no* questions and to second position in *wh*-questions (i.e., there is I-to-C movement) (e.g., *is there fish in the water?*; *where is the sun?*).

Stage 5: Inversion (i.e., I-to-C movement) of *do* and other auxiliaries (e.g., *what's the boy doing?*; *how do you say [proche]?*) Additionally, if Lightbown and Spada are correct in their observation that this sequence is "similar in most respects to first language question development" (p. 64), then we should expect to find that embedded questions also (incorrectly) exhibit subject-auxiliary inversion (e.g., *I don't know why can't he go out*).

Stage 6: Complex questions, including tag questions (e.g., *it's better, isn't it?*), negative questions (e.g., *why can't you go?*) and correct word order in embedded questions (e.g., *can you tell me what the date is today?*).

---

[11] Another error type not mentioned in the Pienemann et al. developmental sequence cited by Lightbown and Spada (1993) but which would perhaps fit into this stage is the incorrect omission of the finite element (copula, modals, or auxiliaries; e.g., *what they doing?*) or the use of the wrong form (e.g., *when will you returning to Boston?*). These examples are from Patty's data.

Lightbown and Spada note that even learners whose L1s have subject-auxiliary inversion nonetheless appear to go through the early stages of those described above in which there is no inversion in their L2 English question formation. Hawkins (2001a) ties these earlier stages (Stages 1–3) to a "modulated structure building" model similar to the "minimal trees" account proposed by Vainikka and Young-Scholten (1994) described earlier. However, for our purposes (since we do not have initial- or early-stage data from Patty that could further illuminate the matter) we will simply conclude that her production of questions exhibiting the characteristics of Stages 4 to 6 entails the availability of the required functional projections (CP) and feature value settings (strong [+wh] in English).

As we might expect given how much exposure she has had to English, Patty readily produces Stage 6 (the most advanced-stage) questions in both her speaking and writing. However, she does not always do so; it is possible to find question forms representative of every one of the prior stages in her data. Of course, it should be noted that native speakers often use intonation minus movement in echo and/or clarification contexts—or what look like Stage 1 and Stage 2 questions, and naturally, so does Patty. However, there are very rare instances of inappropriate Stage 2 question formation as well: *I put here?*; *each of you have bike?*[12]

The following examples in (13) from Patty's data illustrate questions characteristic of each stage (the examples for Stage 1 were completely appropriate in context and thus should not be construed as indicative of a vestigial rudimentary stage of development persisting into the end-state grammar; thus, I have placed it in square brackets).

(13)
[Stage 1:   the maid?
               grade 12?]

Stage 2:   I put here?
               each of you have bike?

Stage 3:   are they feel very content?
               why I was so cruel to him?
               but how you get into my voicemail?

---

[12] I find the second example marginally acceptable in colloquial conversation (aside from the missing indefinite article). As noted earlier in chapter 3, non-inversion or the omission of initial *do* in casual speech is common in *yes/no* questions in the variety of English to which Patty has been exposed (e.g., *you have a charge card?*).

Stage 4:   is he a womanizer?
             isn't it generous gift?
             what is high school here?

Stage 5:   why do you want me to go?
             how can I read in Cantonese?
             have you read "The Memoirs of Geisha"?
             do you want to take a shower?
             should I call you on the phone next time?
             didn't he know that it will get back to me?
             you know what does he # she sell?
             I wonder what are they talking about
             I started to search about what can I do to survive

Stage 6:   I don't know how long we are going to wait
             [she] could not tell us when we can travel to Russia
             I don't know why I understand Chinese [*people*] better when
             they spoke English
             I tried to analysis what kind of a person M. is
             I don't know how they did it
             I didn't understand what he's talking about in the class
             I don't know what they're doing with this system now
             It's funny that you always late when the place you want to go is
             so close, isn't it?
             You don't know who you should associate with[13]

We also find, interestingly, an exclamative with correct subject-auxiliary inversion:

(14)   not in a million year would I stop going to high school

In sum, the data suggest that Patty has indeed acquired I-to-C movement of the copula, modals, auxiliaries, and expletive *do*, implicating the presence of a strong feature in C that triggers the overt movement. This feature value is weak in her L1; presumably she was able to acquire the

---

[13] Embedded clauses such as this one (*who you should associate with*) and *what he's talking about in the class* are examples of free relative constructions (and thus do not exhibit subject-auxiliary inversion). I return to relative clauses in the next section.

strong value for English on the basis of positive evidence in the input—for example, on observing and acquiring *do*-support.

Another possible (but admittedly speculative) explanation for how Patty was able to acquire the strong English *wh* or Q feature may be tied to her acquisition of the lexical differentiation in English between *wh*-question words such as *what* and quantifier expressions such as *anything* or *everything*, which may be conflated in Chinese (e.g., *shenme*, as shown in the following examples from Huang, 1995, p. 171, his examples (170–172a)):

(15) a. ni   xiang mai   *shenme* (ne)?
       you   want   buy   *what*   Q
       'What do you want to buy?'

    b. wo *shenme*   dou   mai
       I   *everything* all   buy
       'I will buy everything'

    c. wo   bu   xiang   mai   *shenme*
       I   not   want   buy   *anything*
       'I don't want to buy anything'

Huang (1995) ties *wh*-in-situ in Chinese (and Japanese) to the possibility that *wh*-phrases are assigned the features of a universal, existential, or interrogative quantifier and must be interpreted within the domain of some appropriate binder (e.g., as an interrogative quantifier in the presence of a question operator or particle such as *ne* in (15a), an existential quantifier in the presence of a negative particle such as *bu* 'not' in (15b), or a universal quantifier in the context of the adverb *dou* 'all' in (15c)).

The fact that Patty uses quantifiers such as *anything, everything, nothing, something, all*, etc., appropriately and with correct polarity in English, as shown in the examples in (16),

(16) a. you don't have to tell *everyone* in the world
     b. you don't have to tell *anyone*
     c. *nobody* like to hear *something* bad
     d. there is *nothing* more I can do
     e. and can't even see *anything*

and never produces *wh*-in-situ questions (except appropriately as in echo or clarification contexts), suggests that she has indeed acquired the featural properties associated with these various lexical items in English versus *wh*-question words such as *what*. Another way to say this is that she has managed to correctly map the syntactic and semantic *features* of quantification and clause type such as interrogative or exclamative—perhaps as available from her L1, but presumably universal—onto the corresponding lexical items in English with the correct resultant syntactic consequences in terms of overt movement.

III. Relative Clauses

Relative Clauses in English and Chinese

In this section we examine Patty's production of English relative clauses, particularly in reference to the claim by Hawkins and Chan (1997) that native Chinese speakers construct alternative (i.e., non-nativelike) representations of relative clauses in English that do not involve movement. According to their Failed Functional Features Hypothesis, this is because the only features available to adult second language learners are those of the L1, and Chinese does not instantiate the strong [wh] feature in C that triggers movement, as we observed in the preceding section. Let us examine their claim and the evidence for it in a bit more detail.

English relative clauses can be introduced by a *wh*-element (a phrase or relative pronoun), by the complementizer *that*, or (in non-subject relativizations) by a covert (null) operator, as shown in (17a–c) respectively (examples based on Hawkins & Chan 1997, p. 190). In brief, Hawkins and Chan assume that the strong [wh] feature of English induces movement of the *wh*-phrase (or null operator) to Spec, CP, leaving behind a trace (t) that functions as a variable. When a *wh*-phrase has moved into Spec, CP, then the head C must be left empty; conversely, if the operator in Spec, CP is null, then the head C may be either filled by *that* or left empty.

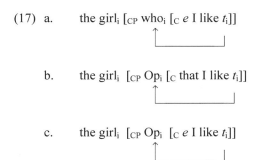

(17) a.   the girl$_i$ [$_{CP}$ who$_i$ [$_C$ e I like t_i]]

       b.   the girl$_i$ [$_{CP}$ Op$_i$ [$_C$ that I like t_i]]

       c.   the girl$_i$ [$_{CP}$ Op$_i$ [$_C$ e I like t_i]]

Within syntactic theory, the main diagnostic for determining whether a *wh*-phrase or null-operator has moved or not is by observing whether such movement exhibits locality effects, i.e., is constrained by subjacency. Operations involving fronted elements such as *wh*-question formation, relativization and topicalization should result in ungrammaticality if they violate certain locality constraints (however these are theoretically formulated). Conversely, when the result appears to violate these constraints but does *not* give rise to ungrammaticality, that operation is assumed not to have been derived by movement to a given position, but rather to result from the base-generation of the relevant item (e.g., a *wh*-phrase or a topic) in that position to begin with. The idea is that subjacency constraints, as constraints on what type of movement may occur, simply do not apply if there is no movement.

In Chinese relative clauses, *wh*/null-operator movement is assumed by Hawkins and Chan not to occur. Instead, Chinese relative clauses are assumed to be a form of topicalization (following Huang, 1984, 1995), involving the base-generation of a null topic that binds a null or resumptive pronoun (following Xu & Langendoen, 1985). (I return to the analysis of Chinese relative clauses shortly.) An example is provided in (18).

(18) $[_{CP}$ Ø-Top$_i$ $[_{IP}$ wo   xihuan $e_i{}^{14}$] de] neige   nuhai
      null topic   I   like   *e*   C   the   girl
    'the girl that I like'

The main point is that if we assume that no movement is involved, then relativization in Chinese is not subject to subjacency constraints, unlike English. Because feature strength is assumed to trigger movement, Hawkins and Chan argue that Chinese has a weak (or absent) value for this feature, and this reflects a parametric difference between the two languages. The prediction made by the Failed Functional Features Hypothesis, then, is that native Chinese speakers acquiring English will fail to acquire the strong feature value that induces movement and gives rise to subjacency violations in English relative clauses, because this feature value is not present in the native language.

---

[14] Huang's (1984) analysis, rejected by Hawkins and Chan in favor of Xu and Langendoen's (1985) approach, is that this empty category is in fact a trace left behind by the movement of the null topic into Spec, CP. Under Hawkins and Chan's analysis, however, it is a null pronoun (*pro*) bound by the null topic base-generated in Spec, CP. We return to the analysis below.

To test this prediction, Hawkins and Chan administered a grammaticality judgment task to native (Cantonese) Chinese and native French speakers acquiring English at three different proficiency levels. They tested a variety of properties related to English relative clauses, including knowledge of the grammatical placement of *wh*-elements, operators and complementizers, as in the examples shown in (17a–c) above, as well as the ungrammaticality of the "doubly filled" CP, as shown below in (19a), resumptive pronouns in various positions as in (19b–c), and subjacency violations as in (19d–e) below (examples from Hawkins & Chan, 1997).

(19) a. *The girl who that lost her way cried.
　　 b. *The man who he lives next door has left.
　　 c. *The patient that I visited him was very sick.
　　 d. *This is the man who Mary told me when she will visit.
　　 e. *This is the boy who Mary described the way that Bill attacked.

The results showed a significant difference in performance between the two L1 groups in favor of the French speakers, whose native language also instantiates movement. However, the advanced Chinese speakers nonetheless performed at 83% accuracy on rejecting ungrammatical doubly filled CP sentences and at 90% accuracy on rejecting ungrammatical resumptive pronouns. Hawkins and Chan note that, with increasing proficiency, they acquire the "main properties of English predicative CP morphology" (p. 207), a finding that White (2003b) points out could be interpreted as problematic for the Failed Functional Features Hypothesis.

Hawkins and Chan's most striking finding, however, was that with increasing proficiency, the ability of the Chinese subjects to detect subjacency violations actually appears to *decrease*. They argue that this result suggests that the beginning proficiency learners, whose accuracy rate on rejecting subjacency violations is surprisingly higher than the advanced proficiency learners, are in fact not responding to a subjacency violation, but rather to the complete absence of resumptive pronouns in English relative clauses, which they expect to find (reflecting L1 transfer, since Chinese relative clauses allow or even require resumptives in certain grammatical contexts). On the other hand, the more advanced learners have learned that overt resumptive pronouns are ungrammatical in English, and are therefore more likely to accept sentences without them, but with little regard to violations of constraints on movement. Hawkins and Chan argue that these sentences are acceptable to the advanced native Chinese speakers precisely because these learners' grammatical representation of English relative clauses does not include movement but rather a null (resumptive) *pro*, thus supporting the Failed Functional Features Hypothesis.

Before moving on to relative clause data from Patty, perhaps a few comments regarding Hawkins and Chan's analysis are in order here. Hawkins and Chan (1997) interpret the Chinese speakers' increasing accuracy on correctly rejecting overt resumptive pronouns as reflecting awareness that English relative clauses have an obligatory [CP ... gap] pattern without necessitating, however, that the gap is being represented as a trace left behind by operator movement. Indeed, as mentioned earlier, they argue that it is not the result of movement, and that the gap is a null resumptive *pro*. As White (2003b) points out, however, this would be a somewhat peculiar representation: "There does seem to be something very odd about a grammar which permits null resumptives and disallows lexical ones; it is not clear that this is in fact a possibility realized elsewhere" (p. 125).

It is also not clear that the Chinese speakers' increasing tendency to reject doubly filled CP structures can be similarly explained away. Hawkins and Chan interpret this result as simply indicating that the Chinese speakers "can acquire the surface morphophonological properties of English predicative CP" (p. 208). But there is little explanation for *why* these sentences are (correctly) rejected, and it is not at all obvious why they should be disallowed if Chinese speakers have not acquired the grammatical properties thought to be associated with them. In brief, Hawkins and Chan assume an analysis for English in which the [+wh] feature of overt *wh*-expressions is incompatible with the [−wh] feature of the overt complementizer that, ruling out the possibility of their co-occurrence in a doubly filled CP (following Rizzi, 1990). Going back to the data, it is not clear why the Chinese speakers are ruling them out if they have not acquired the English [±wh] feature values associated with overt *wh*-expressions versus the complementizer *that*, and realize these are incompatible. If the Chinese speakers were relying on L1 feature values, then these would be left unspecified and there would be no feature mismatch to give rise to ungrammaticality. Although it is certainly possible that some other factor is responsible for their rejecting these sentences, no alternative explanation is offered.

Finally, as noted by Hawkins (2001a) and White (2003b), other studies have produced conflicting findings—namely, that high-proficiency native Chinese speakers do perform accurately on detecting subjacency violations (White & Juffs, 1998) as well as exhibiting sensitivity to different types of violations (Li, 1998; Martohardjono, 1993). The many subjacency studies that have been carried out in the L2 literature have occasionally been muddied by less-than-categorical native speaker judgments as well (although not in Hawkins & Chan's study, where the native-speaker judgments were quite consistent).[15] In fact, the available findings seem to suggest that, as proficiency increases, it is indeed possible for native Chinese speakers to acquire properties associated with *wh*/null-operator movement in English. In the next section, I show that production data from Patty also appear to support this conclusion.

Patty's Production of English Relative Clauses

The first observation we can make is that, in contrast to previous findings suggesting that many Chinese speakers avoid producing English relative clauses to a greater extent than other L1 groups (Schachter, 1974), in Patty's particular case, we find that she produces them quite freely. An examination of the longest spoken recording (Recording 2) indicates that she produces at least as many relative clauses in that recording as her two English native-speaker interlocutors combined (which is likely to be a consequence of the interview format). We find throughout both her spoken and written production data at least 120 relative clauses.[16]

---

[15] I have to admit, however, that as a native speaker, I find all four of Hawkins and Chan's *wh*-island violation test items (their examples 48–51, p. 226), perfectly okay except for the violation of sequence-of-tense harmony (I clearly prefer *would* instead of *will*), which is of course unrelated to subjacency:

(48) *This is the man who(m) Mary told me when she will [/*would*] visit.

This sentence sounds quite acceptable to me, perhaps because the entire clause (*when she would visit x*) does not feel like an adjunct; although introduced by an adverb *when*, the clause itself functions as a subcategorized theme argument of the verb *told* (e.g., *Mary told me x*). Compare this to a true adjunct extraction across an IP boundary (e.g., *??That was the job that Mary left town after she quit*), which for me is indeed much worse.

Interestingly, Hawkins and Chan suggest that subjacency violations can be "rescued" or corrected by adding a resumptive pronoun, as in: *?The man who Mary told me when she will visit **him*** (their example and grammaticality judgment, p. 212). Yet this "correction" feels distinctly worse to me than the original supposedly ungrammatical sentence! Hawkins and Chan do not provide data on native speaker corrections of the subjacency violation test items, and it is of course possible that there are variety differences (e.g., British vs. American English) that partially account for my intuitions versus those of the native controls tested in their study.

[16] This figure includes both restrictive and nonrestrictive relative clauses (Examples i–ii, respectively) as well as free relatives (Examples iii–iv) (all examples from Patty):

    i.   the # the language *that you don't know*
    ii.   I copy it to my friend Lynn, uh, *who is a native.*
    iii.   I got *what I wanted.*
    iv.   You don't know *who you should associate with.*

Some examples are provided of subject, object, and oblique relativization, as shown in (20–22), respectively:

(20) a. you will find someone *who share your belief*
    b. and then they find this place *that will do the catering*
    c. China also send a lot of boat to the refugee *who want to go back to China*
    d. I hear better with the Chinese person *who speak English* than a native
    e. my parents contributed in some way *that shaped me as who I am*
    f. you see a lot of teacher *who # who have a very good education*
    g. they are the one *who clean your bathroom*
    h. I don't have any uh, friend *who spoke English*

(21) a. the mistake *one makes* is only a lesson to learn
    b. the # the language *that you don't know*
    c. there are book club in Hawaii *you may like to join*
    d. one of the two books *that I read* on uh, Chinese history
    e. there's a poem *that you have to memorize*
    f. I was dating a man *that I met in a club previous week*
    g. there is something *I have to tell you*
    h. I got *what I wanted*

(22) a. you have any particular topic *you want to talk about* tonight?
    b. everything *you deal with*
    c. I have a girlfriend *that I can introduce you to*
    d. so there's seven # seven opera *you can only listen to*
    e. I have couple # couple university *that I apply to*
    f. he's the only person *I spoke to*
    g. we finally get a call *we have been waiting for a long time*
    h. you don't know *who you should associate with*

The last set of examples in (22) is particularly interesting, because these illustrate Patty's robust acquisition of preposition stranding in oblique object relativization. Preposition stranding is not allowed in Chinese; indeed, these are the contexts in Chinese in which overt resumptive pronouns are required, suggesting that Patty has acquired operator movement. These examples also demonstrate that Patty's acquisition of relative clauses in English has developed beyond the so-called "null prep" stage argued for by E. Klein (1993, 2001), in which learners from various L1 backgrounds omit required (overt) prepositions in *wh*-questions and relative clauses (e.g., Klein's example: *which bus are the children waiting?*). Because analyses of L2 null-prep phenomena (Dekydtspotter et al., 1998; Klein, 2001) attribute the lack of an overt preposition in these contexts in part to the base-generation of the *wh*-expression in Spec, CP rather than derivation via *wh*-movement, Patty's suppliance of overt prepositions again suggests (although does not prove) that she is not base-generating *wh*-expressions in Spec, CP, but rather deriving them via *wh*-operator movement. In other words, she appears to have acquired English feature values for relative clause formation in her L2 English.

Throughout all the data, we can find only three occurrences of relative clauses with resumptive pronouns:

(23) a.   then they have another # another # another guy who # who, *his* name is Saul, I think
   b.   there's one word that, um, people say *it* differently from me
   c.   one of the Chinese author that I really like *her* a lot

Of the three examples in (23), only (23c) is unambiguously resumptive. Both (23a) and (23b) follow pauses, which could indicate a self-interruption and reformulation. This leaves us with a production rate for resumptive pronouns ranging from 0.8% to 2.5% (depending on how the three examples above are analyzed). In any case, it is a very small, probably negligible proportion. In terms of L1 influence with respect to the use of resumptive pronouns, Patty seems to have correctly determined that these are disallowed in English relative clauses.

There is another type of error in the data that does indeed appear to reflect direct influence from the native language, however. Li and Thompson (1981) describe two serial verb constructions in Chinese. The first is a kind of so-called "pivotal" construction that contains a noun phrase that functions as both the (direct) object of the first verb and subject of the second, as shown in (24) (example from Li & Thompson, 1981, p. 608):

(24) wo   yuanliang   ni   si-huai-le   wode   shu
    I   forgive   you   tear-ruin-ASP   my   book
    'I forgive you for tearing up my book.'

Note that, while the English translation for the second clause above 'for tearing up my book' is nonfinite, the verb is marked with perfective aspect in Chinese (e.g., 'you tore up my book'). The perfective aspectual marking applies only to the second verb in the serial verb construction, not the first. (Of course, the English interpretation of the tearing event also implies aspectual perfectivity.) The entire sentence is pronounced under a single intonational contour with no pauses.

The second serial verb construction is one that Li and Thompson (1981) refer to as a "realis descriptive clause"; it is semantically similar to a relative clause (and is often translated the same as a relative clause in English) in its modification function, but appears to be less restrictive. The structural characteristics of the realis descriptive clause construction are: The verb in the first clause is transitive and takes an object that is described by the second clause, and the direct object must be indefinite. The following Chinese pairs illustrate the comparison between descriptive clause modification (25a) and (26a), and true relative clauses (25b) and (26b) (examples from Li & Thompson, 1981, pp. 611–617):[17]

(25) a. wo   mai-le   yi-jian   yifu   tai   da
      I   buy-ASP one-CL outfit too big

     b. wo mai-le   yi-jian tai da de   yifu
       I   buy-ASP one-CL too big [C][18] outfit

'I bought an outfit that was too big.'

(26) a. ta   yang-le   yi-tiao gou   wo   yao   mai
      s/he raise-ASP one-CL dog   I   want buy

     b. ta   yang-le   yi-tiao wo   yao   mai   de   gou
      s/he raise-ASP one-CL I   want buy [C] dog

'S/he raised a dog that I want to buy'

According to Li and Thompson (1981), although both sentences in (25a–b) above assert that the outfit in question was too big, in (25a) this is an "entirely incidental" property whereas (25b) would be appropriate in a discourse context in which a "pre-established class" of items in question

---

[17] Wu (2002) offers a more formal analysis of Li and Thompson's (1981) "descriptive clause" construction as a CP adjunct to the first verb, in addition to technical arguments against viewing the second clause as either a conjoined or relative clause.

[18] Li and Thompson (1981) do not refer to the *de* particle as a complementizer or relativizer, but rather as a "nominalizer" and they gloss it as NOM (p. 118). The categorial status of *de* is unclear; see Aoun & Li (2003) and especially Simpson (2002) for some discussion. In these examples and others that follow, I've continued to gloss the *de* particle as C for the sake of consistency, following Hawkins and Chan's own glossing convention. Nothing in the discussion here hinges on its exact label (e.g., Aoun & Li, 2003; Li, 2002, simply gloss it as DE).

(e.g., outfits that are too big) is assumed by both interlocutors. The meaning of (25a) is that the speaker bought an outfit that incidentally turned out to be too big, whereas (25b) would be more appropriate in a context in which the speaker and hearer were discussing clothes that were too big or in which the hearer knew that the speaker "was especially looking for an outfit that was too big" (p. 614).

Similarly in (26), (26a) asserts that s/he has raised a dog that the speaker happens to want to buy; Li and Thompson's translation is 'S/he has raised a dog and I want to buy it.' In (26b), on the other hand, the speaker is indicating that there exists for both speaker and hearer "an understood class of dogs" consisting of the kind the speaker would like to buy, and s/he just happens to have raised such a dog. Their translation for this sentence is 'S/he has raised one of those dogs I want to buy' (p. 615), a more restrictive modification.

Li and Thompson also point out that the descriptive clause is both semantically and structurally similar to juxtaposed clauses except that in the former both clauses are included within a single intonation contour. Compare the following examples in (27a–b), which illustrate juxtaposed clauses and the nonrestrictive descriptive clause, respectively (from Li & Thompson, p. 617):

(27) a. ta   you   yi-ge   meimei,   hen   xihuan kan   dianying
      s/he   have   one-CL   younger.sister   very   like   see   movie
      'S/he has a younger sister. (She) likes to see movies.'

    b. ta   you   yi-ge   meimei   hen   xihuan kan   dianying
      s/he   have   one-CL   younger.sister   very   like   see   movie
      'S/he has a younger sister who likes to see movies.'

In Patty's data, we find six errors (about 5% of the total number of relative clauses produced) that appear similar to Chinese serial verb constructions as described in the examples above. These are given in (28):

(28) a. I have friends from Indonesia also speak Hokkien
    b. they have one last name was so long, some of them
    c. there is a girl from Russia has been identify
    d. and have a lawyer works on the case
    e. his buddy at the time was an older lady we hang out a lot together
    f. it is very interesting letter from captain Bill shared his experience

In particular, (28a–e) appear to resemble those constructions described by Li and Thompson as Chinese realis descriptive clauses (note that the NP about which the second clause is predicated is indefinite) and (28f) a pivotal construction (with a definite oblique object functioning as the subject of a finite second clause). Given these constructions' functional similarity to relative clauses, it is perhaps not surprising to find them in an environment where English native speakers would most likely use a relative clause. In these special cases, it appears that a Chinese-based grammatical representation is still available in the L2, even if only infrequently employed. The vast majority (around 90%) of occurrences of relativization, however, appear quite nativelike. But are they? Recall that Hawkins and Chan (1997) have argued that native Chinese speakers rely on an L1 representation that precludes operator movement. We turn next to a consideration of this question.

Grammaticality Judgment Data

To see whether the conclusions suggested by Patty's production data could be further supported and strengthened, a grammaticality judgment task quite similar to that used by Hawkins and Chan (1997) was devised and given to Patty, after being piloted on five native speaker controls. The task consisted of 50 sentences containing relative clauses—20 grammatical and 30 ungrammatical. The ungrammatical sentences included those with doubly filled CP violations (e.g., *The girl who that lost her way cried*, n = 5), resumptive pronouns in various positions (e.g., *The boy who I play with him is my cousin*, n = 11), and ten subjacency violations of two subtypes: extractions from adjuncts (e.g., *I bought the book my professor became famous after he wrote*, n = 5) and extraction from noun complements (e.g., *They want the land which the manager made the decision that we should sell*, n = 5). In addition, four sentences of the error-type produced by Patty resembling serial verb constructions were included (e.g., *She is the classmate always forgets her assignments*, n = 4).

The native speakers rejected the ungrammatical sentences as expected (97.33%), and I will have little else to say about them here.[19] As for the results for Patty from this task, these are in fact highly consistent with the view that she has indeed acquired an English-like representation of relative clauses, as suggested by her production data. She correctly rejected all five doubly filled CP violations (100%), 10/11 of the sentences with resumptive pronouns (91%), and 9/10 of the subjacency violations (90%, 5/5 adjunct extractions and 4/5 of the noun complement extractions). In these cases, the

---

[19] Although a few grammatical sentences were also rejected, for what appear to be prescriptive or stylistic reasons.

findings suggest that she has acquired operator movement that is subject to constraints similar to those represented by native English speakers (and are presumably universal).

But this is not her *only* possible representation. Patty correctly rejected only 1/4 (25%) of the serial verb-type constructions, which is also consistent with her production of these in English. On one of these sentences, which she accepted, she notated that it could also be rendered with the (missing) subject relative pronoun, as would be correct in English. Thus it appears that two analyses—one that is valid in the L1 and one generated by the L2 grammar—co-exist and are available for nominal modification in English.

Relative Clause Analyses Reconsidered

It is difficult to reconcile Patty's apparent knowledge of the features associated with English relative clauses with the claim made by Hawkins and Chan (1997) that native Chinese speakers cannot acquire knowledge of those features that distinguish Chinese from English with respect to relative clause formation. On the one hand, we do find an apparent residue of L1 influence in the resemblance of a small number of Patty's relative clauses to serial verb constructions, although these constructions were not among those examined by Hawkins and Chan. On the other hand, we find little evidence to suggest that the overwhelming majority of her relative clauses are anything other than well-formed structures involving targetlike operator movement.

The study design, findings, and conclusion of Hawkins and Chan (1997) are framed as a test of whether Chinese native speakers can reset a parameter that differs between Chinese and English—namely, whether or not relative clauses in each language involve *wh-* or null-operator movement (p. 189). However, what if there is no such parametric difference, or one that perhaps involves more complex non-binary, intermediate, or overlapping values of the relevant parameter?

Let us briefly return to Hawkins and Chan's (1997) theoretical assumptions in light of more recent work (e.g., Aoun & Li, 2003; Li, 2002; Ning, 1993; Watanabe, 1992) based on closer examination of the descriptive empirical data regarding Chinese relativization. Recall that Hawkins and Chan assume, following Huang (1982), that Chinese relative clauses contain a null topic in Spec, CP based on "a number of properties shared by Chinese [restrictive relative clauses] and topicalized structures" (p. 193). A couple of observations can be made here.

First, there are enough crucial differences between relativization and topicalization in Chinese to undermine the view that these are essentially the same kind of operation and therefore that Chinese relative clauses involve a (null) topic. These differences are explicitly highlighted in Li (2002) and Aoun and Li (2003), citing Huang (1993) and especially Ning (1993). For example, there are some topic structures that are claimed to be licensed without movement via a so-called "aboutness" relation, whereas corresponding relativized structures cannot. The examples in (29a) and (30a) below illustrate topicalized sentences whose topic phrases cannot similarly function as the head of a corresponding relative clause as in (29b) and (30b) (examples from Aoun & Li, 2003, pp. 259–260).

(29) a.   shuiguo,   wo   zui   xihuan   xiangjiao
            fruit   I   most   like   banana
           '(As for) fruit, I like bananas.'

     b. *wo   zui   xihuan   xiangjiao   de   shuiguo
           I   most   like   banana   C   fruit
           'the fruit such that I like bananas most'

(30) a.   tamen,   yiwai   fasheng-le
           them   accident   happen-PERF
           '(As for) them, an accident happened'

     b. *yiwai   fasheng   de   neixie   ren
         accident   happen   C   those   person
         'the people such that an accident happened'

Conversely, relativization is possible in some cases—namely, those involving relativized adjuncts, where topicalization is not. The examples in (31a) and (32a) below show relative clauses whose corresponding topicalized structures in (31b) and (32b) are ungrammatical (examples from Aoun & Li, 2003, pp. 173–174 and Li, 2002, pp. 63–64):

(31) a.   ta   bu   xiu   che   de   yuanyin
          he   not   fix   car   C   reason
          'the reason he does not fix cars'

     b. *na-ge   yuanyin,   ta   bu   xiu   che
         that-CL   reason   he   not   fix   car
         'that reason, he does not fix cars'

(32) a. ta   xiu   hao   na-bu   che de fangfa
   he   fix   well   that-CL   car C   way
   'the way he fixed that car'

  b. *na-ge   fangfa, ta   xiu   hao   le   na-bu   che
    that-CL way   he   fix   well   PERF   that-CL   car
    'that way, he fixed that car'

This contrast has been argued to support the claim that topicalization and relativization structures involve different kinds of movement, with relativization derived via movement of a (null) operator "which is equivalent to a *wh*-operator in English" (Li, 2002, p. 58, citing Ning, 1993).[20] Indeed, Li (2002) and Aoun and Li (2003) argue that operator movement must be available to derive (some) relative clauses in Chinese on the basis of evidence from relativization of adjuncts. The examples in (33a) and (34a) below show that long-distance movement is possible in Chinese, suggesting that such movement should be subject to locality (subjacency) effects and that violations of these constraints should give rise to ungrammaticality. The unacceptability of the sentences in (33b) and (34b) confirm that this is indeed the case (examples from Li, 2002, pp. 58–59, and Aoun & Li, 2003, pp. 177–178). Sentence (33b) is a violation of the complex NP constraint and sentence (34b) violates the adjunct island constraint:

(33) a. zhe jiu   shi [[women juede [ta yinggai qu t_i nianshu] de] difang$_i$]
   this exactly is   we   feel   he should go   study   C   place
   'This is the place where we feel he should go study.'

---

[20] The ungrammatical topicalized structures here in (31b) and (32b) are rescued by the addition of the missing adjunct head (e.g., P or adverb); cf. the following:

  (31b') wei   na   yuanyin,   ta bu   xiu   che
      for   that   reason,   he not   fix   car
      'for that reason, he does not fix cars'

  (32b') yong nage fangfa, ta   xiu   hao   le   nabu   che
      use   that   way   he fix   well   PERF   that   car
      'in that way, he fixed that car'

Li (2002), citing Ning (1993), observes that this suggests that topicalization requires the straightforward fronting of an entire constituent (e.g., an entire adjunct PP), rather than just the object of the P as in the relativized examples in (31a) and (32a) in the text above.

b. *zhe jiu   shi [[[[ta xihuan [t_i nian guo shu] de] ren] de] difang$_i$]
  this exactly is   he like   read ASP book C person C place
  'This is the place where he likes the person that has studied.'

(34) a. zhe jiu   shi [[ta renwei [nimen t_i/(weishenme$_i$) yinggai likai]
     this exactly is   he think   you   (why)   should leave

de] yuanyin$_i$]
C   reason

'This is the reason why he thinks you should leave.'

b. *zhe jiu   shi [[[[ruguo ta t_i shengqi] ni   hui bu gaoxing] de]
  this exactly is   if   he   angry   you will not happy   C

yuanyin$_i$]
reason

'This is the reason (x) that you will not be happy if he gets angry
(because of) x.'

As noted by Hawkins and Chan (citing Xu & Langendoen, 1985), there are indeed sentences in Chinese that do not exhibit island effects; that is, they appear to violate subjacency constraints on movement but nonetheless are acceptable. Li (2002, p. 59) points out that such cases always involve an island in a subject (or topic) position, as shown in (35):

(35) [[[t_i chuan de] yifu]   hen piaoliang de]   na-ge   ren$_i$
       wear C   clothes very pretty   C   that-CL person
  'the person$_i$ that the clothes that (she$_i$) is wearing are pretty'

Li observes that when the island occurs in an object position, however, the island effects reappear, resulting in ungrammaticality:

(36) *[wo xihuan [[t_i chuan de] yifu]   de]   nage   ren$_i$
     I   like   wear C   clothes C   that-CL person
  'the person$_i$ that I like the clothes that (she$_i$) is wearing'

However, the sentence in (36) can be made acceptable with a resumptive pronoun in place of the trace, as in (37):

(37) [wo xihuan [[ta_i chuan de] yifu]   de]   nage   ren$_i$
    I   like   *she* wear C   clothes C   that-CL person
  'the person$_i$ that I like the clothes that she$_i$ is wearing'

Note that this is the same strategy that Hawkins and Chan (1997) suggest rescues subjacency violations in English as well (although this result in English is very marginal to my ears). Subjects in their experiment were:

> ... scored for their ability to recognize this ungrammaticality and to rescue the sentence in some form, typically by using a resumptive pronoun to produce a passable sentence: *?The man who Mary told me when she will visit HIM.* (pp. 211–212)

The overall point to be made here is that English and Chinese, despite clear differences in word order (i.e., head direction) and other properties within relative clauses, also appear to share certain similarities at least for certain types of relative clauses (e.g., adjunct relativization). Moreover, it is not the case that relative clauses are formed in uniform fashion even within a single language (either Chinese or English).[21] Although it is possible (even likely) that knowledge of L1 features influences the development of relativization in a second language, as Hawkins and Chan argue, the differences between those languages appear not to boil down to a single stark parametric choice that divides English-type languages from Chinese/Japanese-type languages. This is precisely the argument made by Aoun and Li (2003, p. 191ff.), who suggest that various relativization strategies may instead be tied to particular morphosyntactic properties of the phrases themselves that are relativized.[22]

---

[21] In recent work, Kuong (2006) demonstrates that different types of topicalization must also be distinguished in Mandarin Chinese (as in other languages, such as many Romance languages). One of the distinguishing characteristics is sensitivity to island constraints. In Mandarin, as in many other languages, one type of topic (Preposed Topic) is indeed subject to constraints on extraction from contexts such as complex NPs and adjuncts, whereas another type of topic (Hanging Topic) is not. Kuong points out that studies that claim that topics in Mandarin Chinese do not show island sensitivity (e.g., Xu & Langendoen, 1985) have not taken into consideration the distinction between different kinds of topics in that language, and thus, a much finer-grained analysis is required.

[22] Aoun and Li (2003) follow the "traditional" semantic literature in decomposing *wh*-question words into three component properties of Question, Quantification, and Restriction. They argue that these features may be morphologically realized in various permutations cross-linguistically (e.g., combined within a single expression or realized discretely in different positions within a clause). Another feature that affects how relativization is realized in a particular language is definiteness. The reader is referred to their work for further details.

Summary

The fact that Patty appears to have acquired English relativization suggests again that, as with English question formation, she has managed to more or less correctly sort out how to map the syntactic *features* associated with relativization (which indeed appear to be available from her L1) onto their corresponding morphological realization in English, with the correct resultant syntactic consequences in terms of overt movement. If this view is correct, it does not falsify Hawkins and Chan's (1997) essential claim that the L1 remains the (only) source for knowledge of L2 features, but it may render that claim to some extent rather vacuous. The learning problem shifts from simply resetting a binary parameter value (claimed to be impossible by Hawkins & Chan) to the far more complex process of teasing apart and re-arranging the language-particular morphological realization of semantic features that are presumably universal.

IV. Passives

On a recent stroll with Patty, we came across a garden with a bunch of day lilies in it. Pointing them out to me, she said, "These flowers can eat." I repeated what she said: These flowers can eat? "Yes, they are edible," she said, reformulating. This little conversational exchange prompted me to examine (briefly) her use of passivization in English. This type of error has been observed in the L2 English of native Chinese speakers, where it is sometimes referred to as a "pseudo-passive" (Han, 2004; Yip, 1995).

Li and Thompson (1981) point out that the translational equivalents of English passive sentences are often non-passive topic-comment structures in Mandarin. They provide the following examples (p. 498):

(38) a.   nei-ben   shu   yijing   chuban le
        that-CL   book   already   publish CRS[23]
        'That book has already been published.'

     b.   ni-de   baoguo   shou-dao   le
        you-GEN   package   receive-arrive CRS
        'Your package has been received.'

---

[23] Li and Thompson (1981) gloss the sentence-final particle *le* as referring to a "Currently Relevant State."

As we observed earlier for Patty in relation to relative clauses, it appears that a Chinese-based grammatical representation for such topic-comment structures has transferred and persists in her L2 English. But is it frequent in proportion to more targetlike passive constructions—in other words, has Patty acquired the English passive?

In quantifiying passive constructions in Patty's data, I eliminated the frequent but idiomatic expressions *was born* and *get/got married/divorced/engaged.* This left only 37 reasonably clear passive examples among both the spoken and written data, including *get*-passives. Some examples are shown in (39):

(39) a. I got yelled at
     b. I was asked to respond to each question
     c. the new cabinet is being installed right now
     d. there is a girl from Russia has been identify
     e. since it got demolished
     f. you were treated like uh[/a?], animal or something
     g. think that my teeth need to # need to be straighted
     h. she was chosen from forty people

Of these 37 examples, three were pseudo-passives, resulting in a targetlike passivization rate of about 81% among the clearly passive constructions in the data. These three exceptions are shown in (40):

(40) a. I thought you may interest
     b. I heard his car has to toll [*sic* = 'tow'] away
     c. you would amaze, how # how he know so many thing

There are some examples which appear to show that Patty actually does productively derive the passive form in English; that is, she can move easily between derivationally related passive and active sentences. These derivational pairs appear within the same discourse context in adjacent or close proximity to each other, so that it is obvious in context that the subjects of the active sentences are the omitted agents in the corresponding passive sentences:

(41) a. I was accepted
     b. only that college accepted me

(42) a. and also glad that I was never spoiled
     b. my parents never spoiled us

(43) a.   maybe we are the one who chosen
     b.   maybe uh, God chose us

In sum, there seems to be little doubt that Patty has productively acquired the passive in English.[24]

The classic analysis for passivization in English is that this operation demotes the external agent argument to an oblique position or suppresses it altogether, and detransitivizes the verb such that it cannot assign (accusative) case. Thus, the theme (or first internal argument) of transitive verbs must move to the subject (or Spec, IP) position in order to receive (nominative) case. Hawkins (2001a) raises the possibility that native Chinese speakers do not truly acquire English-type representations for the passive, but rather misanalyze them as L1-based topic-comment structures in which at least one topic must be overt. This claim is based on Huang's (1984) analysis, according to which topics in Chinese are obligatory, although they can be null. Even the following apparently simple SVO Chinese sentence in (44a) is hypothesized to have the topicalized structure shown in (44b) (from Hawkins, p. 212):

(44) a.   Zhangsan   renshi   Lisi
          Zhangsan   know   Lisi
          'Zhangsan knows Lisi'

     b.   [$_{[topic]}$ Zhangsan$_i$ [e$_i$ renshi Lisi]]

Chinese does have a passive (*bei*) construction, as shown below in (45) (example from Li & Thompson, 1981, p. 496).

(45)   Zhangsan bei   ren   kanjian   le
          Zhangsan BEI   person   see   CRS
          'Zhangsan was seen by people'

---

[24] In addition to these 37 passive constructions, I also came across what appear to be two middle constructions:

   i.   [when your car got hit] it will not *drive* the same
   ii. and the table best *sit* for 12 [= 'and the table best sits/seats 12']

It is not really possible to determine whether these are English-type middles or Chinese-type topic-comment structures.

Li and Thompson (1981) describe its use as "essentially to express an *adverse* situation, one in which something unfortunate has happened" (p. 493; italics in original); thus a likely interpretation of (45) above would be 'Zhangsan was seen by people and shouldn't have or didn't want to be seen' (p. 496).

As a side note, however, Li and Thompson do point out that it has been observed by "practically all Chinese grammarians" that the rate of *bei*-passives that do not express adversity is rising, is clearly due to the influence of Indo-European languages (especially English), and has now been extended from written sources into people's speech (pp. 496–497). They cite Chao (1970), who writes "it is already common in scientific writing, in newspapers, and in schools" (p. 155) and Kierman (1969), who writes:

> [A] markedly increased use of the passive has perhaps been one of the striking syntactic trends in the development of Modern Chinese ... Such patterns become enshrined in ritually-admired literature and thence they are imitated in other literature and are read aloud; and in no time people are speaking that way, with no idea that they are participating in radical linguistic change. (p. 75)

As this increase was already noticeable at least 35 years ago, it is probably safe to assume that the amount of written (and spoken) materials crossing linguistic paths has only exponentially increased since then. In that case, a grammatical re-analysis or re-structuring that eventually admits an English-type passive might not be so surprising. Even if it did not become a (prescriptively) standard construction of Chinese, its greater presence in that language in non-adverse situations might allow an easier "way in" for a native Chinese speaker acquiring English to acquire the passive.

Assuming, however, that Chinese still primarily makes use of a topic-comment sentence in cases where English would use a passive, the structure for the example in (46) is hypothesized to be similar to that in (47) (from Hawkins, 2001a, p. 214).

(46) Ta$_i$, henduo ren xihuan e$_i$
S/he$_i$ many people like e$_i$
'S/he is liked by many people' / 'As for her, many people like her'

(47)

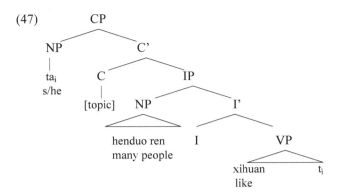

'As for her, many people like her'

Hawkins posits a parametric difference between Chinese and English in which the presence of a [topic] feature in C is obligatory for Chinese, but only optional for English. He suggests that native Chinese speakers are unable to reset their L1 [+ obligatory] value to the L2 [– obligatory] value and therefore produce (only) topicalized structures in English. Although the degree of obligatoriness versus optionality of any construction may constitute part of one's knowledge of a language and may well be susceptible to transfer (as I mentioned earlier in chap. 4), positing "obligatoriness" versus "optionality" as the binary values for the very same feature in a functional category strikes me as a rather peculiar kind of parameter (as opposed to the presence versus absence of the feature itself or of associated features). Moreover, given that the [+ obligatory] value is the more restrictive of the two options, it should probably be delearnable in the face of positive evidence for the less restrictive value.

More to the point, however, since quite a few of Patty's passives occur within embedded clauses whose C nodes are already filled with complementizers or whose Spec, CPs contain *wh*-expressions, it is likely that the subjects of these clauses (which are in fact overtly nominative case-marked in the case of pronominal subjects) are in Spec of IP and not topicalized:

(48) a.   [CP [C before [IP a child will be identify]]]
     b.   [CP [C since [IP it got demolished]]]
     c.   [CP [C that [IP I was never spoiled]]]
     d.   [CP where [C [IP I was brought up]]]
     e.   [CP when [C [IP your car got hit]]]

What the data instead seem to indicate is that an English-like passive has indeed been acquired. However, the L1-based topic-comment structure described by Li and Thompson still apparently persists as an optional clause type in Patty's idiolect, occasionally surfacing instead of the passive. In sum, both options—a true English-like passive and a transferred topic-comment structure—appear to co-exist as part of Patty's mental representation of English. This sort of co-occurrence of L1 and L2 structures appears problematic for a parameter-resetting model that assumes that the selection or setting to one value necessarily results in the relinquishment of another. I return to this issue in chapter 7.

6

Nominal Phrases

In this chapter, we turn to Patty's acquisition of some of the categories and features associated with nouns and noun phrases, particularly the features of number and definiteness. Descriptive data are presented on Patty's use of possessive determiners, plural marking, and definite and indefinite articles. The feature of definiteness is examined in light of proposals that have been made regarding L1 transfer, especially White (2003a); definiteness is interesting in this respect because it is present in both English and Chinese, but expressed rather differently in each of those languages. In the last section of the chapter, I briefly discuss an interesting interaction between number marking and definiteness in Chinese that could hypothetically pose a transfer problem that Patty appears to have overcome (but we would need early-stage developmental data from other speakers to further explore this hypothesis).

Basic Word Order

For English, following Abney (1987) and much subsequent literature, I assume that nominal phrases are actually DPs headed by the functional category D[eterminer], which selects a noun phrase (NP) as a complement, as in the (simplified) diagram shown in (1).

(1)

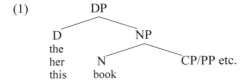

We observed in the preceding chapter that Patty produces complex DPs with relative clauses in English; in general, note that she has clearly acquired the left-headed complementation properties of English nouns (e.g., in the case of CP and PP complements). A few examples from the data are shown in (2):

(2) a. a man that I met in a club previous week
    b. a girlfriend that I can introduce you to
    c. in everything she would like to do or have
    d. the minute I walked out of that office
    e. his attitude toward my family and friends
    f. a good motivation to do well
    g. some charity works helping the elderly
    h. the vineyard overlooking the lake

Because noun complementation in her native Chinese is right-headed, as in the examples shown in (3) below, it is clear that Patty has overcome any transfer in word order that might have influenced her word order in the earlier stages of her English development. There are no traces in the data of the kind of right-headed complementation found in Chinese noun phrases as in (3) (examples from Li & Thompson, 1981, pp. 115, 125).

(3) a. chenggong de   xiwang
       success   DE hope
       'hopes for success'

    b. nimen   xuexiao de cong Zhongguo lai   de   nei-wei kexuejia
       you.PL school DE from China   come DE   that-CL scientist
       'that scientist at your school who came from China'

In short, there is nothing in the data to suggest that Patty has not acquired a nativelike representation for the essential word order of English DPs. Let us turn to a description of some other aspects of her L2 knowledge of DPs, starting with her use of possessive pronominal determiners.

Possession in DPs

With the exception of sometimes mixing up 3SG gender, Patty's use of possessive pronouns is near-nativelike. There are 224 contexts for these across all the data (spoken and written). Although not all of these contexts are strictly obligatory for possessives per se (because some other determiner type might be used), all those that are obligatory are included. Obligatoriness of a possessive instead of some other type of determiner or possibly no determiner at all is, to a large extent, contingent on co-reference or other semantic factors and/or pragmatic intent. Some examples from the data are shown in (4):

(4) a. *her sister* and *my cousin* are friends
     b. I could not speak *my own language* either
     c. but they also spoke Vietnamese in *their household*
     d. *our kitchen* is almost finish
     e. put everything in *her mouth*
     f. I really like *your friends*
     g. *our hostess J.* and *her family*
     h. *his friend* have no money

Out of these 224 possessive contexts, only three are missing a determiner, which would likely be possessive (*the* could also be colloquially appropriate for the first utterance below):

(5) a. I have uh, friends *from family* came over and uh, pick me up
     b. yeah, *front tooth* a little bit black
     c. with aol you can chitchat online *with buddy*

Again, except for choice of gender, there is only one error in pronominal form in all the data (although note that use of the genitive/possessive case is still appropriate):

(6)   and I don't think *mine* score is very high

Moreover, there are no occurrences of inappropriate over-usage.

The most prevalent error—and one that is disproportionately noticeable in Patty's speech since it occasionally leads to genuine comprehensibility problems due to the difficulty of keeping track of her referents—is her occasionally incorrect choice of masculine or feminine pronominal gender for 3SG referents. (Neither of these is ever confused with 3SG neuter *it*.) Within all the data, however, this error appears to be confined to Patty's spoken production. Although there are only 34 3SG possessive contexts in the written data, the fact that all 34 (100%) of these are perfectly correct points to a lexical access (performance) problem in her speech. (She has the same difficulty with choice of gender in subject and object pronouns in her spoken English as well, but these are also completely error-free in her writing.) The spoken gender error goes in both directions, suggesting there is no default gender. Out of 38 3SG possessive determiner contexts in the spoken data, there are 8 gender errors, for an error rate of 21%. Among the 30 instances of correct 3SG gender, three of these were self-corrected in mid-utterance, indicating that she is aware of the mismatch in some cases ('*' indicates mismatched gender, '√' a correct match):

(7) a. *her father* speak better than *her mom* # √*his mom*
    b. we living together with *her sister* # √*his sister*
    c. so then for the first time met uh, *his par* ... # √*her parents*

Aside from this type of error, we find that Patty's knowledge of possessive pronouns is actually quite sophisticated, alternating correctly in distribution with the definite, indefinite, or zero article in modified DPs. For example, consider the following pairs of utterances:

(8) a. *she* play *the* best on that one
       it's the # *her* best one [self-corrected]

    b. *my* lowest point in math
       the highest point in *my* TOEFL

We also find the correct use of possessive determiners with gerund phrases, as shown below in (9):

(9) a. with the issue *my getting pregnant*
    b. *my being well like* in the company
    c. how is *your hunting for condo?*

In sum, Patty appears to have acquired highly proficient knowledge of possessive pronominal determiners in English. We do observe some difficulty in her ability to retrieve the correct 3SG masculine or feminine form while speaking, although this problem is not evident in her writing.

Patty's proficient use of possessive determiners is in contrast to her suppliance of affixal -'s in obligatory contexts, although there are relatively few of the latter in the data—only a total of 12 contexts across Recordings 1–3. Of these, five instances of -'s are supplied and seven are omitted, for a suppliance rate of 41.67%. Suppliance appears to be truly variable, as the following pair of proximal utterances shows:

(10) a.   he's a little bit surprised about *Debbie's father*
    b.   *Debbie brother* was very rich

In the written data, at first glance it is quite orthographically clearcut to see where the possessive affix is supplied, and its application is typically straightforward as an indicator of possession in the determiner position (e.g., *J.'s cell phone*, *A.'s family*, *R.'s office*, etc.). There are 10 of these in the written data, including one correctly "possessive"-marked subject of a deverbal NP: *the doctor's recommendation.*

The instances of omission are trickier because they involve only two contexts for what we might consider prototypical possessive usage (as in the examples above); they rather mostly involve alternative uses such as partitive constructions (there are two of these that are in fact marked for plural: *4 weeks severance pay* and *4 days time*), idiosyncratic constructions (*New Year eve* and *New Year day*), possible compounding (*Anne Lander column*), and possible head noun ellipsis (*and her ears like Adam*). If we include all such contexts as obligatory, then there are 11 instances of omission of *-'s*. In my view, a more nuanced reading of the written data would suggest that Patty has acquired the form-function mapping of the core or more prototypical functions of possessive-marked nouns, but not the more peripheral ones. (This could not be readily discerned from the spoken data, where affixation is as equally likely to be omitted as supplied across prototypical contexts.)

Plural Marking

There are several kinds of contexts for plural marking in English, some clearly obligatory and some not quite as clear. The most unambiguous obligatory contexts for plural marking are quantified expressions requiring plural noun complements (e.g., *7,000 daffodils*; *a lot of ministers*; *both languages*), where we find a convergence of referential plural meaning and formal agreement requirements. Other contexts that are quite clear are unquantified expressions in which the referent is actually plural, and this is somehow obvious in the discourse or from shared knowledge among the interlocutors (e.g., *my parents*; *brown eyes and chubby with red cheeks*; *my tears*) or otherwise idiomatic (*doing taxes*; *sends his regards*; *you guys*). Findings for suppliance in these obligatory contexts are presented below. Other contexts that are not clearly obligatory are unquantified expressions that seem likely to be plural but could possibly also be singular, such as DPs that could be missing an article instead of plural marking (or using an incorrect article), or for which the plurality of the referent is simply un-known to one of the interlocutors (e.g., *when I need to do my composition, we also have newspaper*; *always send me the picture*). In this case, I simply provide some examples of plural marking (or its absence). There are some instances of inappropriate plural use and one instance of plural overregu-larization (*her foots*); I return to these below.

Quantifier Expressions

The use of plural marking in *quantified* expressions is one area of Patty's grammar that shows significant improvement in her spoken production from the first recording to the second ($\chi^2 = 10.226$, $p < .01$), and reaches 84% suppliance in her written data, as shown in Table 6.1. The errors in the data consist almost completely of omissions; there is one instance of mis-placed plural marking, shown in (11):

(11)   along with *three others Asian novelist and poet*

Although spoken production is still far from native-like at the third record-ing, it is possible that this area of grammar is still developing. More data will be needed in the future to determine if further development in this area of her spoken production is ongoing.

TABLE 6.1. Suppliance of Plural Marking in Obligatory Quantified Expressions.

		Suppliance/Contexts	%
Recording	1	2 / 23	08.70
	2	24 / 51	47.06
	3	14 / 24	58.33
Written data		27 / 32	84.38

Some examples of supplied and unsupplied plural marking in quantifier expressions from the data are shown in (12) and (13), respectively:

(12) a.   interview with *couple of agencies*
    b.   every day for *the next five days*
    c.   we spoke *two languages* in our household
    d.   we have done these for *several years*
    e.   for *all the human beings* in the world

    f.   we thought at least *another 6 months*

    g.   I read maybe *one or two books* now a year in Chinese

    h.   actually I have *ten more minutes*

(13) a.   I borrow *a lot of book* from her

    b.   I hear it *so many time*

    c.   but he just ask him *more question* after that

    d.   I have *two cousin*

    e.   A. bought # got his for *twenty-five dollar*

    f.   we are home *most weekend*

    g.   divided into *nine different type*

    h.   and that is *one of the Chinese dialect*[1]

Other Obligatory Plural Contexts

The proportion of suppliance of plurals in unquantified obligatory spoken contexts is roughly similar to that for quantified expressions, although the number of contexts in the spoken data is considerably smaller, making comparisons difficult. The rate of unquantified plural marking is somewhat lower in the written data than it was in quantified contexts. The results are shown in Table 6.2.

---

[1] Patty generally has difficulty with plural marking in this kind of partitive construction, in which the head noun, an object being selected from a set of objects, is actually singular, making it semantically quite different from the other quantified expressions. Out of six such contexts in the data, only one has plural marking, and that is on a quantified set: *I just complete one of the two books that I read on uh, Chinese history.*

TABLE 6.2. Suppliance of Plural Marking in Obligatory (Unquantified) NPs

		Suppliance/Contexts	%
Recording	1	3 / 14[2]	21.43
	2	14 / 37	37.84
	3	5 / 9	55.56
Written data		21 / 30	70.00

Some examples of supplied and unsupplied plural marking in unquantified NPs from obligatory contexts in the data are shown in (14) and (15), respectively:

(14) a. but it's like their *headquarters*
 b. her sister and my cousin are *friends*
 c. so we still exchanging uh, *letters*
 d. I ask my *parents* for like, two years
 e. and *miles and miles* of green plain
 f. can you see Fernando *eyes*?
 g. my *tears* just can't stopping coming down
 h. we would like to watch the *fireworks* at 7 pm on the Common

(15) a. we exchange *journal* every week
 b. every day *the student* just get together
 c. and I have to read *subtitle*
 d. I was applying to come to *United State*[3]
 e. just before *the disciple* going to Jerusalem

---

[2] Of the 11 omissions in Recording 1, seven of these were for the same idiomatic item: *speak in tongue*. It is possible, although a bit difficult to tell, that Patty thinks of "tongue" as a name or kind of language (like *Chinese* or *English*), as suggested by the following utterances: *because it's tongue, the # the language that you don't know*; *he don't know the tongue language*; *he doesn't understand what you talk in tongue*. If that is the case, then we might want to discount the seven instances of *speak in tongue* as obligatory plural contexts. In that case, the percentage of plural marking would be far higher (3/7 = 42.86%), but the number of contexts is probably too small to allow us to draw any firm conclusions.

[3] This error (*United State*) is consistent throughout the spoken production data (there is only one occurrence of *US* in the written data), and it is possible that, because it refers to a single country, Patty's omission of plural marking on this item is semantics-based.

    f.   did you watch *Olympic*?

    g.   I am growing so anxious *these day*

    h.   I also interested to watch the *firework* at Boston Common [cf. (14h) above]

There are a few cases where Patty may be interpreting what native English speakers would consider plural count nouns (from the context) as mass nouns, as indicated by singular agreement with non-plural-marked subjects (e.g., *but the new cabinet is being installed*; *except the building is more modern*; *my allergy was gone*). Because of this uncertainty in the face of the singular agreement marking, these were excluded from the figures in Table 6.2. The opposite condition also occurs in a few places—namely, where Patty pluralizes nouns that (in context) would be treated by native speakers as mass nouns (e.g., *he offered to do her laundries*; and (of a computer:) *old one is a bit slow and not enough memories*).

In addition to the two examples above, there are 11 other occurrences of inappropriate plural overuse. Three of these involve a common error among ESL speakers—pluralization in age-related compounding (e.g., *a normal, healthy 8 months old*) and four are used with the lexical item *time* (e.g., *we have such a good times, it was long times ago*). One (in the written data) is the word *responds* in place of *response*, which Patty may think is the correct form, especially given her tendency toward -*t/d* deletion in final consonant clusters as observed earlier in chapter 4: *thank you for your quick responds*. Two co-occur with *another* and indeed seem to refer to singular referents in context (e.g., *there is another issues concern me*; *there's another words I forgot*), although it is possible that the referents are plural and it is really the use of *another* that is inappropriate. One is just idiosyncratic: *she is such a cuties pie*.

The set of irregular plural nouns in English is quite small, and there are only a few obligatory contexts for these in the data—there is one instance in the spoken data in which Patty produces *woman* (/wʊmən/) instead of the required *women* (/wɪmən/), and one instance where she appropriately uses the plural form *teeth*. As mentioned earlier, there is one case of overregularization (*foots*) used in an obligatorily plural context. These three contexts were included in the data reported above in Tables 6.1 and 6.2.[4]

---

[4] I did not include contexts for the inherently plural noun *people*, although it is clear from the data that Patty realizes it signifies plural referents and uses it appropriately.

Other Plural Contexts

Finally, there are many contexts where it is difficult or impossible to determine the obligatoriness of singular versus plural usage. In some of these, the utterance is ungrammatical, but it is not clear whether the context calls for, say, a generic or specific reading, definite versus indefinite, or mass versus count, etc., which of course would affect whether pluralization should be used as opposed to a particular kind of determiner. These contexts were not included in the tables above, because the obligatoriness of plural use was unclear from the grammatical or discourse context.[5] Some examples of these are shown in (16):

(16) a. we also have *newspaper*
     b. I don't think that God give us *problem*
     c. he spend *extra years*
     d. when I need to do *my composition*
     e. Jewish believe in *sins* also?
     f. he followed *the instruction*
     g. I remember *the past happy times*
     h. I hope it is going to perform *miracles*

Article Usage

In a recent article investigating the role of L1 in fossilization, White (2003a) examined the acquisition of definite and indefinite articles in English by a native Turkish speaker, SD, who moved to Canada from Turkey and had lived in Canada for 10 years at the time she was first recorded (similar to Patty). White hypothesized that, if the L1 played a role in fossilization, then (a) SD's suppliance of English verbal inflection should be significantly higher than that for articles, since Turkish has rich verbal inflection but no articles, and (b) SD's rate of verbal inflection should be significantly higher than Patty's, since Turkish has rich verbal inflection, whereas Chinese does not.

---

[5] In order not to double-count these while still ensuring they are represented somewhere in the data, bare count nouns (i.e., determinerless and unmarked for plural, as in the first two examples in (16) in the text) are considered in the section on articles.

First, regarding (b), White found that indeed, SD's rate of suppliance of tense and agreement morphology on lexical verbs averaged around 80%, considerably higher than Patty's. (In particular, there is a very striking difference between SD's use of 3SG -*s* agreement on lexical verbs, at about 80% suppliance, and Patty's, at about only 4.5%.) In this case, it looks as if there is a significant effect for the L1.[6]

Turning next to SD's article usage and hypothesis (a) above, White also found that there was a significant difference between SD's suppliance of articles versus verbal inflection in obligatory contexts. SD supplied definite articles in about 72% of obligatory contexts but indefinite articles in only about 60%. At this point, let us look a bit more closely at Turkish.

White notes that Turkish has no definite article. Regarding indefiniteness, however, she notes that the numeral *bir* ('one') can be used in indefinite contexts and has been argued to be an article (Kornfilt, 1997) or a "quasi indefinite article" (Lyons, 1999). (Underhill, 1976, argues that it is a numeral.) Because Turkish has something more article-like for indefinite contexts than for definite, we might plausibly expect to find facilitative effects showing up in the form of higher accuracy on indefinite article usage than definite in SD's L2 English; yet, this is the opposite of what White found. In fact, there was a significant difference between SD's accuracy on definite versus indefinite article usage, with higher accuracy on definites. However, it is also possible, as White states, that *bir* is arguably "not a true article" in Turkish (p. 17), in which case no such facilitative effect would be predicted in any case.

White also notes that SD produces plural morphology in English at a rate (about 87%) that is significantly higher than her rate of production of determiners. Because Turkish also has overt plural inflection, this may again be a consequence of a facilitative effect from the L1. In other words, the presence of overt morphology in the L1 "appears to sensitize the L2 speaker to the requirement for overt morphology in the [L2] ... and to facilitate its use" (p. 23). The pluralization data from Patty reported above support White's suggestion. Chinese does not have plural inflectional mor-

---

[6] As mentioned earlier in chapter 4, Hawkins and Liszka (2003) also found a significant effect for the native language in English past-tense marking, with a suppliance rate of only about 77% for native Chinese speakers versus about 93% and 95.6% for native Japanese and native German speakers, respectively, in spontaneous oral production. It might seem a bit surprising that SD's rate of suppliance of past-tense marking is closer to that of Hawkins and Liszka's Chinese speakers than to that of their Japanese speakers, since Turkish is more similar to Japanese than to Chinese with respect to past marking. I return to the issue of L2 learner variability in supplying inflection in the next chapter.

phology except on personal pronouns and, in limited circumstances, on nouns denoting humans. (I return to the issue of plural marking in Chinese in the next section.) Patty's omission rate for plural morphology is higher than that of SD's, at least in her spoken production data. By the same token, Patty's production of demonstrative and possessive determiners in English is quite nativelike, as we might expect, since both these kinds of determiners are also found in Chinese.

It is important to note here that White is arguing for a kind of L1 "surface effect"—that is, "an effect on suppliance [of overt morphology—DL] and *not on underlying representation*" (p. 23; italics added). In the case of articles, for example, it is shown that SD appears to have knowledge of [±definiteness] despite her frequent omission of articles in obligatory contexts. For example, there is no contingency between the absence of definite determiners and absence of verbal inflection (as has been found in L1 acquisition), there is an extremely low rate of violations of the definiteness effect in existential *there* constructions, she makes very few substitution errors such as the use of definite for indefinite articles and vice versa, and she produces many DPs with demonstrative and possessive determiners appropriately. (I return to these issues with respect to Patty's data below.)

However, following White's logic, we should also be able to derive the following prediction: Because Chinese has neither overt verbal tense and agreement nor articles, we should expect Patty to perform about as (in)accurately on articles as on verbal morphology, or at least rather poorly on both. So let us turn now to Patty's production of articles.

First of all, it should be pointed out that Chinese is similar to Turkish in having a quantifier *yi-* ('one') that, when unstressed, appears to be in the process of becoming grammaticalized and "beginning to take on some of the functions" of the indefinite article (Robertson, 2000, citing Li & Thompson 1981, p. 132). Chinese also has demonstrative determiners *nei-* ('that') and *zhei-* ('this'); Robertson also notes that *nei-* similarly appears to be beginning to take on some of the functions of the definite article in English.[7] In his study of the acquisition of English article usage by native Chinese speakers, Robertson (2000) found that, in fact, his participants exhibited a "tendency" in existential sentences to produce *one* where a native English speaker would be likely to produce the indefinite article *a* (p. 167). He also noted a tendency for Chinese speakers to use demonstratives *this*, *that*, *these*, and *those* in contexts where a native English speaker would use

---

[7] Although these were not discussed in White (2003a), Turkish also has demonstrative determiners.

a definite article. (I must admit to finding his subjects' use of *this* in the few examples he provides perfectly appropriate, however.)

To the extent that native Chinese speakers' use of *one* and demonstratives for indefinite and definite articles (respectively) reflects L1 influence, note that the acquisition problem may be further complicated by a "remapping" problem (to use a term from Robertson, although in a different way) in which Chinese speakers must further learn how to differentiate these forms (*one* and *this* or *that*) in English from the articles *a* and *the*. (For some of Robertson's informants, it appears this differentiation had not yet been made.)

The first finding from Patty's article data is that, similar to what has been widely reported in the literature and to White's findings for SD and Robertson's findings for Chinese native speakers (but cf. Leung, 2001), Patty is significantly more accurate on definite than on indefinite articles ($\chi^2 = 7.9$, $p < .01$). There is also much less difference between her written and spoken production data for both definite and indefinite articles, in contrast to what we previously observed of her production of past-tense marking.

Second, her overall rate of suppliance of articles is quite high. Definite articles are supplied at about a rate of 84% and indefinite at about 75.5%, which is in fact significantly higher than SD's rate of suppliance ($\chi^2 = 15.15$, $p < .001$ for definite; $\chi^2 = 21.65$, $p < .001$ for indefinite). This finding is unexpected from the standpoint of assuming that a lack of articles in the L1 should result in greater difficulty in acquiring articles in the L2, as White has suggested for SD. These rates are, of course, far higher than Patty's own rate of verbal agreement marking and (regular) past-tense marking, which runs counter to the expectation that, because Chinese has neither articles nor verbal tense/agreement morphology, we should find approximately the same (low) rates of overt realization for both. The data are shown in Tables 6.3 and 6.4.

TABLE 6.3. Percentage of Definite Article Suppliance in Obligatory Contexts.

DEF Article	Recording 1	Recording 2	Recording 3	Written	Total
Correctly supplied	84.93 (62/73)	78.45 (91/116)	83.33 (50/60)	90.29 (93/103)	84.09 (296/352)
Omitted	15.07 (11/73)	19.83 (23/116)	16.67 (10/60)	06.80 (7/103)	14.49 (51/352)
Wrong form[†]	00.00 (0/73)	01.72 (2/116)	00.00 (0/60)	02.91 (3/103)	01.42 (5/352)

[†] Instances of a different determiner (5/5 = *a*) used in a context where the definite article was required.

TABLE 6.4. Percentage of Indefinite Article Suppliance in Obligatory Contexts.

INDEF Article	Recording 1	Recording 2	Recording 3	Written	Total
Correctly supplied	63.16 (12/19)	76.47 (104/136)	77.19 (44/57)	74.71 (65/87)	75.50 (225/298)
Omitted	26.31 (5/19)	19.12 (26/136)	17.54 (10/57)	22.99 (20/87)	20.13 (60/298)
Wrong form[†]	10.53 (2/19)	04.41 (6/136)[8]	05.26 (3/57)	02.30 (2/87)	04.36 (13/298)

[†] Instances of a different determiner (10/11 = *the*) used in a context where the indefinite article was required.

Some examples of correct definite article use are provided in (17), and incorrect omissions in (18). Included among the contexts for the definite article were those that are idiomatic (e.g., *the tail end*; *the flu*; *on the phone*), and those that occur with superlatives, ordinal numerals, unique referents (e.g., *the sky*, *the world*) including uniquely quantified referents (e.g. *the only/the same/the other...*), and various time expressions (e.g., *in the morning, the winter, the beginning*).

---

[8] This includes one case where *one* was used instead of the indefinite article: *they have one last name was so long, some of them* (interpreted in context to mean something like 'some of their last names were so long' or 'some of them had such long last names').

(17) a.   he's *the* only person I spoke to
    b.   I have *the* most wonderful teacher
    c.   but I just barely pass the uh, the # *the* minimum
    d.   because *the* other sister got marry
    e.   we may have to meet with *the* Minister of Health
    f.   however, I do love *the* people here
    g.   and went back *the* next day
    h.   they born *the* same year
    i.   she got stuck on *the* first piece
    j.   they have four time in *the* bible

(18) a.   in Ø northern part they speak differently from *the* southern
    b.   that we are traveling Ø end of April
    c.   did you watch Ø Olympic?
    d.   taking um, Ø train to Hong Kong together
    e.   and I have to read Ø subtitle
    f.   he came to Ø United State two years before me[9]
    g.   that I met in a club Ø previous week
    h.   we all Ø same size, you know?
    i.   but Ø first year is really a struggle for me
    j.   this kind of appear four time in Ø bible

Similarly, examples of correct and incorrect indefinite article usage are provided in (19) and (20), respectively.

(19) a.   I think there was *a* breakdown in the agency
    b.   M. needed *a* companion to go to Boston Symphony
    c.   I start working at B. as *a* waitress
    d.   he still looking for *a* house
    e.   well maybe at that time mix in *a* little bit English
    f.   do you guys have *a* bike?
    g.   and my # my father's not *a* good writer
    h.   it's *a* gift

---

[9] Patty consistently produces *United State* instead of *the United States* in these data, which accounts for 7 of the 51 total omissions listed in Table 6.3 and, specifically, 6 out of the 23 total omissions listed for Recording 2, explaining why the rate of suppliance for that recording is slightly lower than for the others.

    i.   they don't have *a* accent[10]

    j.   God give # give us, give him *a* problem

(20) a.   it was kind of Ø mutual situation

    b.   he's gonna be Ø bachelor all his life

    c.   like maybe I knew about Ø hundred character

    d.   she is Ø spiritual person

    e.   so I learn Ø little bit um, Vietnamese

    f.   each of you have Ø bike?

    g.   and he is Ø much better Chinese writer

    h.   isn't it Ø generous gift?

    i.   you have Ø accent

    j.   I don't think that God give us Ø problem

Note that in the examples in (19e–j) and (20e–j), we appear to find true variability with respect to indefinite article usage with the same nouns (i.e., *little bit* [language], *bike*, *writer*, *gift*, *accent*, *problem*) in similar syntactic contexts.

Also revealing, I think, are examples showing that Patty is indeed aware of the difference between the functions of definite and indefinite articles in those cases where she accurately discriminates between them in referring to the same noun within the same discourse context, in both her spoken and written data:

(21) a.   I remember my dance company have *a* party … so I invite A. to # to *the* party

    b.   I know D.'s gonna have *a* show … well she's so busy on *the* show

    c.   we have *a* maid … *the* maid uh, pick up a lot of Hokkien from us

    d.   say, um, he have *a* beer … when A. repeat the story to us the other day about *the* beer

---

[10] The incorrect choice of allomorph here is the only one in all the data; although there are too few instances to generalize from, every other instance of an indefinite article occurring before a vowel sound is correctly produced as *an* in both the spoken and written data: *she's an older woman*; *we go over for an hour now*; *to an expert pediatric*; *we also need an invitation letter*; *I also love to talk to an older person*; *his buddy at the time was an older lady*; *it is not an easy solution*; *I hear with an accent?* (The last example is an echo-question response to an interlocutor (her husband): *she also hears with an accent.*)

    e.   he's *a* killer ... he's *the* killer of prophet

    f.   with *the* deal that if we signed up 3 years with MSN (Microsoft) then we only paid for $300, which is *a* great deal.

    g.   I wanted to have *a* house, a car, etc. ... when I have *the* house, I was the most unhappiest person

In addition to accurate suppliance and inaccurate omissions of articles in obligatory contexts as shown in Tables 6.3 and 6.4 above, there were 21 instances of overuse of the definite article in inappropriate contexts, 10 of which occurred in contexts where the indefinite article was contextually more appropriate instead (e.g., *OK, she # he have the fish call Fernando*; *I have the friend who is a florist*) and others where no article (Ø) was contextually more appropriate (*if you do "holy spirit" in the capital # capital letter, it means different*; *a province next to the Siberia*). There were 10 instances of overuse of the indefinite article in inappropriate contexts, 5 of which were used in contexts where a definite article was contextually more appropriate (*and that I make a right decision to tell you this*; *I think at a second year*), and others, such as for noncount nouns, where no article was more appropriate (*she has a black brown hair*; *we have a really good news to share*).

We observed in the previous section that Patty's use of possessive determiners appears near-nativelike. What about her use of demonstratives and, in particular, any indication that she substitutes these for definite articles? In contrast to Robertson's data, we find no tendency for Patty to substitute demonstratives for definite determiners nor *one* for indefinite determiners: There are no examples of the former and only one instance (out of 298 contexts = near-zero percent) of the latter (see Footnote 8). On the contrary, demonstratives are used perfectly appropriately and *one* is used numerically, as shown in the following examples:

(22) a.   but *that* particular day

     b.   to lift our spirit a bit in *this* long winter day

     c.   hope *this* e-mail find you well and happy

     d.   S. and J. visited us *this* past weekend

     e.   only *that* college accepted me

     f.   *one* time they have a clown come to the house

     g.   *one* semester can feed the whole family over there [*speaking of college tuition*]

     h.   we lost over 6,000 people in *one* day

     i.   I read *one* or two books now a year in Chinese

     j.   her vision came in life *one* day

Finally, if we follow White in exploring the data for definiteness effect violations, we find none at all either in Patty's spoken or written production data. Such effects include a well-known constraint prohibiting definite DPs following existential *there*, as shown in the contrast between (23a) and (23b) below (examples (21–22) from White, p. 19, following Lyons, 1999):

(23) a. There is a unicorn in the garden.
    b. *There is the unicorn in the garden.

If Patty (like SD) observes the requirement that the DP in an existential *there* construction must be indefinite, we have even more support for concluding that she has knowledge of the feature [± definite]. What we should expect to find in such constructions are the indefinite article and quantifiers (or no article for noncount nouns). This is in fact what we do find. There are 37 contexts for existential *there* constructions, and *no* definite articles were produced in any of them (despite the fact that Patty tends to overuse definite more than indefinite articles overall, as previously mentioned). Some examples are provided in (24):

(24) a. there's a poem that you have to memorize
    b. there were some changes in my life recently
    c. there is a signal to show you who are on line
    d. there was a breakdown in the agency
    e. there are so many lessons to learn in your lifetime

There are two instances where it is not clear whether the noun following *there* should be plural or not, although she uses a plural-agreeing copula:

(25) a. there were Asian short stories book that I bought
    b. also there are book club in Hawaii you may like to join

There are also two instances of overuse of the plural both following *another* (it is not known whether the intended referents are plural or singular):

(26) a. there's another words I forgot
    b. there is another issues concern me

There is one instance in which Patty uses (nonreferential) *it's* instead of the more contextually appropriate *there's*:

(27) because it's # it's no mistake at all [*speaking of a mistake-free musical performance*]

and one in which she uses *they* instead of *there* (which is likely to be a typo in her e-mail message):

(28) they are so many things I want to do

None of these errors, however, suggests a lack of knowledge of the constraint prohibiting definite DPs in these environments. In this respect the available data are apparently nativelike.

Note, finally, that 37 contexts for existential *there* constructions is a relatively small number compared with the 146 contexts White found in SD's data. In fact, Patty tends to use a subject pronoun + *have* in many utterances for which existential *there* could also be used. Robertson (2000) observed this as well in his data from native Chinese speakers and considered it to be a translational equivalent of the Chinese verb *you* 'have, exist' which is also used to express existential predication in Chinese. Although this is possible, it should be pointed out that this *have* construction is also very commonly used in the colloquial variety of English Patty has been exposed to for so long.

One problem for the researcher is that it is sometimes difficult to determine whether *have* is being used existentially or not. One likely example of existential usage is the following, where Patty is retelling a bible passage:

> And then *they have* another # another # another guy who # who, his name is Saul, I think. ... And then *they have* another Jewish, too, Jewish family who is very rich. He also # he's also speak in tongue that day. *They have* four time in the bible.

However, it is not clear whether the more representative *have*-constructions in the next example, in which Patty is describing her schooling in Hong Kong, should be treated as existential or not, although perhaps they could be:

> *We have* two Chinese # *we have* two uh, in # in English school *they have* two Chinese literature and Chinese history ... *we have* English uh, literature, and then *we have* uh, other arithmetic, algebra, and uh, also *we have* physics, biology ... *You* don't *have* a chance to really speak in English, and I remember *we have* one # maybe one uh # maybe once a week *we have* oral class which *we have* English woman sit around and

then we spoke English to her. And I remember it's really hard for me ...
And then *I have* um # *I have* a math teacher who is English, and I did so
poorly in my math because half the class I didn't understand what he's
talking about in the class, and uh, that's my lowest point in math.

In sum, Patty's use of *have* in the previous excerpts is quite consistent
with the colloquial English that is present in her linguistic environment.
Nonetheless, as Robertson (2000) suggests, it is possible that her apparently
heavy reliance on the use of *have* to express existential predication in English results from L1 transfer of the *you* 'have, exist' existential construction
in Chinese. Because *you* existential predication in Chinese also exhibits a
strong definiteness effect (Huang, 1987; Kuong, 2002; and see Footnote 11
in the next section), we must consider L1 transfer as a possible source of
Patty's knowledge of the existential definiteness effect in English as well.

An Interaction of DP Features: Definiteness and Number

As mentioned earlier, Chinese lacks a definite article. Nonetheless, it has
definiteness, in the expression of its pronouns and demonstratives, of
course, but, unlike English, as also interpreted according to the pre- versus
post-verbal position of nouns, or the co-occurrence of nouns with classifiers
(see Cheng & Sybesma, 1999). As mentioned, existential sentences in Chinese with *you* 'have, exist' exhibit a definiteness effect. Definiteness also
interacts in an interesting way with the co-occurrence of overt plural marking. In this section, I focus on an optional and highly restricted form of plural suffixation of nouns in Chinese, and how this might have affected
Patty's acquisition of plural number marking in English.

Chinese has an overt plural/collective suffix *-men* that is highly restricted in its usage in that it generally only applies to kinds of human referents. Its use is obligatory with personal pronouns (e.g., *wo* 'I/me' vs. *women* 'we/us'), but otherwise optional with other kinds of human nouns,
which may be interpreted in context as plural even without overt plural
marking (e.g., *xuesheng* 'student(s)'). However, when the noun is marked
for plural with *-men*, it can only be interpreted as definite (Aoun & Li,
2003, pp. 165ff.):

(29) ta hui dai *xuesheng-men* hui jia
he will bring student-PL back home
'He will bring *the* students back home.' [*not* 'He will bring (some) students back home.']

The plural suffix -*men* is claimed by Aoun and Li to be the overt realization of a number feature in the head of a Number category, as shown in (30):

(30)

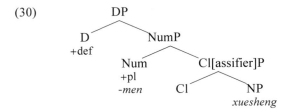

Aoun and Li (2003) argue that as long as the classifier position is empty, a noun can be raised into Number, checking its plural feature, and then is further raised to D to check the definite feature there. Even if D is filled (e.g., with a demonstrative), the noun can still be affixed with -*men* and move up to Number, as long as the Classifier position is empty, and will still be interpreted as definite:

(31) laoshi   dui *zhexie/naxie xuesheng-men* tebie   hao
      teacher to these/those   student-PL   especially good
      'The teacher is especially nice to these/those students.'

However, if the classifier position is filled, it blocks the raising of a noun to Number, so the noun cannot be pluralized with -*men*, as shown in (32):

(32) *laoshi dui (zhe/na) *ji-ge*   *xuesheng-men* tebie   hao
      teacher to this/that several-CL student-PL   especially good
      'The teacher is especially nice to those several students.'

Notice that Chinese nouns, then, cannot be overtly pluralized with -*men* in quantified contexts, such as *ji-ge xuesheng* = several-CL student 'several students' or *san-ge xuesheng* = three-CL student 'three students', as these require classifiers. However, such quantified contexts are exactly the ones that obligatorily require plural marking in English, since plural marking on the noun is required to agree with the plurality of the number (e.g., 'several students' or 'three students'). And of course, plural-suffixed nouns in English are not required to be definite, as they are in Chinese, but rather are definite only if they co-occur with a definite determiner:

(33) He will bring (the/those) three students back home.

This contrast between Chinese and English presents an interesting hypothetical learning problem if we assume L1 influence in second language acquisition. Although positive evidence will readily inform a native Chinese speaker acquiring English that there is no [+human] semantic restriction on overt plural marking, she will still have to dissociate overt plural marking from having a necessarily definite interpretation (in the absence of any definite determiner). She will also have to learn that plural marking is obligatory rather than optional in English, including on nouns in quantified contexts in which such marking would be completely disallowed in Chinese.

Recall that Patty produced no definiteness effect violations in English existential sentences, as discussed in the previous section. The fact that she also produces some plural subjects in this type of sentence suggests that (at least by the end state of L2 acquisition) she has managed to acquire the required dissociation of overt plural marking from definiteness:[11]

(34) a. there were *some changes* in my life recently
     b. there are *so many lessons* to learn in your lifetime
     c. they [sic] are *so many things* I want to do

There are in fact many other instances of indefinite plural-marked nouns throughout the data as well (i.e., in other than existential-*there* contexts). Additional examples are provided in (35):

(35) a. *some Americans* spoke # speak very very well
     b. I read *one or two books* now a year in Chinese
     c. my good fortune to have *good friends*
     d. *women* are more sensitive than *men* in *many ways*

Nonetheless, when we recall from Table 6.1 the significant increase noted earlier between the first and subsequent recordings on Patty's plural marking in quantified contexts—from about 8% to about 50%—it is possible that we are observing lingering transfer effects in the sharply lower rate

---

[11] In fact, Aoun and Li (2003) point out that in Chinese, because nouns affixed with *-men* must be interpreted as definite, they cannot appear in existential sentences since this would incur a definiteness effect violation:

*you	ren-*men*	cf.	you	ren
have	person-PL		have	person
'there are some persons'			'there is/are some person(s)'	

of plural marking of the first recording. Obviously, it is impossible to draw firm conclusions about transfer without earlier-stage data. In general, however, Patty appears to have accomplished the necessary reorganizing or re-clustering of plural and definiteness features from the way they are combined in Mandarin Chinese to the way they need to be de-linked in English.

7

Conclusions

In this concluding chapter, I first provide a brief review of some of the main characteristics of formal aspects of Patty's English idiolect that have emerged from the data. I then turn to a consideration of two (probably related) factors that have been hypothesized to play a crucial role in adult second language acquisition: native language influence and the possibility of decreased sensitivity to the input. Although my main objective is to evaluate the proposals examined in these sections in light of Patty's data specifically, I also consider data from other studies, including a revisiting of Schwartz and Sprouse's (1994, 1996) German L2 acquisition case study of Cevdet. I then conclude by offering some more general thoughts about the possible limitations of parameter resetting as a theoretical mechanism for explaining second language acquisition.

Overview of the Data from Patty

I began this case study of Patty because I was initially struck by the various (and obvious) non-nativelike aspects of her English, especially in light of her relatively favorable acquisition circumstances over a long period of time (immersion, acculturation, level of educational attainment, level of engagement, and professional and personal success in her target language community). Such nontargetlike aspects are evident in her phonology (touched on relatively briefly, mainly in chap. 4) and morphophonology, especially affixal inflection, which tends to be omitted, particularly in her spoken production. For example, in her spoken English, Patty nearly always omits regular past-tense marking (1a) and nonpast 3SG agreement (1b). She also often omits copular and auxiliary *be* forms (1c–d), past-participle inflection (1e), and she occasionally overuses or omits the present participle (-*ing*) form (1f–g). On nouns, she often omits regular plural marking (1h) and affixal possessive marking (1i).

(1) a.   I *call* Bill this morning and nobody *answer*
     b.   because he *understand* better now
     c.   he *ø* around adult a lot
     d.   she *ø* just hanging around
     e.   yeah but we haven't *look* at it carefully
     f.   my tears just can't *stopping* coming down
     g.   try to learn English by # by *read* the dictionary
     h.   I borrow a lot of *book* from her
     i.   *Debbie* brother was very rich

However, over the course of this study, I instead became increasingly impressed by what I had not necessarily expected to find—that much of Patty's knowledge of English, especially in syntactic domains, appears surprisingly targetlike and cannot be easily explained in terms of facilitative transfer from her L1 knowledge. For example, she has apparently perfect knowledge of overall pronominal case marking, and case marking on subjects in particular as a function of clausal finiteness (2a), and various word-order-related phenomena such as the placement of verbs and adverbs (2b–c), robust relative clause formation, and *wh*-movement in general, including the appropriate stranding of prepositions (2d), and subject-auxiliary inversion/*do*-support in questions (2e). She clearly has good knowledge of definiteness: Her use of demonstratives (2f–g) and possessive determiners (2h) is always appropriate (except for occasional mixing of 3SG masculine and feminine forms in her spoken production), and her use of definite and indefinite articles, while not completely nativelike, is nonetheless quite proficient (2i).

(2) a.   maybe they don't want us to use it after office hour
     b.   his brother never came here
     c.   although it was never obvious
     d.   you don't know who you should associate with
     e.   didn't he know that it will get back to me?
     f.   S. and J. visited us this past weekend
     g.   only that college accepted me
     h.   our hostess J. and her family
     i.   say, um, he have a beer … when A. repeat the story to us the other day about the beer

Moreover, her use of overt rather than null subjects is overwhelmingly correct, and she correctly rejects violations of constraints on *wh*-movement (e.g., "subjacency" violations).

We also observed that for at least some aspects of her grammar, Patty's written English is more accurate than her spoken English. This implicates a potentially important role for phonology—an area of which we have barely scratched the surface so far in this case and that obviously warrants looking into in much greater depth in future research. In the next section, we will briefly consider an interesting recent phonological approach that shows promise in accounting for aspects of Patty's difficulty with affixal inflection in her spoken production of English.

The Role of the L1 in Accounting for Divergent L2 Outcomes

It seems entirely plausible that some or all of a learner's native language(s) constitutes a point of departure for second language acquisition, a claim that has been explicitly made with respect to the initial or early stages of L2 development since at least the days of the contrastive analysis hypothesis (see e.g., Corder, 1983; Lado, 1957; Odlin, 1989, 2003; Schwartz & Sprouse, 1996). Within a generative framework of second language acquisition, L1 influence has been articulated in terms of resetting parametric values from those of the native language to those of the target language. For example, in an early discussion of the role contrastive linguistics (i.e., a comparison of the L1 and L2 language systems) should play in SLA research, Haegeman (1988) outlines the basic strategy for investigating L2 competence in terms of UG-constrained parameter resetting:

> To go from the L1 to the L2, learners will often have to reset existing parameters or reassign values to them. Failure to do so will mean that the learner does not attain the L2. The latter possibility seems to be what negative transfer is about. (p. 255)

In a general way, then, the failure of many adult language learners to reach nativelike proficiency could be descriptively modeled in terms of their inability to reset one or more parameters from the L1 value to that of the L2. I return to the issue of parameter setting shortly, but for now focus on models that attempt to predict the conditions under which parameter resetting will likely fail and fossilization will occur. In these proposals, L1 knowledge plays a persistent and, in some cases, a deterministic role in L2 ultimate attainment. This is by no means an exhaustive review, but enough of an overview to provide a flavor of some of the current interesting questions that can be raised with respect to Patty's case.

Representational Deficit/ Failed Functional Features Hypotheses

As discussed in chapters 4 and 5, one approach to accounting for learners' failure to achieve targetlike grammars in adulthood argues that certain morphosyntactic features that are present in the target language but were not previously selected by a learner's L1 will be impossible to acquire beyond a hypothesized critical period for language acquisition. This account is known as the Representational Deficit Hypothesis (Hawkins, 2000, 2003; Hawkins & Liszka, 2003; Tsimpli, 2003a, 2003b; Tsimpli & Roussou, 1991) or, in an earlier version, the Failed Functional Features Hypothesis (Hawkins & Chan, 1997).

Under this account, parametric variation (following Chomsky, 1995) is reducible to morphological properties of functional categories that drive syntactic derivation. The presence or absence of inflectional morphology on lexical items, such as for person, number and gender agreement, case, tense, and so on, is claimed to determine movement for feature checking.[1] Thus, successful parameter resetting in second language acquisition is contingent on the acquisition of those features that are selected by the target language (i.e., by its native speakers), and is demonstrated by the consistent production of their morphophonological reflexes, such as affixes and other functional morphemes. If the learner's L1 also parametrically selects a feature in question, then it should in principle be acquirable in the L2; however, if not, then the learner will be unable to represent it, resulting in fossilization with respect to that feature, its overt realization, and any associated deductive consequences and effects.

In more recent versions of this approach (e.g., Hawkins 2003; Tsimpli 2003a, 2003b), only *uninterpretable* features (i.e., purely formal features devoid of semantic content) that are absent from the learner's L1 are claimed to be unacquirable. In sum then, the acquisition of a second language is argued to be rather severely constrained by properties of the

---

[1] It is not clear to what extent the abstract features associated with inflectional morphology must be overtly realized for such feature-checking to occur. Chomsky (1995) assumes "at least a tendency for phi-features to be overtly manifested" in case of overt movement (p. 277), and others, such as Solà (1996) and Thráinsson (1996), explicitly require it. See Lardiere (2000, 2005, to appear) for further discussion.

L1—namely, the unavailability of any (uninterpretable) features that have not already been parametrically selected in the L1.

In chapter 4, I argued that, although Patty's representation (and overt realization) of past tense does not appear to be nativelike, it is supplied at too high a rate at least in her written production (at about 78%) to simply dismiss as unacquirable. The same point is even more obviously the case for the native Chinese-speaking informants in Hawkins and Liszka's own (2003) study, the most advanced of whom supplied past-tense marking in 77% of obligatory contexts in their spoken production. Moreover, in the instances where Patty does provide past-tense inflection, it is typically correctly and appropriately supplied. In that chapter, I argued that the semantic complexity and multifunctionality of the morphosyntactic feature [past], along with phonological factors and the positive evidence for historical present usage in past temporal contexts in the input, were more likely responsible for Patty's difficulty in acquiring past-tense marking and the gaps in her production. (More on phonological factors directly below.)

Although it is impossible to derive reliably predictive generalizations from case-study data, it is possible to test them. The data suggest that the predictions of the Representational Deficit Hypothesis are not upheld with respect to the L2 acquisition of English past-tense marking by native Chinese speakers (see Goad & White, 2005, for additional experimental confirmation of this). In sum, the Representational Deficit Hypothesis cannot account for the difference between spoken versus written production, why the percentage of suppliance is as high as it is, or the difference between the rate of regular versus irregular past-tense marking.

We observed in chapter 5 that Patty appears to have acquired an English targetlike [+wh] feature that triggers overt *wh*-movement, as well as knowledge of violations of constraints on extraction (e.g., subjacency-type constraints). Other studies involving native Chinese speakers have found this as well, such as Li (1998), Martohardjono (1993), and White and Juffs (1998). I have suggested in chapter 5 and elsewhere (Lardiere, to appear) that the parametric view according to which English is presumed to have a [+] or "strong" value for a [wh] or [Q] feature, whereas Chinese does not, may be too simplistic. However, if we stick with this view, pending further refinement of the syntactic theory underlying it (including, for example, what counts as an uninterpretable feature; see Pesetsky & Torrego, 2001, 2004, for some discussion), then the Representational Deficit approach cannot easily account for the available data.

The Prosodic Transfer Hypothesis

A recent collection of articles has argued that L1 constraints on prosodic structure play a central role in explaining missing inflection in L2 spoken production (Goad & White, 2004a, 2004b, 2005; Goad, White, & Steele, 2003). This approach, called the Prosodic Transfer Hypothesis, goes well beyond my suggestion in chapter 4 that a native language prohibition on consonant clusters could account for a substantial part of Patty's difficulty in producing regular past-tense marking where such inflection would result in a cluster (e.g., *lived* /lɪvd/, *picked* /pɪkt/).

Looking specifically at Mandarin Chinese native speakers acquiring L2 English, Goad et al. (2003) and Goad and White (2005) propose that inflectional morphology is prosodified differently in Mandarin and English. Whereas the perfective aspectual particle *le* in Mandarin is argued to be represented within a prosodic word (PWd), as shown in (3), (regular) inflection in English is instead represented by the adjunction structure shown in (4):

Because Mandarin is claimed to lack the adjunction structure shown for English in (4) above, the Prosodic Transfer Hypothesis predicts that the production of regular past-tense-marking inflection (as well as that of regular past participles) in the L2 English grammars of native Mandarin speakers will be depressed (Goad & White, 2005).[2] Because irregular past-tense

---

[2] Goad and White appear to have selected the prosodic representation for perfective aspectual particle *le* as that which a native Mandarin speaker would be likely to transfer in attempting to build a representation for English past-tense marking. Although this is not an unreasonable assumption from a semantic point of view, there is at least one other affixal particle in Mandarin for which a structure more similar to the English one in (4) above in the text might seem intuitively more plausible (I use the word "intuitively" because I am not a phonologist), or at least for which it is not immediately obvious why the PWd-internal analysis in (3) should be preferred. The highly frequent particle *de* used to indicate possession may attach to stems rather than roots—one of the criteria used to justify PWd-adjunction for English inflection in Goad et al. (2003). For example, it can attach to words productively suffixed with -*men* (see chap. 6) as in the following (my thanks to Joaquim Kuong for this example):
(Continued)

marking in English is PWd-internal (like the Chinese structure in (3)), its representation can be easily accommodated by a native Chinese speaker.

The Prosodic Transfer Hypothesis appears to account rather neatly for some aspects of Patty's omission of inflection. Like Patty, the native Chinese speakers who participated in Goad and White's (2005) study omitted regular past-tense inflection and past-participle inflection at roughly equal rates, as predicted. This sort of explanation would also help explain the discrepancy between Patty's spoken and written production, as well as her much higher rate of past-tense marking on irregular versus regular verbs. Although a constraint against producing consonant clusters is independently still required to account for her overwhelming rate of -t/d deletion in final clusters in monomorphemic words, the Prosodic Transfer Hypothesis could additionally help to explain why Patty also often fails to mark regular past tense in cases of inflection that would not result in a final cluster (such as *cried* or *started*).

Perhaps the main hurdle for Goad and White's account is similar to that of the Representational Deficit Hypothesis—namely, explaining why rates of inflectional marking for the participants in their studies are as high as they are if those learners are unable to build an English-like representation for regular inflection. However, unlike Representational Deficit proponents, Goad and White (2005) do not claim that targetlike prosodic structures can *never* be acquired. They write:

> While we assume that the adjunction structure can ultimately be acquired, as the necessary building blocks are present in the L1 grammar (see Goad & White 2004a), at intermediate stages in development, suppliance should be relatively low. (p. 218)

(i) Jiaokeshu,   xuesheng-men-*de* wo na-le,   laoshi-men-*de* wo hai mei na.
   Textbook(s) student-PL-DE   I   take-PERF teacher-PL-DE   I   still not take
   'As for textbooks, I've taken the students', (but) I haven't taken the teachers.'

Furthermore, it is not clear whether the English adjunction structure in (4) is intended to cover all regular bound inflection in English, although this appears to be the claim. If so, it seems surprising that the English affix -*ing* is so much more readily produced in comparison to regular past-tense or past-participle affixation by English learners in general and by Patty in particular.

Thus, there is seemingly no presumption in this approach that fossilization with respect to the production of inflectional morphology is inevitable. [3]

However, although Goad and White (2005) argue convincingly that the Prosodic Transfer Hypothesis predicts and accounts for the available data better than the Representational Deficit Hypothesis, there is one sense in which the two hypotheses appear quite compatible: the persistent constraining nature of the L1 representation (phonological in the case of the Prosodic Transfer Hypothesis vs. syntactic in the case of the Representational Deficit Hypothesis). Note the following excerpt from the quote cited above: "… *as the necessary building blocks are present in the L1 grammar…*" and continuing further: "However, for stimuli of certain shapes … English past and perfective can be organized PWd-internally, *consistent with Mandarin prosodic constraints,* thereby allowing the relevant forms to be produced without adjunction" (Goad & White, 2005, p. 218, italics added). In other words, although learner output may appear to be targetlike, the prosodic representation may nonetheless differ from that of an English native speaker. It is not clear whether there are L2 learning situations in which the L1 does not consist of the relevant "building blocks" (which could be interpreted as akin to features within the Representational Deficit approach), but this is what would be needed to determine whether learners can truly acquire new features or structures in the L2 for which there are no corresponding ones in the L1.

Despite these open and interesting questions (see also Footnote 2), the Prosodic Transfer Hypothesis offers considerable promise in accounting for several aspects of missing inflection in spoken production as in the case of Patty, by situating what appear to be morphophonological production problems in the phonological component rather than in the syntax.

The Multiple Effects Principle

In attempting to better account for fossilization by coming up with "a theory-driven list of potentially fossilizable IL structures," Selinker and Lakshmanan (1993) propose that "*when two or more* SLA factors work in

---

[3] White (2003a) and Goad and White (2004a, 2004b) do extend their prosodic analysis to SD, an end-state L2 acquirer of English whose L2 representations of articles and inflectional morphology are argued to be likely constrained by prosodic characteristics of her L1 Turkish. In a more recent paper, Goad and White (to appear) suggest that in SD's case, the building blocks will not be available from the L1 for articles, but they will be available for tense, agreement, and plural inflection, so that there should in fact be fossilization of article usage, which is what they find.

tandem, there is a greater chance of stabilization of interlanguage forms leading to possible fossilization" (p. 198; italics in the original). They dub this proposal the Multiple Effects Principle A (MEP). The second part of the MEP (B) states that language transfer will likely—or even necessarily—be one of the multiple factors. In its strong form, the MEP claims that "whenever the MEP is applicable, one of the SLA factors will *always* be language transfer" (p. 198; italics in the original).

In particular regard to Patty, Lakshmanan (2006) has suggested that Patty's difficulties with affixal inflection for tense and agreement may be a result of the MEP—specifically:

> [A]s Lardiere has indicated, Patty's history of acquisition of other languages prior to her exposure to English encompasses Mandarin, Indonesian and Hokkien. One aspect that is common to all three languages is that the verb forms are not inflected for tense and agreement. It is possible that Patty's difficulties with suffixal inflectional forms in her steady state grammar may be the result of the Multiple Effects Principle. In addition to the complexities involved in the morphophonological mapping of [an] abstract feature of Tense in a language such as English [citing Lardiere 1998a—DL], a triple co-factor involved in causing permanent stabilization of her non-native-like verb inflectional morphology may be the influence exerted independently and jointly by each of her three other languages: Mandarin, Indonesian and Hokkien ... . (p. 109)

I completely agree (as I have earlier mentioned in chap. 4 and elsewhere, e.g., Lardiere, 1998, 2003b) that it is highly likely that prior language knowledge (including Patty's knowledge of Cantonese, in addition to the three languages mentioned above) affects Patty's production of past-tense marking in English. This is especially likely to be true for her spoken production, because all four of her previously acquired languages prohibit the sort of final consonant clusters that would result from past-tense affixation onto English verbs ending in consonants. Moreover, it clearly makes excellent common sense *not* to assume that we could explain end-state fossilization by appealing to a single factor. After all, different constructions, areas, and sub-areas of an L2 grammar may fossilize in different ways for different learners who, as mentioned in chapter 1, have very different initial-state conditions and learning situations. The role of prior language knowledge in acquiring another language has long been, and continues to be, recognized as critically important by many researchers even if particular transfer proposals vary considerably in scope and detail. One might ask, however, whether or not something like the MEP should really be accorded the status of a principle or a theory.

Regarding their strong hypothesis that language transfer is a necessary co-factor in explaining fossilization, Selinker and Lakshmanan (1993) write: "we should *not* be understood to say that fossilization happens only when language transfer occurs" because empirical data exist for which fossilization without transfer has been claimed to occur (p. 212; italics original). Later on the same page, they write: "certain linguistic structures (but not others) tend to fossilize even without severely restricted input. We hypothesized ... that this can only occur in a narrow range of structures where language transfer is a co-factor, when the MEP applies." The apparent hedges here are phrases such as "whenever the MEP is applicable" (p. 198) and "when the MEP applies" (p. 212). Also: "It is our hypothesis that *in every case where the MEP is at work*, language transfer appears to be involved" (p. 199; italics added). If the MEP is proposed as even a partial explanation for fossilization, however, then the arguments here seem a bit problematic. Are there ever instances of fossilization in which multiple factors are *not* at work? What constitutes a possible factor, at what level of specificity? The problems become more apparent when we look at some of the factors other than L1 transfer proposed by Selinker and Lakshmanan to support the MEP:

• "certain input" (p. 200, citing Jain, 1974);
• "universal processes" (p. 200, citing several studies);
• "UG effects" or "the UG factor," including an apparent default strategy for tenseless clauses and empty categories (pp. 201–202), violation of the case filter (p. 207), or non-operation of the subset principle (p. 211);
• "symmetry of structure" (p. 202, citing Kellerman, 1989);
• "affect" to be understood here (somewhat unconventionally) as "trying to make the TL better or more precise" (p. 202, citing Kellerman, 1989; Selinker & Lakshmanan, 1990)
• learners' perception that the L2 "is very similar to their NL" and the "existence of a fair number of cognate words (shared vocabulary)" in both the L1 and L2 [it is rather difficult to see exactly how these two factors should be viewed as distinct from each other or from "transfer"—DL] (p. 203, citing data from Dušková, 1984);
• "morphological factor"—specifically, a failure on the part of the learner to analyze *Its* [*sic*] as consisting of *it* and *is* (p. 206, citing Gerbault, 1978; Lakshmanan, 1989);
• "positive evidence from the target language," by which is meant the existence of semantically related or similar words with different subcategorization properties that the learner incorrectly analogizes from (e.g., treating the verb *want* as analogous to *hope* or *wish* in terms of finite complemen-

tation; p. 207) [although this particular instantiation of this factor seems to conflict with the preference for "tenseless clauses" cited earlier—DL];
• "the TL facts. The evidence from the target language may be misleading" (p. 211). In the case of restrictions on adverb placement, for example, the apparent lack of restrictions on adverbs appearing in various positions in English (other than between the verb and object) may mislead the learner into thinking they should also be able to appear in the unacceptable *SVAO order as well—a classic poverty of the stimulus problem.

Looking over this mixed bag of a list, there is nothing to suggest that there are any restrictions or constraints on what might constitute a possible factor, or over what domains or levels of analysis to formulate such effects, or how to more precisely define them or extend them to cover other situations in order to make testable predictions. An example from Patty's data further illustrates the problem.

Let us try to consider how the MEP would account for different kinds of 3SG pronominal specification in English—distinctions for case (e.g., *he* vs. *him*), gender (e.g., *he* vs. *she*), and number (*he* or *she* vs. *they*).[4] Regarding Patty, let us note that her native Chinese languages Mandarin and Hokkien (as well as Indonesian and Cantonese) have no morphological marking on pronouns for either case or gender, although they do for number. The MEP would seemingly predict that Patty would completely acquire number marking. However, both gender and case marking would likely be equal candidates for fossilization in Patty's English idiolect: Specifically, she should fail to acquire these distinctions because they are not present in her L1. (Whether this would be the right prediction, however, is admittedly not even clear, because one of the possible co-factors for stabilization leading to fossilization listed above is perceived similarity between native and target languages, with similarity having a detrimental, or fossilizing, effect.)

Patty's number marking on pronouns in English is indeed fine, as predicted. She does mix up pronominal gender (e.g., using *he* for *she* and vice versa), and this error appears to have fossilized, as also predicted. However, her overt case marking on pronouns is completely targetlike (as observed in chap. 3), contrary to expectation. How can the MEP explain this mixed result?

---

[4] I have omitted discussion of the 3SG neuter pronoun *it*. Patty does not confuse it with the other genders or with plural, and it has no case distinctions.

First, we have to determine whether the MEP applies. Selinker and Lakshmanan suggest, for example, that if researchers come across tense-less clauses and empty categories in the L2 data, then "our explanations begin with *seeing if the MEP applies*" (p. 202; italics added). But if the only way to see whether it applies is to look for L1 transfer and any other ill-defined, poorly delimited possible effect at virtually any level of analysis, then of course the principle is circular and ultimately unfalsifiable. There are no independent criteria proposed for deciding whether it applies, other than to see if language transfer has occurred. (However, this is un-fortunately also a part of the MEP we would want to test—its part B.)

In Patty's case, (spoken) Chinese does not distinguish between gender on pronouns, so it would be quite easy to chalk up her confusion to L1 transfer—a lack of overt gender marking.[5] Because case, gender, and number are all synthetically fused in English pronouns, we have a reasonably good control on the relative quantity of input for each morpho-syntactic feature—if Patty is exposed to positive evidence (overt marking) for case, for example, then she is also simultaneously exposed to evidence for gender and number as well. The problem, however, is that case should be the hardest feature to acquire if we are basing our MEP predictions on the occurrence of similarly overt marking in the native language. As argued in chapter 3, case distinctions on subjects in English are determined as a function of another formal feature—finiteness. Chinese does not have overt morphological reflexes for either case or finiteness (and perhaps, predictably, Patty's finiteness inflection on verbs has also fossilized well below target norms). Nonetheless, pronominal case is perfectly realized, including on subjects as a function of finiteness.

---

[5] Actually, the situation is even more complex and, with respect to Patty's English, a little more interesting. Although spoken Chinese does not distinguish gender on 3SG pronouns, it does in writing, and Patty is literate in Chinese. Whereas gender confusion (i.e., substitution) is a frequent error in her spoken English, there are no such errors in her written English. In this case, is something like knowledge of spoken versus written modality (i.e., a "literacy factor") transferring from the native language? Or is this error simply performance-related in terms of language-processing pressures that exist in spoken but not written L2 production situations? Patty's performance in written versus spoken production is higher in some aspects of her data, such as past-tense marking, a feature that is thought by many researchers to be nonexistent (to an equal extent) in both spoken and written Chinese. Although either the different modality/literacy factor or the performance factor (or both) could be potential "multiple effects" in the MEP model, that model provides us with no a priori way to determine this in principle, especially when compared with Patty's perfect performance in both speaking and writing on pronominal case, which is also in no way overtly marked in Chinese.

We could appeal to a UG-based explanation that makes use of abstract, non-overtly realized features such as [+finite] (as in Lardiere, 1998a; chap. 3 of this volume), and/or complexity of the morphological derivation (or mapping) (as in Lardiere, 1998a, 2000, 2005, to appear). However, both the "UG factor" and the "morphological factor" have been proposed as among those multiple effects leading to fossilization as applied to the specific cases outlined in Selinker and Lakshmanan (1993). How in principle, then, could we predict whether such factors will facilitate or hinder acquisition? (Whether we should even try to make such predictions, i.e., whether or not this is a realistic research goal is another matter I will have a little more to say about later. At the least, it seems likely to me that each individual case will in fact require its own customized post-hoc analysis, of the sort carried out in some of the studies cited by Selinker & Lakshmanan, 1993.[6])

Finally, we might ask what the MEP was formulated to be a principle or theory *of*. Positing that fossilization results from more than one factor is not a language-acquirer-centered theory, in the sense that it does not seem designed to account for learner knowledge states (or I-language)—that is, how a learner is actually mentally representing an IL grammar. In sum, the MEP is currently too vaguely formulated and unconstrained to be elevated to the status of a principle that can be of much theoretical use to us in explaining L2 fossilization (or fossilizability). It may, however, be rather more useful in offering a (very) broad heuristic or strategy for researchers who are attempting to investigate L2 knowledge: Start with the L1 to see whether anything has appeared to transfer. Although this research tactic is more appropriate and likely to yield higher dividends for earlier stages of acquisition, rather than for end-state idiolects, L1 effects are indeed often claimed to persist among individual learners (see, for example, the Prosodic Transfer and Representational Deficit hypotheses just discussed).

---

[6] But independently of the issue of fossilization per se. It is not clear that any of the studies cited by Selinker and Lakshmanan (1993) involved end-state L2 grammars; indeed, some involved studies of L2 acquisition by young children for which claims of fossilization would be absurdly premature. Selinker and Lakshmanan (1993) of course realize this, writing: "But in contrast to what we proposed in the case of the adult L2 speakers, in the case of the child L2 speakers, we predict that the MEP will result in stabilization leading to possible *development* (and not fossilization)" (p. 207; italics original). How stabilization leads to development in children is not discussed. But if the very same multiple effects can lead to completely different outcomes for child L2 versus adult L2 acquirers, then fossilization would appear to have little to do with the purported effects under consideration, including L1 transfer, and rather much more to do with the difference(s) between learning a language as a child or as an adult.

For some additional discussion on trying to characterize the learnability conditions under which L1 effects are likely to persist, we turn next to another case study.

More on Full Transfer/Full Access and Fossilization

As discussed earlier in chapter 3, another way to account for fossilization that also heavily privileges the role of native language transfer was suggested by Schwartz and Sprouse (1994, 1996) as a consequence of their Full Transfer/Full Access (FT/FA) hypothesis. Assuming that knowledge of the L1 grammar constitutes the initial state of second language acquisition, Schwartz and Sprouse hypothesize that grammar restructuring, in terms of moving from the L1 properties and feature values to those of the target language, requires positive evidence. That is, without evidence from the input that the TL differs from the L1 in some relevant respect, the learner might simply hang on to the L1 property or alternatively come up with some other nontargetlike representation of the L2 grammar. (It seems that both paths are possible, although it is not yet clear why. I return to this point below.) In that case, they suggest, fossilization will result:

> In brief, given that the starting point is not simply open (or set to learning-theoretically delearnable 'defaults'), it may be that the L2 acquirer (L2er) will never be able to arrive at the TL grammar: either the data needed to force restructuring simply do not exist... or the positive data needed are highly obscure, being very complex and/or rare. This view can then account for (aspects of) fossilization in L2 acquisition... (Schwartz & Sprouse, 1996, p. 42).

We asked earlier (in chap. 3) what the authors meant by the term *Full Access* if fossilization could result due to the absence (obscurity, etc.) of the positive data needed to force restructuring—a poverty-of-the-stimulus problem that had led researchers to posit the necessity of UG in the first place. Let us now turn to that question in a little more detail, taking a closer look at Schwartz and Sprouse's analysis. Although the discussion that follows is somewhat technical, the general conclusion I hope to convince the reader of is that the explanation for fossilization advanced by Schwartz and Sprouse is at best incomplete, and would not nearly suffice to account for Patty's end-state L2 outcome. Another objective will be to step back momentarily from Patty's case in particular, in order to take a broader and more critical look at the usefulness of parameter (re)setting in general as a theoretical construct for explaining acquisition (or acquisition failure).

Cevdet: A case study of the acquisition of L2 German word order

The relevant data that gave rise to Schwartz and Sprouse's (1994, 1996) suggestion about fossilization came from a longitudinal (early-state) case study of Cevdet, an adult native Turkish speaker acquiring German. Schwartz and Sprouse (1994) investigated Cevdet's acquisition of word order in German, specifically finite V2 placement in main clauses. They examined declarative clauses with two or more nonverbal constituents; thus, the correct order in German would be either $SV_{[+fin]}X$ or $XV_{[+fin]}S$ (where X could be either an object or another constituent such as an adverb or prepositional phrase).

Three distinct developmental stages were observed over the course of approximately 2 years.[7] In Stage 1, subjects always preceded verbs in Cevdet's production data. This would not be inconsistent with German V2 order if these subjects were always the first element in the clause; however, in 22% of these utterances, there was another constituent preceding the subject, yielding an incorrect *XSV order, or what we refer to as *V3. An example from Cevdet's data at this stage is shown in (5):

(5) *jetzt   er   hat   Gesicht ...   (Schwartz & Sprouse, 1994, p. 335)
     now   he   has   face ...
     'now he makes a face...'

Schwartz and Sprouse analyze Cevdet's IL grammar at this stage as having the structure shown in (6):

(6)

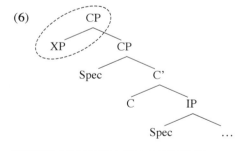

---

[7] In addition to these three stages, Schwartz and Sprouse posit an initial unobserved stage that occurred before data collection began. They hypothesize that, during this stage, which they call Stage 0, Cevdet's word order in main finite clauses would have been SOV, similar to his L1 Turkish. By the time of Stage 1, Cevdet was consistently raising finite verbs out of clause-final position in matrix clauses.

At Cevdet's Stage 1, the subject moved (invariably) into Spec, CP and the finite verb into C. What makes this representation different from German (and accounts for *V3 in Cevdet's production data) is that the subject is always preverbal at this stage, and that another constituent XP (such as an adverb or prepositional phrase) may be optionally adjoined to CP, as shown in the circled part of the tree in (6). Because German is a so-called strict V2 language, such optional CP-adjunction is disallowed.

During the second stage, which lasted nearly one year, Cevdet continued producing incorrect *V3 utterances; however, he also began to produce correct XVS order, but *only when the subjects were pronouns* (7). Nonpronominal (lexical) subjects, in contrast, were still nearly always preverbal (8):

(7) XVS$_{+pron}$ …
     dann   trinken   *wir*   bis   neun   Uhr
     then   drink   we   until   nine   o'clock
     'then we will drink until nine o'clock'

(8) *XSV …
     in der Türkei   *der Lehrer*   kann den Schüler   schlagen
     in the Turkey   the teacher   can   the   pupil to.beat
     'in Turkey the teacher can hit the pupil'

Schwartz and Sprouse argue that, in Cevdet's Stage 2, the asymmetrical split between pronominal and nonpronominal subjects could be analyzed in terms of a UG-constrained option—namely, that Cevdet was essentially representing a French-like grammatical option, in which pronouns but not lexical NPs appear to invert with the verb (in some French interrogative clauses), as in (9):[8]

(9) voit-il   un   chat?
     sees-he   a   cat
     'does he see a cat?'

At Stage 3, the latest stage for which the data are reported, Cevdet had begun to produce post-verbal nonpronominal subjects in correct XVS (i.e.,

---

[8] More precisely, their analysis is that the subject clitic in French incorporates into the verb in cases where the verb has moved from I to C (as in some French questions).

genuine V2) order. At this stage, Schwartz and Sprouse posited a V2-like representation for clauses with nonpronominal subjects (i.e., finite verb in C with an unincorporated subject in Spec, IP that was case-marked under government, as in German). However, this V2 pattern occasionally co-varied with persistent nontargetlike *V3 representations. Because of this, Schwartz and Sprouse argued that Cevdet's IL was still not "German," as he apparently continued to allow illicit CP-adjunction, as shown earlier for Stage 1.

On learnability and parameter resetting: Analyzing the data from Cevdet

We are now in a better position to understand what Schwartz and Sprouse (1994, 1996, 2000) appear to have in mind in regard to the Full Access part of the FT/FA hypothesis: In a learning environment characterized by some poverty of the stimulus, the learner will be able to choose from among (any) options made available by UG. Schwartz and Sprouse (2000) argue that Cevdet's Stage 2 word order has in fact arisen within a poverty-of-the-stimulus situation, since neither the L1 grammar nor the L2 input can account for the asymmetry between pronominal and nonpronominal subjects produced during this stage. Moreover, they argue, they find it "rather implausible" that this asymmetry would arise from a general problem-solving ability on the basis of Cevdet's exposure to German (Schwartz & Sprouse, 2000, p. 175). Regarding their claim of Full Access to UG, they write:

> Central to our claim that this analysis of the L2 data constitutes an argument for the Strong UG hypothesis is the fact that the inversion asymmetry is mirrored in at least one natural language grammar, viz., French. This observation is crucial because no matter what mechanisms syntactic theory may offer in the future to account for the asymmetry in French, these same mechanisms can be relied on to account for Cevdet's Stage 2 data. We therefore conclude that regardless of the precise formulation of syntactic theory, Cevdet's Interlanguage behavior can be accounted for only by assuming that his Interlanguage hypotheses are guided by UG. This is because it instantiates a UG-derived poverty-of-the-stimulus problem. (p. 175)

A couple of interesting issues now arise for us with respect to fossilization. First, we find on examining his production data that, even at Stage 3, Cevdet was about as likely to produce the incorrect *V3 (XSV) order as the correct V2 (XVS) order if the clause had a nonpronominal subject (11.5%

*V3 vs. 13% V2 in clauses with nonpronominal subjects).[9] Recall that, to account for persistent *V3 in the data, it was argued that Cevdet retained the possibility of adjunction to CP—an option not allowed in German. Schwartz and Sprouse (1996) offer a prediction that the persistence of *V3 might well fossilize in Cevdet's German, because there is nothing available in the input (specifically, neither any sort of negative or positive evidence) that could inform him that such CP-adjunction is ungrammatical. They write:

> Under such an analysis, we predict that [Cevdet's IL] will be subject to fossilization. There seem to be no input data that could force the delearning of adjunction to CP [...] Cevdet will not hear any utterances indicating that V3 is ungrammatical. On the assumption that negative data cannot ever effect the restructuring of grammar [...], XSV[+F] is a prime candidate for fossilization. Thus it is predicted that in regard to the strict V2 constraint, Cevdet's Interlanguage will never mirror that of the TL, German. By contrast, acquirers of German as a native language do not find themselves in this situation because they do not bring the full set of fixed UG parameters to the task of acquisition. (p. 49)

Let us consider this point more carefully for a moment. First, the implication here seems to be that optional CP-adjunction appears to be a *parametric* value that Cevdet's IL instantiates but German does not, and that this setting is part of Cevdet's full set of fixed UG parameters that he brings to the L2 acquisition of German from his L1. However, Schwartz and Sprouse (1994) themselves point out that adjunction to CP is *not* allowed in Turkish, Cevdet's L1.[10] So then where did this (particular) setting come from? If it is a developmental error, as they also suggest might be possible,[11] then it is

---

[9] The remaining 75% of relevant clauses were subject-initial clauses (SVX), which are uninformative with respect to V2 or non-V2 analyses (being compatible with both).

[10] They write: "On the basis of his analysis of scope facts, Kural (1992) argues that scrambling in Turkish may adjoin phrases to AGRP, *but not to CP*" (1994, pp. 323–324; italics added). In their later (1996) paper, they write that CP-adjunction is perhaps "a carry-over from the L1 (Turkish allows general scrambling)" (p. 47); thus, the relevant L1 analysis is unclear.

[11] Such adjunction might be "a standard mechanism for creating structure in the process of acquiring language" (Schwartz & Sprouse, 1996, p. 47, following Hoekstra & Jordens, 1994).

unclear what would prevent *native* language acquirers (of either German or Turkish) from positing it and what would cause them to subsequently delearn it. In this case, given full access to UG, we would not necessarily expect Cevdet's German IL to inevitably fossilize.

Furthermore, if the L1 is not the source of CP-adjunction, then under a Full Access approach within a principles-and-parameters framework, why wouldn't the L2 acquisition of nonpronominal XVS (posited in Stage 3) more or less automatically rule out (i.e., somehow push out of the grammar) the possibility of V3, as it does for native acquirers? Although each of these options presumably conforms to UG, one might wonder whether both V2 and V3 can legitimately (i.e., under a Full Access account) mutually co-exist under our current parameter-setting models.[12]

Whatever the correct technical details turn out to be, under a parameter-setting model of acquisition, some parameterized feature or combination of features would distinguish strict V2 languages from non-V2 languages (or non-strict V2 languages). It presumably excludes the opposite value from being simultaneously operative, and must necessarily be detectable in the input in order for parameter setting to take place (under any learning condition, i.e., for both L1 and L2 acquisition). Precisely because parameter setting must be input-driven, we would not expect this type of variable word-order fossilization to occur. Instead, the acquisition of the German V2 parameter setting(s) should in theory trigger the elimination of the non-V2 setting, including CP-adjunction. (Recall that this problem was brought up earlier in chap. 5 with respect to verb raising; see Schwartz & Gubala-Ryzak, 1992; White, 1991, 1992b). Parameter setting in principle would seem to entail all-or-nothing, mutually exclusive grammars (although more on this point below), and we do not observe this in the data from Cevdet over the particular developmental period reported on.

As a methodological issue, it is obvious that we would need to gather later-stage or end-state data in order to find out whatever ultimately became of Cevdet's German idiolect, so to speak. Thus, any discussion of fossilization, such as that by Schwartz and Sprouse in relation to Cevdet, is bound to be speculative (and in any case was not the primary focus of their investi-

---

[12] For example, under (somewhat) more recent theoretical assumptions, presumably there is a (parameterized) [+strong] feature in C in German, but not French (or Turkish), that attracts the finite verb to C in matrix declarative clauses. As Cevdet has reliably acquired this movement from the earliest stage observed, even his Stage 1 grammar could not now accurately be characterized as Turkish-like, as Schwartz and Sprouse (1996, p. 46) previously argued.

gation). Perhaps Cevdet was ultimately able to completely replace *V3 with strict V2, although of course we do not know this.

We do know that even in L1 acquisition, the acquisition of constructs associated with parameter setting is not necessarily instantaneous, and children go through stages of development in which their grammars appear to vary between the constructs of different stages and/or parameter values. Schwartz and Sprouse (2000) cite a longitudinal L1A case study by Schönenberger (1996) of two children acquiring Lucernese Swiss German, in which the children often and persistently produce verbs in embedded clauses in an incorrect position (although matrix clause verb placement is correct).[13] Schwartz and Sprouse (2000) refer to this type of error as a "developmental poverty-of-the-stimulus effect" in which children create intermediate grammars that diverge from the input; that is, "L1 children pass through stages that evince syntactic and semantic phenomena that are not solely input driven" (p. 170).

In Cevdet's case, since SVX order is not part of his L1 (in other words, he is not stuck with his L1 value), we might in this instance expect Full Access to mean that he would in fact eventually converge on the correct word-order target, as the children studied by Schönenberger presumably eventually do. But for those word orders hypothesized to be associated with particular parameter settings, such convergence depends on the theoretical assumption that a setting to one value will necessarily preclude the word-order possibilities associated with an alternative or opposite setting (even if this process takes some time over the course of development). Of course, this is also assuming that parameter setting is the correct way to model all word-order differences found across (and within) languages—not a trivial assumption and one that has turned out to be rather difficult to implement in actual practice.

Let us digress momentarily to illustrate and follow up on this point with native language data taken from Schönenberger's (1996) study cited above, as it has interesting implications for parameter-setting models of acquisition in general. According to Schönenberger, verb placement in embedded clauses in Swiss German is quite complex. The finite embedded verb appears in first (V1) position in cases of hypotheticals (with no com-

---

[13] This result is in sharp contrast to what had been previously reported in the literature for German L1 acquisition, which is that as soon as children begin producing embedded clauses, verb placement in them is nearly invariably correct. As is seen directly below, the input for embedded clauses provided to children acquiring Swiss German appears to be rather more ambiguous than for German.

plementizer present), under "emotive factive" matrix verbs (e.g., *gern ha* 'to like,' *bereue* 'to regret,' *hasse* 'to hate,' *sich freue* 'to be glad,' etc.), and in embedded questions (although this is marked for some speakers). It appears in V2 position under matrix bridge verbs when no complementizer is present (e.g., *säge* 'to say,' *meine* 'to believe,' *bhoupte* 'to claim,' etc.), or under certain matrix verbs expressing a wish or desire (e.g., *wöle* 'to want,' *gern ha* 'to like') when these are in the conditional form (the embedded verb is also put in the conditional form). In sentences introduced by *weisch* 'do you know,' V2 is also possible in embedded questions if the question is rhetorical (i.e., can be answered by the speaker). Otherwise (for genuine questions), the embedded verb appears clause-finally. In general, embedded clauses introduced by a complementizer, except for *wüu/weil* 'because,' require verbs in clause-final position; however, complement clauses introduced by *wüu/weil* allow verbs in third position (V3). Schönenberger notes that some of these conditions for embedded verb placement in Swiss German are similar to those in German, whereas others are different. In general, she observes, Swiss German is much more liberal than German in allowing V2 in embedded clauses; unlike German, it also allows doubly filled COMP and does not exhibit *that*-trace effects.

For purposes of theoretical syntactic analysis, these differences set up an analytical situation involving the necessity of fine-grained comparative "microparameters"—namely, those parameters that differentiate two closely related languages (Kayne, 2005)—and a learning situation that requires the mapping of various lexico-semantic and pragmatic features (e.g., "emotive factive predicate" or "rhetorical intent") and/or individual lexical items (e.g., *wüu/weil* 'because') to distinct microparametric values in particular languages.

Although I believe that this fine-grained mapping procedure is what the learning of a language actually does entail, it would seem to weaken the overall utility of the notion of *parameter* as a theoretical construct originally posited to ameliorate the difficulty of this very learning process. Kayne (2005), for example, writes: "I freely use the term 'parameter' to characterize all cross-linguistic syntactic differences, independently of the degree of 'drama' or range of effects associated with any particular parameter" (p. 6); furthermore, "every parameter is a microparameter" (p. 10). This view effectively weakens the mutual exclusivity requirement mentioned earlier. Or more precisely, it confines each (mutually exclusive) setting to such a tiny ("micro") domain that parameterization as a learnability-theoretical mechanism is reduced to a mere descriptive device for cataloguing small differences between languages, especially if no range of effects must be associated with them. For an expression of alarm regarding such microparameter-proliferation with respect to learnability, see Lightfoot

(1997, pp. 253–254). For arguments for the existence of macroparameters with deductive consequences (as opposed to only microparameters), see Baker (1996). For arguments that parameters are essentially metaphorical rather than psychologically real, see Haider (1993). In sum, there is little current agreement on the nature of parameters, a point I return to a little later in the chapter.

Now, returning to Cevdet's case and the likelihood that his L2 representations of German word order had fossilized, an interesting problem with what I will call the "French-representation" scenario is that it again does not appear to be inherited in any way from Cevdet's L1. Recall that, for Schwartz and Sprouse (1994, 1996, 2000), establishing the UG-constrained nature of Cevdet's grammar in the face of a poverty-of-the-stimulus problem was of primary importance. This was accomplished by their arguing that the curious asymmetry with the clauses with pronominal subjects was analyzable in terms of an existing natural language—namely, French—and therefore was the expression of an option made available by UG.

Going beyond Schwartz and Sprouse's original goal for a moment, however, one might well ask: Why French? It is difficult to see how this particular option could have been predicted. Cevdet's native language was Turkish, a language with SOV word order that is very different from that of French. Indeed, the fact that Cevdet's IL data were *not* like his L1, nor like the (totality of the) target language input, was used by Schwartz and Sprouse (2000) to argue for the existence of poverty-of-the-stimulus effects. Yet if neither the L1 nor the input could have given rise to the different representations for pronominal versus nonpronominal subjects, then it is also not clear whether there is anything in principle that could predictably rule out the same sort of French-representation analysis for *native* German speakers as well.[14] Is it the case, then, that any learner could, in principle, pull any UG-option for any language out of a hat?

A major disadvantage of this sort of "any UG-option" analysis is that it can only be determined after the fact by looking at the data and then finding some natural language that the data resemble. Although the data are UG-constrained, we are left without any explanation for why a particular language option was chosen and, just as problematically, why only a small piece of a parameter setting for a particular language can be surgically excised without regard for its place in the larger intricate system of that lan-

---

[14] Although there might be independent reasons for why young children would acquire pronouns later than lexical NPs, such as later acquisition of knowledge about how deixis works.

guage's own interacting parameter values or features, presumed deductive consequences, and associated effects.[15]

Although Schwartz and Sprouse are correct in arguing that there is no asymmetry between pronouns and non-pronouns either in Turkish or in the German target language environment taken as a whole, in fact, the input is not really poor. Cevdet's production data reflect his analysis of a proper subset of the input (i.e., main clauses with pronominal subjects, as Schwartz & Sprouse, 1994, point out). The fact that there is an asymmetry in the data can be taken as evidence for Cevdet's having isolated (for whatever reasons, e.g., frequency, processing constraints on length, etc.) such a subset. Why should he analyze this particular subset of clauses as being like *French* rather than German, given both his prior L1 knowledge and the particular target language environment?

Schwartz and Sprouse (1994) suggest that the answer to this is that the French-like subject-clitic incorporation option allows this subset of sentences to be separated out from the others in the first place, by providing a way to assign them a representation (pp. 353–354). They prefer this account, on grounds of learner conservatism, to one that would assign a more German-like representation from the start (in this case, at Cevdet's Stage 2) to just a portion of the data (in this case, to main clauses with pronominal subjects), since there would then be no way to explain why the rest of the data did not reflect it more generally. Their account would seem to predict that even native German acquirers would assign the same sort of French-like representation to this subset of the data at the relevant developmental stage, although we don't really know this (Schwartz & Sprouse leave the possibility open).

It seems likely that pronominal subjects are present at a considerably higher frequency than nonpronominal subjects in the target language environment; Cevdet himself produces pronominal subjects at nearly twice the rate of lexical ones. Other studies (e.g., Hoekstra & Jordens, 1994), have found that movement operations such as scrambling are acquired gradually, applying only to certain subsets of the data at a time—in this case, to pronouns first as well (p. 137). If we assume that the learner's analysis can proceed in this rather stepwise or piecemeal sort of fashion over some parts

---

[15] Assuming Schwartz and Sprouse's French-like analysis for Cevdet's Stage 2, for example, we would have to explain further why Cevdet has adopted this analysis for *declarative* clauses, since in French, such I-to-C movement of verbs with incorporated subject clitics occurs in interrogative rather than in declarative clauses, entailing some interaction with a [+wh] or [+Q] feature.

of the data but not others (an assumption I am admittedly more comfortable with than the "French" option), then the poverty-of-the-stimulus problem for Cevdet's case drops away, as utterances with pronominal subjects are most definitely in the input.

This approach suggests that *some parts of the input are attended to and (re-)analyzed sooner or more readily than others* (at least for some period of time). This seems to me to be consistent with what we observe in language acquisition, and especially in adult second language acquisition. It would be consistent with Patty's data in the sense that many of the characteristics of her English idiolect that appear to have fossilized are indeed present in the target language environment. Thus, poverty-of-the-stimulus effects are not obviously at issue in her case. An explanation along the lines of a lack of, or differential, sensitivity to different parts of the input at different developmental stages offers a potentially more unified way to approach both the problem of why Cevdet treats pronominal subjects differently from nonpronominal ones at a certain point in time, and also why Patty has difficulty with inflectional affixes such as nonpast 3SG -*s* that are nonetheless clearly available in the linguistic environment.

Finally, there is nothing in Schwartz and Sprouse's (1994, 1996) approach to fossilization that would seem to account for or predict differences in ultimate attainment between child L2 acquirers and adults, at least if they share the same L1. Specifically, if Cevdet's German L2 word order were to fossilize and this was fully determined by his L1 representation for which no disconfirming data were available in the input, we would have no reason to predict that this outcome would differ from that of a child native Turkish speaker acquiring L2 German. Yet most researchers would be very reluctant to predict this, on the basis of numerous studies that have implicated some degree of maturational constraints on ultimate attainment in language acquisition. Schwartz and Sprouse (1996) write that "the problem with an explanation of fossilization based on a critical period is that it does not offer a sufficiently articulated theory of precisely which aspects of the TL can be acquired and which cannot" (p. 49). In fact, I think this is true.

I completely agree with Schwartz and Sprouse that a highly-articulated linguistic theory is needed to provide a framework for accurately describing these precise aspects and learners' mental representations of their L2 grammars in general. (This would be a property theory as discussed, for example, by Carroll, 2001, and Gregg, 1993.) I also think that studies of the sort conducted by Schwartz and Sprouse (and others) have established that L2 grammars are likely to be UG-constrained at all stages of development. However, a better-articulated psycholinguistic theory is also needed, in order to explain why fossilization happens at all even in the face of abundant positive evidence, and why its likelihood does appear to be roughly correlated with age (with exceptions, albeit typically involving intensive formal study), at least for certain linguistic domains (see e.g., Birdsong, 1999; Birdsong & Molis, 2001; Johnson & Newport, 1989; Johnson, Shenkman, Newport, & Medin, 1996; Long, 1990; Weber-Fox & Neville, 1999, among others).

In terms of learnability, Schwartz and Sprouse may be correct that learners bringing a full set of fixed UG parameters to the L2 acquisition task from the L1 will get stuck if there is no positive evidence available that could force restructuring or resetting. (See also White, 1989, for an earlier similar claim.) This conclusion depends to some extent on one's theory of parameters and their role in learnability—specifically, whether parameter values are mutually exclusive, whether positive evidence for one particular parameter setting will preclude another, and whether this kind of knowledge constitutes part of Full Access. (If so, learners should *not* get stuck on features involving mutually exclusive parameter values.) In any case, however, we will still require an additional independent explanation for why certain aspects of language that are obviously present in the linguistic environment may nonetheless fail to be successfully or categorically acquired—a learning problem that largely characterizes Patty's particular case.

Summary

L1-oriented explanations of L2 ultimate attainment—whether taking the form of contrasts in L1–L2 feature strength, parameter (re-)setting, or in how features or structures are combined and expressed in different languages—all comprise a renewed form of comparative or contrastive analysis that has an important role to play in determining exactly which aspects of a particular grammatical representation are likely to be affected, just in case fossilization does occur.[16] That is, were fossilization to occur, speakers

---

[16] This variant of contrastive analysis is hopefully more on the right track—that is, presumably operates on a more explanatory level of analysis (representational, as constrained by a highly-articulated linguistic theory)—than the arguably more superficial contrastive comparisons of previous research (e.g., that of Fries, 1945; Lado, 1957) subsequently labeled *Contrastive Analysis*. The inability of the Contrastive Analysis Hypothesis to accurately predict fossilization was eventually perceived as a fatal flaw of CAH research, which equated L1–L2 similarity with ease of acquisition and differences with difficulty (Lado, 1957). As I argue below, however, even current L1-based approaches are not necessarily able to predict whether fossilization will or will not occur (or at least, so far, they have not succeeded). For interesting arguments in the service of "rectify[ing] our understanding" and "misrepresentation" of Fries and Lado's ties to linguistic and psycholinguistic theory, particularly behaviorism, see Thomas (2005). *(Continued)*

of one language may well be more likely to represent XYZ than speakers of a different language with diametrically (or perhaps parametrically) opposed feature values.

Under the Full Transfer/Full Access Hypothesis, fossilization is predicted in principle by any lack of available disconfirming evidence in the input for learners' existing L1 representations—a classic poverty of the stimulus approach. For Representational Deficit and Prosodic Transfer approaches, learners are predicted to fail even if positive evidence for a feature or structure that the L1 lacks is available in the input. (This is more categorically so for the Representational Deficit approach, which does tie the permanent inability to acquire new features to maturational factors.) None of these approaches, however, can really tell us the *extent* to which individual speakers within any particular L1 group will succeed or fail in achieving targetlike L2 representations, or cope with the problem of individual variability.

In Patty's case, the evidence for many properties of English is clearly available in the target language environment, but her production (at least) of these remains highly variable. It is still not clear why certain forms are produced less readily than others, at certain percentages of suppliance in obligatory contexts, or differently in speaking versus writing, for individual learners. I do agree with my colleagues that L1 transfer is likely to play a substantial role here. Yet I have personally met other native Chinese speakers whose adult-acquired English is truly near-nativelike, exhibiting near-categorical suppliance of inflections in obligatory contexts in spoken production, for example. Patty herself, recall, is highly literate in both Chinese and English. Despite her variable morphosyntactic omissions and pronunciation difficulties, a richly developed patina of literacy suffuses both her spoken and written English, which may well have aided her on, say, processing the complex sentences involved in rendering acceptability judgments for subjacency violations.

These observations suggest that L1-based representations do not necessarily ultimately determine the L2 end-state grammar, although they almost surely do constrain it in some ways at various points in development, perhaps including at the end state. The data moreover suggest that some L1

Suffice it to say that the approaches outlined in the sections above—the Representational Deficit/Failed Functional Features Hypotheses, the Prosodic Transfer Hypothesis, the Multiple Effects Principle, and the Full Transfer/Full Access Hypothesis—amply demonstrate that the role of L1 transfer in SLA research has since been fully rehabilitated. This is a welcome development from my early grad student days when one could scarcely even utter the word "transfer" in polite generative company.

representations can concurrently co-exist with fully developed targetlike representations in the L2, as we saw, for example, in the case of relative clause formation and passivization in Patty's English idiolect. A role for input sensitivity that takes several factors into account in addition to the L1, such as age-related maturational constraints and type of input, is also required, as has been argued by Long (2003), for example. (I turn to this issue in the next section.) Even so, it may never be possible to accurately predict when fossilization of certain forms will actually occur, or the rate of variability of any given construction, for any given learner.

Variability and Sensitivity to Input in Adult Language Acquisition

For German V2 acquisition, as mentioned earlier, the relevant positive evidence to which learners must be exposed consists of XVS (i.e., non-subject-initial) sentences. According to Lightfoot (1994, 1997), statistical counts show that about 30% of V2 clauses in the input in German are of this type. In historical language contact situations, where the incidence of XVS sentences in the environment has dropped below this level, the strict V2 property was lost. Thus, Lightfoot (1997) argues, we can hypothesize that about 30% XVS input is the critical threshold needed to determine (and maintain, in historical terms) the V2 property (or parameter setting), at least for child acquirers (p. 265). But what about for adult acquirers? What if a 30% rate of occurrence is not a high enough threshold for deducing a categorical V2 requirement? Perhaps adults are more attuned to the possibility that 30% represents some sort of exception to a different generalization—exemplified in the remaining 70% (or so) of the input—that subjects must precede verbs. We do not know. Positive evidence informs adult learners that XVS-order sentences are indeed possible in the target language, but also that such sentences are outnumbered by SVX ones by more than a two-to-one margin.

In an interesting study that sought to test to what extent child and adult language learners reproduced inconsistency or instead categorically regularized the inconsistency in the input they were exposed to (as might occur in a creolization context), clear differences were claimed to be observed between children and adults (Hudson & Newport, 1999; Hudson Kam & Newport, 2005). In their first experiment, the authors randomly assigned adult native English speakers learning a miniature artificial language to one of four exposure conditions, in which learners were presented with different percentages of determiners. (These were actually more like noun-class suffixes of two class-types that co-occurred—or not—with nouns that had been randomly assigned to either class.)

The incidence of co-occurrence of a determiner with a noun for the four conditions was 45%, 60%, 75%, and 100%, respectively. In the absence of any detectable semantic, morphological, or phonological cues that could guide learners as to the source of the inconsistency (a situation obviously quite different from the learning of an actual natural language), most of the adults ended up closely matching on a sentence-production task whatever rate of determiner omission they had been exposed to. In other words, adults generally used determiners in their production about as often as they heard them in the input. Only those learners exposed to the perfect (100%) condition produced them categorically.

Moreover, the results of a sentence-judgment task corroborated those of the production task: Learners accepted sentences with missing determiners if they had been exposed to the variable input conditions, and this rate of acceptance increased the lower the rate of occurrence of determiners had been in the exposure condition. Interestingly, learners in all conditions judged sentences with missing determiners to be better than sentences in which the determiners occurred in the wrong position (preceding instead of following the noun). This particular result mirrors several production data findings in both the L1 and L2 acquisition literature (see Lardiere, 2000, for some discussion). It is also compatible with the past-tense-marking data of Patty reported in chapter 4, where it was observed that, although she omits such marking frequently, it is typically correct when she supplies it.

In contrast to the adults tested, when this experiment was (partially) replicated by Hudson Kam and Newport (2005) with child learners (ages 5–7), the authors reported that most of the children systematically regularized their output, either producing or omitting the determiner, or even imposing patterns on their own output that simply did not exist in the input, such as supplying determiners depending on whether the sentential verb was transitive or intransitive. The authors concluded that, whereas adults do not regularize perceived variability as they learn a language, children "prefer regularity in language and sometimes perceive or produce such regularity even when it is not present in their input" (Hudson Kam & Newport, 2005, p. 184). Children also judged determiner use "more categorically" than adults (p. 184), and also preferred sentences with missing determiners to those with incorrectly positioned ones. However, because the number of subjects tested in this experiment was very small (only four adults in each of two input conditions), these results must be viewed as preliminary and interpreted with caution.[17]

Now, an obvious question arises for us in regard to equating regular versus variable production with language knowledge: Does inconsistent production necessarily reflect a lack of knowledge of a particular linguistic structure or feature? Hudson and Newport (1999) offer an interesting answer to our question, pointing out that "the source of the *structures* may not be the same as the source of the *consistency* and *obligatoriness*" (p. 266; italics original). They view the drive for categorical consistency as part of non-language-specific processing or general learning mechanisms that are likely to be distinct from the (possibly innate) language-specific notions the mechanisms employ (such as *verb transitivity*).

If confirmed by further study, these findings would suggest that a strong preference for categorical consistency is a characteristic of children, but not adults. Indeed, judging from these experiments, adults appear quite "comfortable" with non-conditioned (i.e., random) variability, but this might not reflect anything having to do with a UG-constrained operation. In sum, it looks as if indeed there is a strong maturational component in adult L2 ultimate attainment, and when purely linguistic factors are removed from the picture, we might be able to predict the likely rate of variability quite precisely.

Clearly, however, linguistic factors *are* part of the picture in real language-learning situations. Adult second language learners must acquire the complex conditioning factors for the appropriate suppliance of some form, since such forms—while they may occur variably in the input—do not typically occur randomly within the natural languages being acquired. Take, for example, the acquisition of real determiners in a real natural language such as English. Learners will have to acquire (or transfer) knowledge of (in)definiteness, specificity, quantification and the count/mass distinction, pragmatic ability to take an interlocutor's point of view into account, allophonic variation, clitic-like morphological behavior in suffixing to the first element in a DP, and weird lexically conditioned idiosyncrasies such as the tendency to co-occur with the names of larger bodies of water (*the Atlantic Ocean, the Baltic Sea*), but not smaller ones (*Lake Erie, Walden Pond,*

---

[17] In the second Hudson Kam and Newport (2005) experiment, there were only two input conditions for determiner suppliance: 100% (no variability) and 60%. As a reviewer has pointed out to me, children in the 100% input condition were actually less systematic than the adults, who all responded systematically. In the variable input condition, children were more likely to be systematic than the adults (71.3% vs. 50%, respectively). Thus, replication studies with larger sample sizes would be most welcome.

Puget Sound, Gloucester Harbor), among other factors I have probably neglected to mention. (In fact it is this latter category of lexical idiosyncrasy that accounts for much of Patty's variability in producing determiners. Since such occurrence in the linguistic environment *is* largely unpredictable, then, given Hudson and Newport's results, perhaps we should not be at all surprised by Patty's variable usage in this respect.)

The Representational Deficit and the Prosodic Transfer Hypotheses are in fact hypotheses implicating a diminished sensitivity to properties of the input—namely, to certain linguistic features that do not already exist in the L1 (or perhaps exist in some different sort of configuration). In effect, the representation of L1 properties appears to (at least partially) "blind" the learner to alternative ways of perceiving or analyzing the data to which they are exposed.

Long (2003) cites sensitivity to input as "the most likely explanation for fossilization" (p. 516), a critical factor in accounting for the individual variation we find among learners in ultimate attainment and a "key component" of language aptitude, which he claims is one of the better predictors of success in SLA:

> Sensitivity to input is arguably a key component of aptitude…. In fact three of the four components which [J.B.] Carroll proposed made up language aptitude could be viewed as involving input sensitivity: phonetic coding ability, grammatical sensitivity, and inductive language learning ability…. A thorough test of the current hypothesis would require a validated measure of sensitivity to input, with scores predicted to be lower for learners whose ILs revealed longer periods of stabilization. (p. 517)

But as Long points out, because the degree of input sensitivity is presumably a stable characteristic of any individual learner's aptitude, it cannot account for why only some forms and structures are affected, but not others. Therefore, he argues, we also need a theory that distinguishes the different degrees of perceptual salience of target structures, comprising factors such as frequency, communicative value, and semantic weight. "In sum," he writes, "the interaction of *input sensitivity* (a constant within the individual, but varying across individuals) with *perceptual saliency* (which varies across structures) has the potential to account for stabilization or fossilization of some structures, but not others, observed in some individuals, but not others" (p. 517, italics original). This combination, he argues, "should predict accurately which classes of linguistic elements are more likely to stabilize (or fossilize) than others" (p. 517).

Here again we encounter the possibility, as I mentioned earlier, that we can make broad predictions about "which elements are more likely to stabilize or fossilize" *if such fossilization were to occur* for those particular elements. Unfortunately, however, we still cannot predict whether or not it actually will, or precisely to what extent—that is, what percentages of variability we are likely to expect—for any particular learner. I remain rather pessimistic that the various factors cited by Long as comprising perceptual salience can be objectively quantified or operationalized in a way such that they would actually be perceived equally by all learners (or at least those with the same MLAT score), as if they were entities "out there" in the world rather than a function of individual learners' own perceptions filtered through the lens of their own experience, processing capacities, and preexisting linguistic representations. Thus, a native speaker of a language that does not allow consonant clusters or prosodic word-internal adjunction structures might well perceive the English data differently than one whose native language does, no matter how frequently such clusters are present in the linguistic environment.[18]

Moreover, given the complexity of the constellation of linguistic correlates from various domains that might be associated with any particular target structure, as sketched above for English determiners, it is not at all clear that we could assign to each of them a relative weight in calculating predictions of variability. (And that is assuming we have described all these correlates accurately, which is questionable.) In short, the ability to accurately predict fossilization—whether and to what exact extent or degree of variability it will occur for particular target structures in the L2 idiolects of particular learners, beyond simply stating (theoretically motivated) tendencies for certain L1–L2 pairings—may simply be an unrealistic goal.[19]

---

[18] Carroll (2001) makes a similar point, noting that "we will not understand the nature of SLA by studying the putatively objective properties of the stimulus. What matters for language acquisition is how such stimuli are analyzed" (pp. 15–16).

[19] Aside from the value such statements might bring to supporting or disconfirming various linguistic or psycholinguistic analyses, as discussed in the next section, it may also be useful to establish such tendencies for pedagogical purposes, as appeared to be one of the goals of the original Contrastive Analysis program. Regarding the predictive power (or lack thereof) of the myriad variables cited in his paper, Long (2003) writes:

> Some might claim that while very few, if any, variables can successfully predict stabilization or fossilization, a variety … can genuinely account for individual cases after the fact. Put another way, stabilization and/or fossilization might be caused by different factors in different individuals and/or grammatical subsystems and/or discourse domains. Quite apart from the unwelcome enormous increase in

(Continued)

A Different Goal?

What, then, should be the goal of the study of ultimate attainment in adult second language acquisition? Hawkins (2001b) suggests that focusing on the differences (and also, I would suggest, the similarities) in outcomes between L1 and (adult) L2 acquisition from within a UG perspective can lead to "real progress in understanding the nature of SLA and may even shed light on the structure and organization of the innate language faculty" (p. 346). Recall from chapter 1 that, following Caramazza (1986), one of the ultimate goals toward which nearly all acquisitionists strive to contribute is the (collective) formulation of a functional architecture of the human mind/brain that specifies the componential structure of a cognitive system (p. 47). I take these goals to be ones that the data from Patty could potentially make a small contribution to, at least in terms of trying to determine the right questions to ask for future research. I think that a review of the data from Patty (and also from other cases, such as Wes and Cevdet) leads us to a partial list of logically possible conclusions that include the following:

• Although all stages of L2 development are UG-constrained, the notion of "full access" might not necessarily include full knowledge of parameter setting, or at least that the setting to one value should automatically preclude another. Alternatively (and frankly more likely, in my view), something is wrong with our formulation of particular parameters, or perhaps with our parameter-setting model in general. The existence of micro- vs. macro-parameters, associated clustering effects, constraints on what constitutes a possible parameter, how parameters are set, and so on are all still unresolved matters of considerable theoretical debate.

---

the power of the theory such a stance allows ... with data potentially being "explicable" after the fact by any variables the theorist likes—anything goes and no claim is falsifiable—to take this stance is to forget that fossilization is supposedly a cognitive mechanism affecting all L2 learners, albeit manifesting itself in a variety of linguistic domains in different learners. (pp. 527–528)

Now, Long proceeds to make it quite clear that he is skeptical of fossilization as a "cognitive mechanism" and so am I. But I also think—however unfortunate for our theory-building hopes—that divergent outcomes in L2 ultimate attainment are indeed exactly likely to be caused by "different factors in different individuals and/or grammatical subsystems." At the very least, as a small first step it would be helpful to amass several more long-term longitudinal case studies in the literature for which detailed after-the-fact analyses and subsequent meta-analyses could be carried out.

• For both L1 and L2 acquisition, the particular knowledge of a language attained includes large portions of that language that lie outside the scope of UG, especially if this is defined in minimalist terms as narrow computation in the syntax. If so, we require additional models to account for this other kind of knowledge.

• Maturational changes in the learner may influence the ability to perceive or statistically calculate the criterial percentage of information needed for deriving a categorical generalization, resulting in variability. (The degree of variability for any particular learner appears to be unpredictable.)

• Native language effects may persist into the L2 end state. Although L1 influence may indeed inhibit the eventual acquisition of some aspects of the target language by some learners, this is apparently not a necessary outcome. It also appears that L1 representations (where these have not been completely supplanted by the L2) can continue to co-exist alongside fully developed (nativelike) L2 representations, and that these are not necessarily mutually exclusive.

These conclusions pose questions that are not by any means answered by the available data—only raised—and chart a potential course for further research within the generative paradigm.

Additionally, data from adult second language learners provide us with a window onto the human language faculty that is not necessarily afforded to us by child language acquirers. For example, one well-known hypothesis about the language faculty is that it consists of autonomous levels of representation. (For a highly detailed exposition with particular relevance to SLA, see Carroll, 2001, following Jackendoff, 1987, 1992; see also Jackendoff, 1997). Because children ultimately acquire everything in the languages they are exposed to, and within a relatively condensed period of time, it is more difficult to differentiate these various components and tease apart their properties.

In terms of these components, Patty's data appear to support the modularity of grammatical subsystems (e.g., knowledge of phonology, morphology, syntax, lexicon, semantics, pragmatics, etc.) and the interface "translation" procedures for mapping one area to another. The data show that some domains are more susceptible to fossilization than others. In Patty's case, the mapping or translation procedures from abstract syntactic features to the morphophonological spell-out of (affixal) inflection seems most vulnerable, whereas the development of clausal phrase structure and knowledge of the features responsible for structural configurations and movement (e.g., non-raising of lexical verbs vs. raising of *be*, use of *do*-support, subject-aux inversion or I-to-C movement, placement of adverbs and negation, *wh*-movement and relative clause formation, preposition stranding, etc.) have been largely successfully acquired. In short, the lack of fully successful or categorical acquisition in one or more formal domains (phonology, morphology) has not hindered or precluded further development in another (syntax). This result suggests that these domains are not linked in the way that linguistic theory has previously suggested, as discussed in chapter 3.

In addition to the support the data lend to a modularity hypothesis, we might ask what the presence of consistency where it *does* exist in the data can tell us. One very strong (probably too strong) conjecture is the following: For end-state idiolects in which we observe both highly variable and highly consistent degrees of performance, those areas that are acquired perfectly or near-perfectly are the best candidates for being most closely tied to UG-constrained knowledge, whereas the more highly variable ones are not. Assuming optimal exposure conditions, as in Patty's case, this might be because the format of UG-constrained language knowledge can scarcely be otherwise. On the other hand, in those areas where we encounter pervasive omissions, this might be due to non-language-specific processing mechanisms as suggested by Hudson and Newport's research, discussed above. Clearly, both parts of the picture—a theory of UG-constrained representation and a processing theory—are needed to explain the data. (See Carroll, 2001, for a particularly heroic effort.)

Perhaps this conjecture will turn out to be completely mistaken. The field clearly needs additional long-term case studies. To my knowledge, there is not a single long-term study of adult second language acquisition from initial to steady state under optimal exposure conditions. Thus, I hope the interested reader will consider doing one.

Postscript

I wanted the last words in this book to be about Patty, rather than about linguistic or psycholinguistic theory. I am often asked whether Patty realizes the extent to which her English is non-nativelike. The answer is yes and, in a way, no. Patty is well aware that her pronunciation is different from that of native speakers and that she often omits morphological inflection. She herself feels that she writes more accurately than she speaks. As we have observed, this self-assessment is largely borne out by the data examined in these pages. What she lacks is any "non-nativelike" sense of limitation or expectation that her expressive capacity in her adopted language will be compromised. Again, she is largely right about this, too.

Several years ago, Patty sent me an essay entitled "Mother Tongue," by the novelist Amy Tan (1995), because she thought it would interest me and prove relevant to my study of her English idiolect. I decided I would try to work it into this book somewhere, and this seems like the right place.

In this essay, Tan, a first-generation American, describes the evolution of her own perceptions of the limitations of her immigrant mother's "broken" L2 English. She points out that her mother "reads the *Forbes* report, listens to *Wall Street Week*, converses daily with her stockbroker, reads all of Shirley MacLaine's books with ease—all kinds of things I can't begin to understand." On giving more thought to the kind of English her mother speaks, she realizes she finds it "perfectly natural … vivid, direct, full of observation and imagery" (p. 316). In Tan's own writing, she explains, she tries to imagine the essence of her mother's internal language—what her mother's own translation of her native Chinese would be if only she could speak in "perfect" English.

I like this essay, and the fact that Patty also found it moving and meaningful enough to send to me, and I sometimes use it in my classes. For those who wonder whether Patty is aware of "what her English sounds like," Tan's words, sent via Patty, are the closing ones I would like to pass along: "I wanted to capture what language ability tests can never reveal: her intent, her passion, her imagery, the rhythms of her speech and the nature of her thoughts."

References

Abney, S. (1987). *The English noun phrase in its sentential aspect*. Unpublished doctoral dissertation, Massachusetts Institute of Technology.

Alexiadou, A. (1997). *Adverb placement: A case study in anti-symmetric syntax*. Amsterdam: John Benjamins.

Andersen, R. W. (1991). Developmental sequences: The emergence of aspect marking in second language acquisition. In T. Huebner & C. A. Ferguson (Eds.), *Crosscurrents in second language acquisition and linguistic theories* (pp. 305–324). Amsterdam: John Benjamins.

Andersen, R. W. & Shirai, Y. (1996). The primacy of aspect in first and second language acquisition: The pidgin-creole connection. In W. C. Ritchie & T. K. Bhatia (Eds.), *Handbook of second language acquisition* (pp. 527–570). San Diego, CA: Academic Press.

Aoun, J. & Li, Y.-H. A. (2003). *Essays on the representational and derivational nature of grammar*. Cambridge, MA: MIT Press.

Archibald, J. (1993). *Language learnability and L2 phonology: The acquisition of metrical parameters*. Dordrecht: Kluwer.

Archibald, J. & Young-Scholten, M. (2003). The second language segment revisited. *Second Language Research* 19, 163–167.

Aronoff, M. (1994). *Morphology by itself*. Cambridge, MA: MIT Press.

Atkinson, M. (1996). Now, hang on a minute: Some reflections on emerging orthodoxies. In H. Clahsen (Ed.), *Generative perspectives on language acquisition* (pp. 451–485). Amsterdam: John Benjamins.

Bailey, N., Madden, C., & Krashen, S. (1974). Is there a "natural sequence" in adult second language learning? *Language Learning* 24, 235–243.

Baker, M. C. (1988). *Incorporation*: *A theory of grammatical function changing*. Chicago: University of Chicago Press.

Baker, M. C. (1996). *The polysynthesis parameter*. New York: Oxford University Press.

Baker, M. C. (2003). *Lexical categories: Verbs, nouns, adjectives*. Cambridge: Cambridge University Press.

Bardovi-Harlig, K. (1995). A narrative perspective on the development of the tense/aspect system in second language acquisition. *Studies in Second Language Acquisition* 17, 263–291.

Bardovi-Harlig, K. (1998). Narrative structure and lexical aspect: Conspiring factors in second language acquisition of tense-aspect morphology. *Studies in Second Language Acquisition* 20, 471–508.

Bardovi-Harlig, K. (2000). *Tense and aspect in second language acquisition: Form, meaning and use.* Malden, MA: Blackwell.

Bardovi-Harlig, K. & Reynolds, D. W. (1995). The role of lexical aspect in the acquisition of tense and aspect. *TESOL Quarterly* 29, 107–131.

Bayley, R. J. (1991). Variation theory and second language learning: Linguistic and social constraints on interlanguage tense marking. Unpublished doctoral dissertation, Stanford University.

Bayley, R. J. (1996). Competing constraints on variation in the speech of adult Chinese learners of English. In R. J. Bayley & D. Preston (Eds.), *Second language acquisition and linguistic variation* (pp. 97–120). Amsterdam: John Benjamins.

Beard, R. (1995). *Lexeme-morpheme base morphology.* Albany, NY: SUNY Press.

Beck, M.-L. (1997). Regular verbs, past tense and frequency: Tracking down a potential source of NS/NNS competence differences. *Second Language Research* 13, 93–115.

Beck, M.-L. (1998). L2 acquisition and obligatory head movement: English-speaking learners of German and the Local Impairment Hypothesis. *Studies in Second Language Acquisition* 20, 311–348.

Belletti, A. & Hamann, C. (2000). *Ça on fait pas!* On the L2 acquisition of French by two young children with different source languages. In S. C. Howell, S. A. Fish, & T. Keith-Lucas (Eds.), *Proceedings of the 24th annual Boston University Conference on Language Development* (pp. 116–127). Somerville, MA: Cascadilla Press.

Bialystok, E. & Hakuta, K. (1994). *In other words: The science and psychology of second-language acquisition.* New York: Basic Books.

Bialystok, E. & Hakuta, K. (1999). Confounded age: Linguistic and cognitive factors in age differences for second language acquisition. In D. Birdsong (Ed.), *Second language acquisition and the critical period hypothesis* (pp. 161–181). Mahwah, NJ: Lawrence Erlbaum Associates.

Bickerton, D. (1996). A dim monocular view of Universal Grammar access. *Behavioral & Brain Sciences* 19, 716–717.

Birdsong, D. (1989). *Metalinguistic performance and interlanguage competence.* New York: Springer.

Birdsong, D. (1999). Introduction: Whys and why nots of the critical period hypothesis for second language acquisition. In D. Birdsong (Ed.), *Second language acquisition and the critical period hypothesis* (pp. 1–22). Mahwah, NJ: Lawrence Erlbaum Associates.

Birdsong, D. (2004). Second language and ultimate attainment. In A. Davies & C. Elder (Eds.), *The handbook of applied linguistics* (pp. 82–105). Malden, MA: Blackwell.

Birdsong, D. (2006). Why not fossilization. In Z-H. Han & T. Odlin (Eds.), *Studies of fossilization in second language acquisition* (pp. 173–188). Clevedon: Multilingual Matters.

Birdsong, D. & Molis, M. (2001). On the evidence for maturational constraints in second language acquisition. *Journal of Memory & Language* 44, 235–249.

Bley-Vroman, R. (1983). The comparative fallacy in interlanguage studies: The case of systematicity. *Language Learning* 33, 1–17.

Bobaljik, J. D. (1999). Adverbs: The hierarchy paradox. *Glot International* 4 (9/10), 27–28.

Bobaljik, J. D. (2001). The implications of rich agreement: Why morphology doesn't drive syntax. In K. Megerdoomian & L. A. Bar-el (Eds.) *Proceedings of WCCFL 20*. Somerville, MA: Cascadilla Press.

Bobaljik, J. D. (2002). Realizing Germanic inflection: Why morphology does not drive syntax. *Journal of Comparative Germanic Linguistics* 6, 129–167.

Bodman, N. C. (1987). *Spoken Amoy Hokkien*. Ithaca, NY: Spoken Language Services, Inc.

Borer, H. (1996). Access to Universal Grammar: The real issues. *Brain & Behavioral Sciences* 19, 718–720.

Borer, H. & Rohrbacher, B. (1997). Features and projections: Arguments for the full competence hypothesis. In E. Hughes, M. Hughes, & A. Greenhill (Eds.), *Proceedings of the 21st annual Boston University Conference on Language Development* (pp. 24–35). Somerville, MA: Cascadilla Press.

Bromberg, H. S. & Wexler, K. (1995). Null subjects in child *wh*-questions. *MIT Working Papers in Linguistics* 26, 221–247.

Brown, C. (2000). The interrelation between speech perception and phonological acquisition from infant to adult. In J. Archibald (Ed.), *Second language acquisition and linguistic theory* (pp. 4–63). Malden, MA: Blackwell.

Brown, R. (1973). *A first language: The early stages*. Cambridge, MA: Harvard University Press.

Caramazza, A. (1986). On drawing inferences about the structure of normal cognitive systems from the analysis of patterns of impaired performance: The case for single-patient studies. *Brain and Cognition* 5, 41–66.

Carroll, J. B. (1965). The prediction of success in foreign language training. In R. Glaser (Ed.), *Training, research, and education* (pp. 87–136). New York: Wiley.

Carroll, J. B. (1981). Twenty-five years of research on foreign language aptitude. In K. Diller (Ed.), *Individual differences and universals in language learning aptitude* (pp. 83–118). Rowley, MA: Newbury House.

Carroll, S. E. (2001). *Input and evidence: The raw material of second language acquisition*. Amsterdam: John Benjamins.

Chao, Y.-R. (1970). *Language and symbolic systems*. Cambridge: Cambridge University Press.

Chapelle, C. & Green, P. (1992). Field independence/dependence in second language acquisition research. *Language Learning* 42, 47–83.

Cheng, L. L.-S. & Sybesma, R. (1999). Bare and not-so-bare nouns and the structure of NP. *Linguistic Inquiry* 30, 509–542.

Chomsky, N. (1986). *Knowledge of language: Its nature, origin and use.* New York: Praeger.

Chomsky, N. (1995). *The Minimalist Program*. Cambridge: MA, MIT Press.

Chomsky, N. (1998). Minimalist inquiries: The framework. *MIT Working Papers in Linguistics*, 15, 1–56.

Chomsky, N. (1999). Derivation by phase. *MIT Occasional Papers in Linguistics*, 18.

Cinque, G. (1999). *Adverbs and functional heads: A crosslinguistic perspective*. Oxford: Oxford University Press.

Clahsen, H. (1990/1991). Constraints in parameter setting: A grammatical analysis of some acquisition stages in German child language. *Language Acquisition* 1, 351–391.

Clahsen, H., Eisenbeiss, S., & Penke, M. (1996). Lexical learning in early syntactic development. In H. Clahsen (Ed.), *Generative perspectives on language acquisition* (pp. 85–118). Amsterdam: John Benjamins.

Clahsen, H. & Penke, M. (1992). The acquisition of agreement morphology and its syntactic consequences. In J. Meisel (Ed.), *The acquisition of verb placement: functional categories and V2 phenomena in language acquisition* (pp. 181–223). Dordrecht: Kluwer.

Clahsen, H., Penke, M., & Parodi, T. (1993/1994). Functional categories in early child German. *Language Acquisition* 3, 395–429.

Clément, R, Dörnyei, Z., & Noels, K. A. (1994). Motivation, self-confidence, and group cohesion in the foreign language classroom. *Language Learning* 44, 417–448.

Comrie, B. (1976). *Aspect*. Cambridge: Cambridge University Press.

Corder, S. P. (1983). A role for the mother tongue. In S. Gass & L. Selinker (Eds.), *Language transfer in language learning* (pp. 18–31). Amsterdam; John Benjamins.

de Haan, G. R. (1987). A theory bound approach to the acquisition of verb placement in Dutch. In G. R. de Haan & W. Zonneveld (Eds.), *Formal parameters of generative grammar III*. Utrecht: University of Utrecht.

DeKeyser, R. M. (2000). The robustness of critical period effects in second language acquisition. *Studies in Second Language Acquisition* 22, 499–533.

Dekydtspotter, L., Sprouse, R. A., & Anderson, B. (1997). The interpretive interface in L2 acquisition: The process-result distinction in English-French interlanguage grammars. *Language Acquisition* 6, 297–332.

Dekydtspotter, L., Sprouse, R. A., & Anderson, B. (1998). Interlanguage A-bar dependencies: Binding construals, null prepositions and Universal Grammar. *Second Language Research* 14, 341–358.

deVilliers, J. G. & deVilliers, P. A. (1973). A cross-sectional study of the acquisition of grammatical morphemes in child speech. *Journal of Psycholinguistic Research* 2, 267–278.

Döpke, S. (1998). Competing language structures: The acquisition of verb placement by bilingual German-English children. *Journal of Child Language* 25, 555–584.

Dörnyei, Z. (1994). Motivation and motivating in the foreign language classroom. *The Modern Language Journal* 78, 273–283.

Dulay, H. & Burt, M. (1974) Natural sequences in child second language acquisition. *Language Learning* 24, 37–53.

duPlessis, J., Solin, D., Travis, L., & White, L. (1987). UG or not UG, that is the question: A reply to Clahsen & Muysken. *Second Language Research* 3, 56–75.

Dus&kova, L. (1984). Similarity—an aid or hindrance in foreign language learning? *Folia Linguistica* 18, 103–115.

Eubank, L. (1993/1994). On the transfer of parametric values in L2 development. *Language Acquisition* 3, 183–208.

Eubank, L. (1994). Optionality and the initial state in L2 development. In T. Hoekstra & B. D. Schwartz (Eds.), *Language acquisition studies in generative grammar* (pp. 369–388). Amsterdam: John Benjamins.

Eubank, L. (1996). Negation in early German-English interlanguage: More valueless features in the L2-initial state. *Second Language Research* 12, 73–106.

Eubank, L., Bischoff, J., Huffstutler, A., Leek, P., & West. C. (1997). "Tom eats slowly cooked eggs": Thematic verb-raising in L2 knowledge. *Language Acquisition* 6, 171–199.

Eubank, L., Cliff, S., Collins, G., Ellis, M., Seo, E.-J., Tamura, A., & Yates, K. (1998). Grammaticality judgments and verb raising: If it feels good, raise it. Paper presented at the Second Language Research Forum (SLRF), University of Hawaii, October.

Eubank, L. & Grace, S. T. (1998). V-to-I and inflection in non-native grammars. In M.-L. Beck (Ed.), *Morphology and its interface in L2 knowledge* (pp. 69–88). Amsterdam: John Benjamins.

Eubank, L. & Gregg, K. R. (1995). 'Et in amygdala ego'?: UG, (S)LA, and neurobiology. *Studies in Second Language Acquisition* 17, 35–57.

Eubank, L. & Gregg, K. R. (1999). Critical periods and (second) language acquisition: Divide et impera. In D. Birdsong (Ed.), *Second Language Acquisition and the Critical Period Hypothesis* (pp. 65–99). Mahwah, NJ: Lawrence Erlbaum Associates.

Flege, J. E. (1999). Age of learning and second language speech. In D. Birdsong (Ed.), *Second Language Acquisition and the Critical Period Hypothesis* (pp. 101–131). Mahwah, NJ: Lawrence Erlbaum Associates.

Francis, W. N. & Kuc&era, H. (1982). *Frequency analysis of English usage: lexicon and grammar.* Boston: Houghton Mifflin.

Freidin, R. (1999). Cyclicity and minimalism. In S. D. Epstein & N. Hornstein (Eds.), *Working minimalism* (pp. 95–126). Cambridge, MA: MIT Press.

Fries, C. C. (1945). *Teaching and learning English as a second language.* Ann Arbor, MI: University of Michigan Press.

Gardner, R. C. (1985). *Social psychology and second language learning: The role of attitudes and motivation.* London: Edward Arnold.

Gavruseva, L. & Lardiere, D. (1996). The emergence of extended phrase structure in child L2 acquisition. In A. Stringfellow, D. Cahana-Amitay, E. Hughes, & A. Zukowski (Eds.), *Proceedings of the 20th annual Boston University Conference on Language Development* (pp. 225–236). Somerville, MA: Cascadilla Press.

Gerbault, J. (1978). *The acquisition of English by a five-year-old French speaker.* Unpublished master's thesis, UCLA.

Giorgi, A. & Pianesi, F. (1997). *Tense and aspect: From semantics to morphosyntax.* Oxford: Oxford University Press.

Goad, H. & White, L. (2004a). Ultimate attainment of L2 inflection: Effects of L1 prosodic structure. In S. Foster-Cohen, M. Sharwood Smith, A. Sorace, & M. Ota, (Eds.), *Eurosla Yearbook 4* (pp. 119-145). Amsterdam: John Benjamins.

Goad, H. & White, L. (2004b). (Non)nativelike ultimate attainment: The influence of L1 prosodic structure on L2 morphology. In A. Brugos, L. Micciula, & C. E. Smith (Eds.), *Proceedings of the 28th annual Boston University Conference on Language Development* (pp. 177–188). Somerville, MA: Cascadilla Press.

Goad, H. & White, L. (2005). Representational 'deficits' in L2: Syntactic or phonological? In A. Brugos, M. R. Clark-Cotton, & S. Ha (Eds.),

Proceedings of the 29th annual Boston University Conference on Language Development (pp. 216–227). Somerville, MA: Cascadilla Press.

Goad, H. & White, L. (to appear). Ultimate attainment in interlanguage grammars: A prosodic approach. *Second Language Research.*

Goad, H., White, L., & Steele, J. (2003). Missing inflection in L2 acquisition: Defective syntax or L1-constrained prosodic representations? *Canadian Journal of Linguistics* 48, 243–263.

Golinkoff, R. M., Hirsh-Pasek, K., & Schweisguth, M. A. (2001). A reappraisal of young children's knowledge of grammatical morphemes. In J. Weissenborn & B. Höhle (Eds.), *Approaches to bootstrapping: Phonological, syntactic and neurological aspects of early language acquisition* (pp. 167–188). Amsterdam: Benjamins.

Gregg, K. R. (1993). Taking explanation seriously; or, let a couple of flowers bloom. *Applied Linguistics* 14, 276–294.

Grondin, N. & White, L. (1996). Functional categories in child L2 acquisition of French. *Language Acquisition* 5, 1–34.

Guy, G. (1980). Variation in the group and the individual: The case of final stop deletion. In W. Labov (Ed.), *Locating language in time and space* (pp. 1–36). New York: Academic Press.

Haegeman, L. (1988). The categorial status of modals and L2 acquisition. In S. Flynn & W. O'Neil (Eds.), *Linguistic theory in second language acquisition.* Boston: Kluwer.

Haegeman, L. (1995). Root infinitives, tense and truncated structures. *Language Acquisition* 4, 205–255.

Haider, H. (1993). Principled variability—parametrization without parameter fixing. In G. Fanselow (Ed.), *The parametrization of Universal Grammar* (pp. 1–16). Amsterdam: John Benjamins.

Hale, K. (1988). Linguistic theory: Generative grammar. In S. Flynn & W. O'Neil (Eds.), *Linguistic theory in second language acquisition* (pp. 26–33). Dordrecht: Kluwer,.

Halle, M. & Marantz, A. (1993). Distributed morphology and the pieces of inflection. In K. Hale & S. J. Keyser (Eds.), *The view from Building 20: Essays in linguistics in honor of Sylvain Bromberger* (pp. 111–176). Cambridge, MA: MIT Press.

Hamann, C. & Plunkett, K. (1998). Subjectless sentences in child Danish. *Cognition* 69, 35–72.

Han, Z.-H. (2004). *Fossilization in adult second language acquisition.* Clevedon: Multilingual Matters.

Hannahs, S. J. & Young-Scholten, M. (Eds.). (1997). *Focus on phonological acquisition.* Amsterdam: John Benjamins.

Hawkins, R. (2000). Persistent selective fossilization in second language acquisition and the optimal design of the language faculty. *Essex Research Reports in Linguistics* 34, 75–90.

Hawkins, R. (2001a). *Second language syntax: A generative introduction.* Malden, MA: Blackwell.

Hawkins, R. (2001b). The theoretical significance of Universal Grammar in second language acquisition. *Second Language Research* 17, 345–367.

Hawkins, R. (2003). 'Representational deficit' theories of adult SLA: Evidence, counterevidence and implications. Plenary paper presented at EuroSLA, Edinburgh, September.

Hawkins, R. & Chan, Cecelia Y.-H. (1997). The partial availability of Universal Grammar in second language acquisition: The 'Failed Functional Features Hypothesis.' *Second Language Research* 13, 187–226.

Hawkins, R. & Liszka, S. (2000). More on the source of defective L2 past tense morphology. Paper presented at the 5th Generative Approaches to Language Acquisition Conference (GASLA 5), MIT, March–April.

Hawkins, R. & Liszka, S. (2003). Locating the source of defective past tense marking in advanced L2 English speakers. In R. van Hout, A. Hulk, F. Kuiken, & R. Towell (Eds.), *The lexicon-syntax interface in second language acquisition* (pp. 21–44). Amsterdam: John Benjamins.

Haznedar, B. (1997). L2 acquisition by a Turkish-speaking child: Evidence for L1 influence. In E. Hughes, M. Hughes, & A. Greenhill (Eds.), *Proceedings of the 21st annual Boston University Conference on Language Development* (pp. 245–256). Somerville, MA: Cascadilla Press.

Haznedar, B. (2001). The acquisition of the IP system in child L2 English. *Studies in Second Language Acquisition* 23, 1–39.

Haznedar, B. & Schwartz, B. D. (1997). Are there optional infinitives in child L2 acquisition? In E. Hughes, M. Hughes & A. Greenhill (Eds.), *Proceedings of the 21st annual Boston University Conference on Language Development* (pp. 257–268). Somerville, MA: Cascadilla Press.

Herschensohn, J. (2000). *The second time around: Minimalism and L2 acquisition.* Amsterdam: John Benjamins.

Hilles, S. (1991). Access to Universal Grammar in second language acquisition. In L. Eubank (Ed.), *Point counterpoint: Universal Grammar in the second language* (pp. 303–338). Amsterdam: John Benjamins.

Hoekstra, T. & Jordens, P. (1994). From adjunct to head. In T. Hoekstra & B. D. Schwartz (Eds.) *Language acquisition studies in generative grammar* (pp. 119–149). Amsterdam: John Benjamins.

Huang, C.-T. J. (1982). *Logical relations in Chinese and the theory of grammar.* Unpublished doctoral dissertation, Massachusetts Institute of Technology.

Huang, C.-T. J. (1984). On the distribution and reference of empty pronouns. *Linguistic Inquiry* 15, 531–574.

Huang, C.-T. J. (1987). Existential sentences in Chinese and (in)definiteness. In E. J. Reuland & A. G. B. ter Meulen (Eds.), *The representation of (in)definiteness* (pp. 226–253). Cambridge, MA: MIT Press.

Huang, C.-T. J. (1993). Reconstruction and the structure of VP. *Linguistic Inquiry* 24, 103–138.

Huang, C.-T. J. (1995). Logical form. In G. Webelhuth (Ed.), *Government and Binding theory and the Minimalist Program* (pp. 125–175). Malden, MA: Blackwell.

Huang, Y. (1994). *The syntax and pragmatics of anaphora: A study with special reference to Chinese.* Cambridge: Cambridge University Press.

Hudson, C. L. & Newport, E. L. (1999). Creolization: Could adults really have done it all? In A. Greenhill, H. Littlefield, & C. Tano (Eds.), *Proceedings of the 23rd annual Boston University Conference on Language Development* (pp. 265–276). Somerville, MA: Cascadilla Press.

Hudson Kam, C. L. & Newport, E. L. (2005). Regularizing unpredictable variation: The roles of adult and child learners in language formation and change. *Language Learning and Development* 1, 151–195.

Hyams, N. (1996). The underspecification of functional categories in early grammar. In H. Clahsen (Ed.), *Generative perspectives on language acquisition: Empirical findings, theoretical considerations, crosslinguistic comparisons* (pp. 91–127). Amsterdam: John Benjamins.

Iatridou, S. (1990). About AgrP. *Linguistic Inquiry* 21, 551–557.

Ionin, T. & Wexler, K. (2001). L1-Russian children learning English: Tense and overgeneration of 'be'. In X. Bonch-Bruevich et al. (Eds.), *The past, present and future of second language research: Selected proceedings of SLRF 2000* (pp. 76–94). Somerville, MA: Cascadilla Press.

Ionin, T. & Wexler, K. (2002). Why is 'is' easier than '-s'?: Acquisition of tense/agreement morphology by child second language learners of English. *Second Language Research* 18, 95–136.

Ioup, G. & Weinberger, S. (Eds.). (1987). *Interlanguage phonology.* Cambridge, MA: Newbury House.

Jackendoff, R. (1972). *Semantic interpretation in generative grammar.* Cambridge, MA: MIT Press.

Jackendoff, R. (1987). *Consciousness and the computational mind.* Cambridge, MA: MIT Press.

Jackendoff, R. (1992). *Languages of the mind.* Cambridge, MA: MIT Press.

Jackendoff, R. (1997). *The architecture of the language faculty*. Cambridge, MA: MIT Press.

Jain, M. (1974). Error analysis: Source, cause and significance. In J. C. Richards (Ed.), *Error analysis: perspectives on second language acquisition* (pp. 189–215). London: Longman.

Johnson, J. & Newport, E. L. (1989). Critical period effects in second language learning: The influence of maturational state on the acquisition of English as a second language. *Cognitive Psychology* 21, 60–99.

Johnson, J. & Newport, E. L. (1991). Critical period effects on universal properties of language: The status of subjacency in the acquisition of a second language. *Cognition* 39, 215–258.

Johnson, J., Shenkman, K., Newport, E. L., & Medin, D. (1996). Indeterminacy in the grammar of adult language learners. *Journal of Memory & Language* 35, 335–352.

Kanno, K. (1997). The acquisition of null and overt pronominals in Japanese by English speakers. *Second Language Research* 13, 265–287.

Kayne, R. S. (2005). Some notes on comparative syntax, with special reference to English and French. In G. Cinque & R. S. Kayne (Eds.), *The Oxford handbook of comparative syntax* (pp. 3–69). Oxford University Press.

Kellerman, E. (1989). The imperfect conditional: Fossilization, crosslinguistic influence, and natural tendencies in a foreign language setting. In K. Hyltenstam & L. Obler (Eds.), *Bilingualism across the lifespan* (pp. 87–115). Cambridge: Cambridge University Press.

Kierman, F. A. (1969). Night-thoughts on the passive. *Unicorn* 5, 72–78.

Klein, E. C. (1993). *Toward second language acquisition: A study of null prep*. Dordrecht: Kluwer.

Klein, E. C. (2001). (Mis)construing null prepositions in L2 intergrammars: A commentary and proposal. *Second Language Research* 17, 37–70.

Klein, W. (1994). *Time in language*. London: Routledge.

Klein, W. (1998). The contribution of second language acquisition research. *Language Learning* 48, 527–550.

Klein, W. (2000). An analysis of the German Perfekt. *Language* 76, 358–382.

Klein, W. & Purdue, C. (1997) The basic variety or, couldn't language be much simpler? *Second Language Research* 13, 301–347.

Koptjevskaja-Tamm, M. (1993). *Nominalizations*. London: Routledge.

Koptjevskaja-Tamm, M. (1994). Finiteness. In R. E. Asher (ed.), *The encyclopedia of language and linguistics* (pp. 1254–1248). New York: Pergamon.

Kornfilt, J. (1997). *Turkish*. London: Routledge.

Krämer, I. (1993). The licensing of subjects in early child language. In C. Phillips (Ed.), *Papers on case and agreement* (Vol. 2), *MIT Working Papers in Linguistics* 19, 197–212.

Kuhn, S. T. & Portner, P. (2002). Tense and time. In D. Gabbay & F. Guenther (Eds.), *Handbook of philosophical logic* (Vol. 7) (pp. 277–346). Dordrecht: Reidel.

Kuong, I.-K. (2002). On existential *you* in Chinese. In F.-H. Liu (Ed.), *Proceedings of the 14th North American Conference on Chinese Linguistics (NACCL-14)* (pp. 158–175). GSIL, University of Southern California.

Kuong, I.-K. (2006). Clausal peripheries and resumptives: A cross-linguistic study of topic-comment structures. Unpublished doctoral dissertation, Georgetown University.

Kural, M. (1992). Properties of scrambling in Turkish. Unpublished manuscript, University of California, Los Angeles.

Labov, W. (1989). The child as linguistic historian. *Language Variation and Change 1*, 85-98.

Lado, R. (1957). *Linguistics across cultures: Applied linguistics for language teachers.* Ann Arbor, MI: University of Michigan Press.

Laenzlinger, C. (1996). Adverb syntax and phrase structure. In A.-M. di Sciullo (Ed.), *Configurations: essays on structure and interpretation* (pp. 99–127). Somerville, MA: Cascadilla Press.

Lakshmanan, U. (1989). *Accessibility to Universal Grammar in child second language acquisition.* Unpublished doctoral dissertation, University of Michigan.

Lakshmanan, U. (2006). Child second language acquisition and the fossilization puzzle. In Z.-H. Han & T. Odlin (Eds.) *Studies of fossilization in second language acquisition* (pp. 100–133). Clevedon: Multilingual Matters.

Lardiere, D. (1998a). Case and tense in the 'fossilized' steady state. *Second Language Research* 14, 1–26.

Lardiere, D. (1998b). Dissociating syntax from morphology in a divergent end-state grammar. *Second Language Research* 14, 359–375.

Lardiere, D. (1999). Suppletive agreement in second language acquisition. In A. Greenhill, H. Littlefield, & C. Tano (Eds.), *Proceedings of the 23rd annual Boston University Conference on Language Development* (pp. 386–396). Somerville, MA: Cascadilla Press.

Lardiere, D. (2000). Mapping features to forms in second language acquisition. In J. Archibald (Ed.), *Second language acquisition and linguistic theory* (pp. 102–129). Malden, MA: Blackwell.

Lardiere, D. (2003a). Revisiting the comparative fallacy: A reply to Lakshmanan and Selinker, 2001. *Second Language Research* 19, 129–143.

Lardiere, D. (2003b). Second language knowledge of [±past] vs. [±finite]. In J. M. Liceras, H. Zobl, & H. Goodluck (Eds.), *Proceedings of the 6th Generative Approaches to Second Language Acquisition Conference (GASLA 2002)* (pp. 176–189). Somerville, MA: Cascadilla.

Lardiere, D. (2005). On morphological competence. In L. Dekydtspotter, R. A. Sprouse, & A. Liljestrand (Eds.) *Proceedings of the 7th Generative Approaches to Second Language Acquisition Conference (GASLA 2004)* (pp. 178–192). Somerville MA: Cascadilla Press.

Lardiere, D. (2006). Establishing ultimate attainment in a particular second language grammar. In Z.-H. Han & T. Odlin (Eds.), *Studies of fossilization in second language acquisition* (pp. 35–55). Clevedon: Multilingual Matters.

Lardiere, D. (to appear). Feature-assembly in second language acquisition. In J. Liceras, H. Zobl & H. Goodluck (Eds.), *The role of features in second language acquisition*. Mahwah, NJ: Lawrence Erlbaum Associates.

Larsen-Freeman, D. (2006). Second language acquisition and the issue of fossilization: There is no end, and there is no state. In Z.-H. Han & T. Odlin (Eds.), *Studies of fossilization in second language acquisition* (pp. 189–200). Clevedon: Multilingual Matters.

Lasnik, H. (1981). Restricting the theory of transformations: A case study. In N. Hornstein & D. W. Lightfoot (Eds.), *Explanations in linguistics* (pp. 152–173). London: Longman.

Leung, Y.-K. I. (2001). The initial state of L3A: Full transfer and failed features? In X. Bonch-Bruevich et al. (Eds.), *The past, present and future of second language research: Selected proceedings of SLRF 2000.* Somerville, MA: Cascadilla Press.

Li, C. & Thompson, S. (1981). *Mandarin Chinese: A functional reference grammar.* Berkeley, CA: University of California Press.

Li, X. (1998). Adult L2 accessibility to UG: An issue revisited. In S. Flynn, G. Martohardjono, & W. O'Neil (Eds.), *The generative study of second language acquisition* (pp. 89–110). Mahwah, NJ: Lawrence Erlbaum Associates.

Li, Y.-H. A. (1990). *Order and constituency in Mandarin Chinese.* Dordrecht: Kluwer.

Li, Y.-H. A. (2002). Word order, structure, and relativization. In S.-W. Tang & C.-S. L. Liu (Eds.), *On the formal way to Chinese languages* (pp. 45–73). Stanford: CSLI Publications.

Lightbown, P. & Spada, N. (1993). *How languages are learned.* Oxford: Oxford University Press.

Lightfoot, D. W. (1994). Degree-0 learnability. In B. Lust, G. Hermon, & J. Kornfilt (Eds.), *Syntactic theory and first language acquisition: crosslinguistic perspectives* (Vol. 2). Mahwah NJ: Lawrence Erlbaum Associates.

Lightfoot, D. W. (1997). Shifting triggers and diachronic reanalyses. In A. van Kemenade & N. Vincent (Eds.), *Parameters of morphosyntactic change* (pp. 253–272). Cambridge: Cambridge University Press.

Lightfoot, D. W. & Hornstein, N. (1994). Verb movement: An introduction. In D. W. Lightfoot & N. Hornstein (Eds.), *Verb movement* (pp. 1–17). Cambridge: Cambridge University Press.

Liszka, S. (2000). Explaining divergent tense marking in advanced L2 speakers. Unpublished manuscript, University of Essex.

Locke, J. L. (1995). Development of the capacity for spoken language. In P. Fletcher & B. MacWhinney (Eds.), *The handbook of child language* (pp. 278–302). Oxford: Blackwell.

Long, M. H. (1990). Maturational constraints on language development. *Studies in Second Language Acquisition* 12, 251–285.

Long, M. H. (2003). Stabilization and fossilization in interlanguage development. In C. J. Doughty & M. H. Long (Eds.), *Handbook of second language acquisition* (pp. 487–535). Malden, MA: Blackwell.

Ludlow, P. (1999). *Semantics, tense and time.* Cambridge, MA: MIT Press.

Lyons, C. (1999). *Definiteness.* Cambridge: Cambridge University Press.

Major, R. C. (2001). *Foreign accent: The ontogeny and phylogeny of second language phonology.* Mahwah NJ: Lawrence Erlbaum Associates.

Marantz, A. (1995). The minimalist program. In G. Webelhuth (Ed.), *Government and Binding theory and the Minimalist Program* (pp. 349–382). Malden, MA: Blackwell.

Martohardjono, G. (1993). *Wh-movement in the acquisition of a second language: A crosslinguistic study of three languages with and without movement.* Unpublished doctoral dissertation, Cornell University.

Meisel, J. M. (1994). Getting FAT: Finiteness, agreement and tense in early grammars. In J. M. Meisel (Ed.), *Bilingual first language acquisition: French and German grammatical development* (pp. 89–129). Amsterdam: John Benjamins.

Meisel, J. M. (1997). The acquisition of the syntax of negation in French and German: Contrasting first and second language acquisition. *Second Language Research* 13, 227–263.

Moyer, A. (2004). *Age, accent, and experience in second language acquisition: An integrated approach to critical period inquiry.* Buffalo, NY: Multilingual Matters.

Müller, N. (1998). UG access without parameter setting: A longitudinal study of (L1 Italian) German as a second language. In M.-L. Beck (Ed.), *Morphology and its interfaces in L2 knowledge* (pp. 115–161). Amsterdam: John Benjamins.

Newport, E. L. (1990). Maturational constraints on language learning. *Cognitive Science* 14, 11–28.

Ning, C. (1993). *The overt syntax of relativization and topicalization in Chinese.* Unpublished doctoral dissertation, University of California, Irvine.

Nunes, J. (1999). Linearization of chains and phonetic realization of chain links. In S. D. Epstein & N. Hornstein (Eds.), *Working minimalism* (pp. 217–249). Cambridge, MA: MIT Press.

Odlin, T. (1989). *Language transfer: Cross-linguistic influence in language learning.* Cambridge: Cambridge University Press.

Odlin, T. (2003). Cross-linguistic influence. In C. J. Doughty & M. H. Long (Eds.), *Handbook of second language acquisition* (pp. 436–486). Malden, MA: Blackwell.

Papafragou, A. (1998). Modality and misrepresentation. In A. Greenhill, M. Hughes, H. Littlefield, & H. Walsh (Eds.), *Proceedings of the 22nd annual Boston University Conference on Language Development* (pp. 610–620). Somerville, MA: Cascadilla Press.

Papafragou, A. & Li, P. (2002). Evidential morphology and theory of mind. In B. Skarabela, S. Fish, & A. H.-J. Do (Eds.), *Proceedings of the 26th annual Boston University Conference on Language Development* (pp. 510–520). Somerville, MA: Cascadilla Press.

Parrott, J. (2005). Beyond you and I: Distributed morphological mechanisms of pronoun variation. Paper presented at NWAV–34, New York University, October.

Pesetsky, D. & Torrego, E. (2001). T-to-C movement: Causes and consequences. In M. Kenstowicz (Ed.), *Ken Hale: A life in language* (pp. 355–426). Cambridge, MA: MIT Press.

Pesetsky, D. & Torrego, E. (2004). Tense, case, and the nature of syntactic categories. In J. Guéron & J. Lecarme (Eds.), *The syntax of time* (pp. 495–537). Cambridge, MA: MIT Press.

Phillips, C. (1995). Syntax at age two: Crosslinguistic differences. In C. Schütze, J. Ganger, & K. Broihier (eds.), *MIT Working Papers in Linguistics* 26, 325–382.

Phillips, C. (1996). Root infinitives are finite. In A. Stringfellow, D. Cahana-Amitay, E. Hughes, & A. Zukowski (Eds.), *Proceedings of the*

20th annual Boston University Conference on Language Development (pp. 588–599). Somerville, MA: Cascadilla Press.

Pienemann, M., Johnston, M., & Brindley, G. (1988). Constructing an acquisition-based procedure for second language assessment. *Studies in Second Language Acquisition* 10, 217–243.

Pierce, A. (1992). *Language acquisition and syntactic theory: A comparative analysis of French and English child grammars.* Dordrecht: Kluwer.

Pinker, S. & Prince, A. (1988). On language and connectionism: Analysis of a parallel distributed processing model of language acquisition. *Cognition* 28, 73–193.

Platzack, C. (1990). A grammar without functional categories: A syntactic study of early Swedish child language. *Nordic Journal of Linguistics* 13, 107–126.

Platzack, C. & Holmberg, A. (1989). The role of AGR and finiteness. *Working Papers in Scandinavian Syntax* 43, 51–76.

Plunkett, K. & Strömqvist, S. (1992). The acquisition of Scandinavian language. In D. I. Slobin (Ed.), *The crosslinguistic study of language acquisition* (Vol. 3) (pp. 457–556). Hillsdale, NJ: Lawrence Erlbaum Associates.

Poeppel, D. & Wexler, K. (1993). The full competence hypothesis of clause structure in early German. *Language* 69, 1–33.

Pollock, J.-Y. (1989). Verb movement, Universal Grammar and the structure of IP. *Linguistic Inquiry* 20, 365–424.

Prévost, P. (1997). *Truncation in second language acquisition.* Unpublished doctoral dissertation, McGill University.

Prévost, P. (2001). Morphological variability in child SLA: An account integrating truncation and missing inflection. In A. H.-J. Do, L. Domínguez, & A. Johansen (Eds.), *Proceedings of the 25th annual Boston University Conference on Language Development* (pp. 633–644). Somerville, MA: Cascadilla Press.

Prévost, P. & White, L. (1999). Finiteness and variability in SLA: More evidence for missing surface inflection. In A. Greenhill, H. Littlefield & C. Tano (Eds.), *Proceedings of the 23rd annual Boston University Conference on Language Development* (pp. 575–586). Somerville MA: Cascadilla Press.

Prévost, P. & White, L. (2000). Truncation and missing inflection in second language acquisition. In M. A. Friedmann & L. Rizzi (Eds.), *The acquisition of syntax* (pp. 202–235). London: Longman.

Progovac, L. (1993). Long-distance reflexives: Movement to Infl vs. relativized subject. *Linguistic Inquiry* 24, 755–772.

Pulvermüller, F. & Schumann, J. H. (1994). Neurobiological mechanisms of language acquisition. *Language Learning* 44, 681–734.

Pye, C. (2001). The acquisition of finiteness in K'iche' Maya. In A. H.-J. Do, L. Domínguez, & A. Johansen (Eds.), *Proceedings of the 25th annual Boston University Conference on Language Development* (pp. 645–656). Somerville, MA: Cascadilla Press.

Radford, A. (1990). *Syntactic theory and the acquisition of English syntax.* Oxford: Blackwell.

Radford, A. (1995). Children—architects or brickies? In D. MacLaughlin & S. McEwen (Eds.), *Proceedings of the 19th annual Boston University Conference on Language Development* (pp. 1–19). Somerville, MA: Cascadilla Press.

Radford, A. (1996). Phrase structure and functional categories. In P. Fletcher & B. MacWhinney (Eds.), *The handbook of child language* (pp. 483–507). Oxford: Blackwell.

Ramsey, S. R. (1987). *The languages of China.* Princeton, NJ: Princeton University Press.

Rice, K. (2000). *Morpheme order and semantic scope: Word formation in the Athapaskan verb.* Cambridge: Cambridge University Press.

Rizzi, L. (1990). *Relativized minimality.* Cambridge, MA: MIT Press.

Rizzi, L. (1993/1994). Some notes on linguistic theory and language development: The case of root infinitives. *Language Acquisition* 3, 371–393.

Robertson, D. (2000). Variability in the use of the English article system by Chinese learners of English. *Second Language Research* 16, 135–172.

Robison, R. E. (1990). The primacy of aspect: Aspectual marking in English interlanguage. *Studies in Second Language Acquisition* 12, 315–330.

Robison, R. E. (1995). The aspect hypothesis revisited: A cross-sectional study of tense and aspect marking in interlanguage. *Applied Linguistics* 16, 344–370.

Sano, T. & Hyams, N. (1994). Agreement, finiteness, and the development of null arguments. *Proceedings of NELS* 24 (pp. 543–558). Amherst, MA: GLSA.

Santelmann, L. & Jusczyk, P. (1998). 18-month-olds' sensitivity to relationships between morphemes. In A. Greenhill, M. Hughes, H. Littlefield, & H. Walsh (Eds.), *Proceedings of the 22nd annual Boston University Conference on Language Development* (pp. 663–674). Somerville, MA: Cascadilla Press.

Sato, C. (1984). Phonological processes in second language acquisition: Another look at interlanguage syllable structure. *Language Learning* 34, 43–57.

Sato, C. (1990). *The syntax of conversation in interlanguage development.* Tübingen: Gunter Narr.

Schachter, J. (1974). An error in error analysis. *Language Learning* 24, 205–214.

Schiffrin, D. (1981). Tense variation in narrative. *Language* 57, 45–62.

Schmidt, R. W. (1983). Interaction, acculturation, and the acquisition of communicative competence: a case study of an adult. In N. Wolfson & E. Judd (Eds.), *Sociolinguistics and language acquisition* (pp. 137–174). Rowley, MA: Newbury House.

Schmidt, R. W., Boraie, D., & Kassabgy, O. (1996). Foreign language motivation: internal structure and external connections. In R. L. Oxford (Ed.), *Language learning motivation: Pathways to the new century* (pp. 9–70). Honolulu, HI: University of Hawai'i at Manoa: Second Language Teaching and Curriculum Center.

Schönenberger, M. (1996). Why do Swiss-German children like verb movement so much? In A. Stringfellow, D. Cahana-Amitay, E. Hughes & A. Zukowski (eds.), *Proceedings of the 20th annual Boston University Conference on Language Development* (pp. 658–669). Somerville, MA: Cascadilla.

Schumann, J. H. (1978). The acculturation model for second language acquisition. In R. Gingras (Ed.), *Second language acquisition and foreign language learning* (pp. 27–50). Arlington, VA: Center for Applied Linguistics.

Schumann, J. H. (1986). Research on the acculturation model for second language acquisition. *Journal of Multilingual and Multicultural Development* 7, 379–392.

Schumann, J. H. (1995). Ad minorem theoriae gloriam: A response to Eubank and Gregg. *Studies in Second Language Acquisition* 17, 59–63.

Schumann, J. H. (1997). *The neurobiology of affect in language.* Malden, MA: Blackwell.

Schwartz, B. D. & Eubank, L. (1996). What is the L2 initial state? Introduction. *Second Language Research* 12, 1–5.

Schwartz, B. D. & Gubala-Ryzak, M. (1992). Learnability and grammar reorganization in L2A: Against negative evidence causing unlearning of verb movement. *Second Language Research* 8, 1–38.

Schwartz, B. D. & Sprouse, R. A. (1994). Word order and nominative case in nonnative language acquisition: A longitudinal study of (L1 Turkish) German interlanguage. In T. Hoekstra & B. D. Schwartz (Eds.), *Language acquisition studies in generative grammar* (pp. 317–368). Amsterdam: John Benjamins.

Schwartz, B. D. & Sprouse, R. A. (1996). L2 cognitive states and the Full Transfer/Full Access model. *Second Language Research* 12, 40–72.

Schwartz, B. D. & Sprouse, R. A. (2000). When syntactic theories evolve: Consequences for L2 acquisition research. In J. Archibald (Ed.), *Second language acquisition and linguistic theory* (pp. 156–186). Malden, MA: Blackwell.

Schwartz, B. D. & Tomaselli, A. (1990). Some implications from an analysis of German word order. In W. Abraham, W. Kosmeijer, & E. Reuland (Eds.), *Issues in Germanic syntax* (pp. 251–274). New York: Mouton de Gruyter.

Selinker, L. (1972). Interlanguage. *IRAL* 10, 209–231.

Selinker, L. & Lakshmanan, U. (1993). Language transfer and fossilization: The Multiple Effects Principle. In S. M. Gass & L. Selinker (Eds.), *Language transfer in language learning* (pp. 197–216). Amsterdam: John Benjamins.

Selinker, L. & Lamendella, J. (1979). The role of extrinsic feedback in interlanguage fossilization. *Language Learning* 29, 363–375.

Simpson, A. (2002). On the status of modifying DE and the structure of the Chinese DP. In S.-W. Tang & C.-S. L. Liu (Eds.), *On the formal way to Chinese languages* (pp. 74–101). Stanford: CSLI Publications

Slabakova, R. (2001). *Telicity in the second language*. Amsterdam: John Benjamins.

Smith, C. (1990). *The parameter of aspect*. Amsterdam: John Benjamins.

Smith, N. & Tsimpli, I.-M. (1995). *The mind of a savant*. Oxford: Blackwell.

Solà, J. (1996). Morphology and word order in Germanic languages. In W. Abraham, S. D. Epstein, H. Thráinsson, & C. J.-W. Zwart (Eds.), *Minimal ideas: Syntactic studies in the minimalist framework* (pp. 217–251). Amsterdam: John Benjamins.

Sorace, A. (2003). Near-nativeness. In C. Doughty and M. H. Long (Eds.), *The handbook of second language acquisition* (pp. 130–161). Malden, MA: Blackwell.

Sprouse, R. A. (1998). Some notes on the relationship between inflectional morphology and parameter setting in first and second language acquisition. In M.-L. Beck (Ed.), *Morphology and its interfaces in second language knowledge* (pp. 41–67). Amsterdam: John Benjamins.

Stowell, T. (1981). *Origins of phrase structure*. Unpublished doctoral dissertation, Massachusetts Institute of Technology.

Strange, W. (1995). *Speech perception and linguistic experience: Issues in cross-language research*. Timonium, MD: York Press.

Tan, A. (1995). Mother tongue. In G. Hongo (Ed.), *Under western eyes: Personal essays from Asian America* (pp. 313–320). New York: Anchor.

Thomas, M. (1991a). Do second language learners have "rogue" grammars of anaphora? In L. Eubank (Ed.), *Point counterpoint: Universal Grammar in the second language* (pp. 375–388). Amsterdam: John Benjamins.

Thomas, M. (1991b). Universal Grammar and the interpretation of reflexives in a second language. *Language* 67, 211–239.

Thomas, M. (2005). The "Ebeling Principle" in the historiography of generative second language acquisition theory. Unpublished manuscript, Boston College.

Thráinsson, H. (1996). On the (non-)universality of functional categories. In W. Abraham, S. D. Epstein, H. Thráinsson. & C. J.-W. Zwart (Eds.), *Minimal ideas: Syntactic studies in the minimalist framework* (pp. 253–281). Amsterdam: John Benjamins.

Tincoff, R., Santelmann, L. & Jusczyk, P. (2000). Auxiliary verb learning and 18-month-olds' acquisition of morphological relationships. In S. Howell, S. Fish, & T. Keith-Lucas (Eds.), *Proceedings of the 24th annual Boston University Conference on Language Development* (pp. 726–737). Somerville, MA: Cascadilla Press.

Tomaselli, A. & Schwartz, B. D. (1990). Analyzing the acquisition stages of negation in L2 German: Support for UG in adult SLA. *Second Language Research* 6, 1–38.

Trahey, M. & White, L. (1993). Positive evidence and preemption in the second language classroom. *Studies in Second Language Acquisition* 15, 181–204.

Trask, R. L. (1993). *A dictionary of grammatical terms in linguistics*. New York: Routledge.

Travis, L. (2003). Lexical items and zero morphology. In J. M. Liceras, H. Zobl, & H. Goodluck (Eds.), *Proceedings of the 6th Generative Approaches to Second Language Acquisition Conference (GASLA 2002)* (pp. 315–330). Somerville, MA: Cascadilla.

Travis, L. (2005). Articulated vPs and the computation of Aktionsart. In P. Kempchinsky & R. Slabakova (Eds.), *Aspectual inquiries* (pp. 69–94). New York: Springer.

Tremblay, P. F. & Gardner, R. (1995). Expanding the motivation construct in language learning. *Modern Language Journal* 79, 505–520.

Tsang, C.-L. (1981). *A semantic study of modal auxiliary verbs in Chinese*. Unpublished doctoral dissertation, Stanford University.

Tsimpli, I.-M. (2003a). Clitics and determiners in L2 Greek. In J. M. Liceras, H. Zobl, & H. Goodluck (Eds.), *Proceedings of the 6th Generative Approaches to Second Language Acquisition Conference (GASLA 2002)* (pp. 331–339). Somerville, MA: Cascadilla.

Tsimpli, I.-M. (2003b). Features in language development. Invited plenary talk presented at EuroSLA, Edinburgh, September.

Tsimpli, I.-M. & Roussou, A. (1991). Parameter resetting in L2? *UCL Working Papers in Linguistics* 3, 149–169.

Ullman, M. T. (2001a). The declarative/procedural model of lexicon and grammar. *Journal of Psycholinguistic Research* 30, 37–69.

Ullman, M. T. (2001b). The neural basis of lexicon and grammar in first and second language: The declarative/procedural model. *Bilingualism: Language & Cognition* 4, 105–122.

Underhill, R. (1976). *Turkish grammar*. Cambridge, MA: MIT Press.

Vainikka, A. (1993/1994). Case in the development of English syntax. *Language Acquisition* 3, 257–325.

Vainikka, A. & Young-Scholten, M. (1994). Direct access to X'-theory: evidence from Turkish and Korean adults learning German. In T. Hoekstra & B. D. Schwartz (Eds.), *Language acquisition studies in generative grammar* (pp. 265–316). Amsterdam: John Benjamins.

Vainikka, A. & Young-Scholten, M. (1996a). Gradual development of L2 phrase structure. *Second Language Research* 12, 7–39.

Vainikka, A. & Young-Scholten, M. (1996b). The early stages of adult L2 syntax: Additional evidence from Romance speakers. *Second Language Research* 12, 140–176.

Vainikka, A. & Young-Scholten, M. (1998). Morphosyntactic triggers in adult SLA. In M.-L. Beck (Ed.), *Morphology and its interfaces in second language knowledge* (pp. 89–113). Amsterdam: John Benjamins.

Valian, V. (1991). Syntactic subjects in the early speech of American and Italian children. *Cognition* 40, 21–81.

Vendler, Z. (1967). Verbs and times. In Z. Vendler (Ed.), *Linguistics and philosophy* (pp. 97–121). Ithaca, NY: Cornell University Press.

Verrips, M. & Weissenborn, J. (1992). Verb placement in early German and French: The independence of finiteness and agreement. In J. M. Meisel (Ed.), *The acquisition of verb placement: Functional categories and V2 phenomena in language acquisition* (pp. 283–331). Dordrecht: Kluwer.

Watanabe, A. (1992). Subjacency and S-structure movement of *wh*-in-situ. *Journal of East Asian Linguistics* 1, 255–291.

Weber-Fox, C. M. & Neville, H. J. (1999). Functional neural subsystems are differentially affected by delays in second language immersion: ERP and behavioral evidence in bilinguals. In D. Birdsong (Ed.), *Second language acquisition and the critical period hypothesis* (pp. 23–38). Mahwah, NJ: Lawrence Erlbaum Associates.

Weerman, F. (1997). On the relation between morphological and syntactic case. In A. van Kemenade & N. Vincent (Eds.), *Parameters of morpho-*

syntactic change (pp. 427–459). Cambridge: Cambridge University Press.

Weverink, M. (1990). *The subject in relation to inflection in child language.* Unpublished master's thesis, University of Utrecht.

Wexler, K. (1994). Optional infinitives, head movement and the economy of derivations. In D. Lightfoot & N. Hornstein (Eds.), *Verb movement* (pp. 305–350). Cambridge: Cambridge University Press.

Wexler, K. (1998). Very early parameter setting and the unique checking constraint: A new explanation of the optional infinitive stage. *Lingua* 106, 23–79.

Wexler, K. & Manzini, M. R. (1987). Parameters and learnability in binding theory. In T. Roeper & E. Williams (Eds.), *Parameter setting* (pp. 41–76). Dordrecht: Reidel.

White, L. (1989). *Universal Grammar and second language acquisition.* Amsterdam: John Benjamins.

White, L. (1990/1991). The verb-movement parameter in second language acquisition. *Language Acquisition* 1, 337–360.

White, L. (1991). Adverb placement in second language acquisition: Some effects of positive and negative evidence in the classroom. *Second Language Research* 7, 133–161.

White, L. (1992a). Long and short verb movement in second language acquisition. *Canadian Journal of Linguistics* 37, 273–286.

White, L. (1992b). On triggering data in L2 acquisition: A reply to Schwartz & Gubala-Ryzak. *Second Language Research* 8, 120–137.

White, L. (1996). Universal grammar and second language acquisition: Current trends and new directions. In W. Ritchie & T. Bhatia (Eds.), *Handbook of language acquisition* (pp. 85–120). New York: Academic Press.

White, L. (2000). Second language acquisition: From initial to final state. In J. Archibald (Ed.), *Second language acquisition and linguistic theory* (pp. 130–155). Malden, MA: Blackwell.

White, L. (2003a). Fossilization in steady state L2 grammars: Persistent problems with inflectional morphology. *Bilingualism: Language & Cognition* 6, 129–141.

White, L. (2003b). *Second language acquisition and Universal Grammar.* Cambridge: Cambridge University Press.

White, L. & Genesee, F. (1996). How native is near-native? The issue of ultimate attainment in adult second language acquisition. *Second Language Research* 11, 233–265.

White, L. & Juffs, A. (1998). Constraints on wh-movement in two different contexts of non-native language acquisition: Competence and processing. In S. Flynn, G. Martohardjono, & W. O'Neil (Eds.), *The gen-*

erative study of second language acquisition (pp. 111–129). Mahwah, NJ: Lawrence Erlbaum Associates.

Williams, E. (1994). A reinterpretation of evidence for verb movement in French. In D. Lightfoot & N. Hornstein (Eds.), *Verb movement* (pp. 189–205). Cambridge: Cambridge University Press.

Wolfram, W. (1985). Variability in tense marking: A case for the obvious. *Language Learning* 35, 229–253.

Wolfram, W. & Hatfield, D. (1984). *Tense marking in second language learning: Patterns of spoken and written English in a Vietnamese community.* Washington DC: Center for Applied Linguistics.

Wolfson, N. (1979). The conversational historical present alternation. *Language* 55, 168–182.

Wu, C.-H. T. (2002). Serial verb construction and verbal compounding. In S.-W. Tang & C.-S. L. Liu (eds.), *On the formal way to Chinese languages* (pp. 143–162). Stanford: CSLI Publications.

Xu, L. & Langendoen, T. (1985). Topic structures in Chinese. *Language* 61, 1–27.

Yin, R. K. (1994). *Case-study research design and methods* (2nd ed.). Thousand Oaks, CA: Sage.

Yip, V. (1995). *Interlanguage and learnability: From Chinese to English.* Amsterdam: John Benjamins.

Zanuttini, R. (1997). *Negation and clausal structure: A comparative study of Romance languages.* Oxford: Oxford University Press.

Zobl, H. & Liceras, J. (1994). Functional categories and acquisition orders. *Language Learning* 44, 159-180.

Author Index

A

Abney, S., 180
Alexiadou, A., 152
Andersen, R. W., 113
Anderson, B., 7
Aoun, J., 166, 169, 170, 171,
  173, 199, 200, 201
Archibald, J., 104
Aronoff, M., 5, 64, 127
Atkinson, M., 55

B

Bailey, N., 86
Baker, M. C., 18, 142, 224
Bardovi-Harlig, K., 64, 113, 117,
  118
Bayley, R. J., 97, 104, 105, 106,
  107, 113, 126
Beard, R., 64
Beck, M.-L., 73, 145
Belletti, A., 67
Bialystok, E., 35
Bickerton, D., 9
Birdsong, D., 2, 3, 5, 14, 15, 16,
  35, 39, 70, 227
Bischoff, J., 144, 145
Bley-Vroman, R., 115
Bobaljik, J. D., 53, 140, 152
Bodman, N. C., 154
Boraie, D., 40
Borer, H., 9, 10, 52
Brindley, J., 155

Bromberg, H. S., 58
Brown, C., 132
Brown, R., 87, 90, 101
Burt, M., 65

C

Caramazza, A., 10, 11, 12, 13,
  14, 234
Carroll, J. B., 37, 232
Carroll, S. E., 9, 15, 18, 132,
  138, 144, 226, 233, 235, 236
Chan, C. Y.-H., 126, 153, 154,
  159, 160, 161, 162, 163, 168,
  169, 172, 173, 174, 206
Chao, Y. R., 177
Chapelle, C., 12
Cheng, L., 199
Chomsky, N., vii, 5, 6, 8, 14, 56,
  57, 87, 142, 152, 153, 154,
  206
Cinque, G., 141, 152
Clahsen, H., 54, 55, 71, 89
Clément, R., 40
Cliff, S., 144, 145, 150
Comrie, B., 113
Corder, S. P., 205

D

de Haan, G. R., 54
DeKeyser, R., 12
Dekydtspotter, L., 7, 164
de Villiers, J., 87

Subject Index

A

acceptability judgment task, *see* grammaticality judgment task
acculturation, 33–37, 44, 203
adverb placement, 48, 141, 143–144, 147–152, 204, 213, 236
age of arrival, 2, 12, 26, 35, 43
age-related effects, 35, 39, 41, 43, 47, 68, 229–230, *see also* critical period
agreement (Agr), 49–56, 59, 62, 74–77, 85, 144–146, 184, 190, 206
    agreement marking, Patty's, 79–81, 146–147, 188, 190, 192, 203, 211
    rich, 140, 142, 152
    strength of Agr, *see* feature strength
aptitude, language, 12, 37–39, 41, 43, 45, 232
    Modern Language Aptitude Test (MLAT), 233
aspect (Asp), 88, 124
    experiential (in Chinese), 61, 131
    perfective (vs. imperfective), 51, 99, 102, 104, 113, 124, 128, 132–133, 165, 208
    telic (vs. atelic), 102, 113–115, 132
Aspect Hypothesis, 64, 102, 104, 113–115

B

be (copula/auxiliary), 58, 78–80, 82–84, 87–90, 95–96, 110, 142, 146, 151, 155, 197, 203
    contractible/incontractible, 87–88, 90
    overgeneration of, 90–92, 107, 110
behaviorism, 227

C

Cantonese, 24–28, 41–42, 103, 107, 161, 211, 213, *see also* Chinese
case, 57–58, 63–64, 66, 68, 75, 77–78, 81, 87–88, 94, 176, 178, 182, 204
    exceptional case marking (ECM), 57
case filter, 212
Chinese, 4, 7, 8, 21–23, 27, 28, 30, 49, 63, 97, 103–105, 107, 114, 117, 125, 131–133, 145–146,